Instructional Effectiveness
of Video Media

Instructional Effectiveness of Video Media

C. Douglas Wetzel
Paul H. Radtke
Hervey W. Stern

Navy Personnel Research and Development Center, San Diego

LAWRENCE ERLBAUM ASSOCIATES, PUBLISHERS
1994   Hillsdale, New Jersey   Hove, UK

Copyright © 1994 by Lawrence Erlbaum Associates, Inc.
All rights reserved. No part of the book may be reproduced in any form, by photostat, microform, retrieval system, or any other means, without the prior permission of the publisher. Portions of this book result from the work of U.S. Government employees done as part of their official duties. No copyright is available for those portions of this work.

Lawrence Erlbaum Associates, Inc., Publishers
365 Broadway
Hillsdale, New Jersey, 07642

Cover design by Roz Orland

Library of Congress Cataloging-In-Publication Data

Wetzel, C. Douglas.
    Instructional effectiveness of video media / C. Douglas Wetzel, Paul H. Radtke, Hervey W. Stern.
        p.   cm.
    Includes bibliographical references and indexes.
    ISBN 0-8058-1698-4
    1. Video tapes in education. 2. Video recording—Production and direction. I. Radtke, Paul H. II. Stern, Hervey W.
LB1044.75.W48   1994
371.3'358—dc20   94-25424
                                                        CIP

Books published by Lawrence Erlbaum Associates are printed on acid-free paper, and their bindings are chosen for strength and durability.

Printed in the United States of America
10 9 8 7 6 5 4 3 2 1

Contents

	Foreword *Harold F. O'Neil, Jr.*	ix
	Acknowledgments	xi
1	Introduction	1
	Instructional Issues	1
	Scope of the Review	3
2	Forms of Educational Television	6
	Reviews of the Effectiveness of Educational Television	6
	Achievement and Educational Television	7
	Attitudes and Educational Television	12
	Extensions of Television-Centered Education	13
	Telecourses	14
	Tutored Videotape Instruction	18
	Interactive Television and Video Teletraining	19
	Supplementary Classroom Use of Videotapes and Films	22
	Other Practical Characteristics	24
	Economics of Television-Centered Education	27
	Cost Analysis	27
	Representative System Costs and Characteristics	29
3	Processing Visual and Verbal Information	40
	Processing Visual and Verbal Information in Dynamic Presentations	40
	Comparing Components of Visual–Verbal Presentations	41
	Learning from Television News Broadcasts	52

vi   CONTENTS

	Attention and Comprehension	57
	Processing Visual and Verbal Information in Static Materials	61
	Generalizations Relevant to Video	61
	Studies of Illustrated Text	62
4	**Dynamic Visual Presentations**	**73**
	Motion Attributes and Functions	73
	General Studies Involving Motion	75
	Studies of Motion and Procedural Learning	77
	Modeling Movements, Feedback, and Sports	84
	Video Feedback in Teacher Education	88
	Studies of Animated Graphics	89
	Uses of Animation in Instruction	89
	The Instructional Effectiveness of Animation	91
	Discussion of Animation	97
	Realism and Fidelity in Visual Instruction	98
	Continua of Realism	98
	Realism in Pictures, Simulations, and Motion	99
	Discussion	103
5	**Computer-Based Interactive Video**	**105**
	Meta-Analyses of Interactive Video	105
	Instructional Designs in Interactive Video	108
6	**Video Production Methods and Tradecraft**	**111**
	Overview of Tradecraft and Instructional Production Methods	111
	Professional Tradecraft	113
	Camera Technique	113
	Composition	119
	Lighting	123
	Movement	125
	Editing Techniques	125
	Audio	128
	Words on the Screen	130
	Animation	130
	Human Factors Guidance	132
	Discussion	133

7	Production Methods and Learning	134
	Using Production Techniques to Enhance Learning	134
	Research Findings	135
	General Presentation Format	135
	Presentation Pace and Length Effects	137
	Instructional Video Strategies, Techniques, and Devices	139
	Attention-Getting Devices	141
	Increasing Attention and Learning Through Cuing	147
	Presenting Verbal Material	153
8	Learning, Mental Effort, and the Perception of Media	158
	Commercial Television's Effect on General Learning	158
	The Effect on Reading	159
	The Effect on Educational Achievement and Aspirations	161
	Commercial Television's Effect on Learning from Televised Media	162
	Popular Attitudes Toward Commercial Television	163
	Student Attitudes Toward Television and Learning	165
	Student Attitudes Toward Television, Mental Effort, and Learning	167
	Salomon's Theory	169
	Related Research	177
	Discussion	179
9	Symbol Systems and Media	181
	Dimensions of Symbol Systems	181
	Symbol Systems Used in Film and Television	183
	Decoding and Elaboration of Information from Symbol Systems	185
	Aiding and Cultivating the Use of Mental Skills	186
10	Perspectives on Video Media	188
	Historical Trends and Critical Perspectives	188
	Media as Vehicles	190
	Media Attributes	192
	Cognitively Relevant Clusters of Media Capabilities	194
	Discussion	198
11	Discussion and Conclusions	200
	Educational Television and Video	200

Learner Involvement and Participation	**203**
Capability of Conveying a Wide Range of Information	**205**
Teaching Methods, Production Practices, and Effects of Video Media	**207**
Video Capabilities and Effectiveness	**209**
References	**211**
Author Index	**239**
Subject Index	**247**

Foreword

As indicated by annual training surveys (e.g., *Training Magazine*), video technology is either the most frequently used medium in industry or second in use to instructor-led classrooms. Furthermore, video is also used extensively in education, both K-12 and postsecondary. The use of video technology is probably the most prevalent in homes (e.g., TVs and VCRs). However, a major impediment to the effective use of media technologies in education and training is the lack of a credible research-based synthesis of the media and learning findings. Newcomers to the field tend to repeat the history of the field. In particular, with the hype that is associated with each new technological media invention for education and training, a resource is needed to separate myths from wisdom. The authors of this book provide such a resource. The volume is an excellent blend of media research, cognitive science research, and tradecraft knowledge regarding video production techniques.

The research that the authors review involves the following topics: visual learning, verbal–auditory information, news broadcasts, the value of motion and animation in film and video, simulation (including fidelity), the relationship of text and graphics, computer-based learning using video and animated graphics, the role of effort in learning from media, and the concept of media symbol systems. Where available, results from various meta-analyses are also reviewed. The authors discuss media systems in terms of instructional effectiveness and cost benefits. Media systems include educational television, distance learning, and teacher education. Many of the benefits of video are practical ones, for example, convenience, access, standardization, and efficiency.

The authors are scientists at the Navy Personnel Research and Development Center. This center conducts some of the best inhouse behavioral and social science research in the Department of Defense. Since the mid-1970s, I have been an avid consumer of their ideas (at Advanced Research Projects Agency, U.S. Army Research Institute for the Behavioral and Social Sciences, and now at the University of Southern California). Their work has been predominantly for military customers, where the utility of a technology-based approach to education and training has been long recognized. Therefore, their publications have been mainly in technical report form, available from the National Technical Information Service. This book offers a means for wider dissemination of their excellent work.

The research covered in this book is a must for those interested in multimedia instruction.

Harold F. O'Neil, Jr.
University of Southern California

Acknowledgments

This book reviews previous research bearing on the use of dynamic video in instruction. It is our hope that researchers and instructional developers will find this background material of use in conducting new work in this area. This book is an updated version of material that was initially part of a literature review on the effectiveness of video-based instruction conducted at the Navy Personnel Research and Development Center, San Diego, California 92152-7250. The initial review of this literature was conducted as part of an Exploratory Development project entitled Videographic Interface Technology funded by the Office of Naval Research (Program Element 0602233N, Training Technology Project No. RM33T23.03). We are indebted to Bill Montague, Jan Dickieson, Ruth Ireland, Wally Wulfeck, Dick Sorenson, Janette Faust, and John Ellis for their encouragement and assistance during the preparation of this work. The opinions expressed in this book are those of the authors, are not official, and do not necessarily reflect the views of the Department of the Navy.

1 Introduction

Visual forms of instruction are increasingly used as a result of the broader availability of technologies such as broadcasts, teleconferencing, videotapes, videodiscs, and emerging multimedia combinations of computer and digital audio–video technologies. The attractiveness of these media has grown as the technology to produce and use video has become less expensive and less complicated. An accompanying trend toward the use of visual materials to supplement or replace traditional verbal forms of instruction (textbooks and lectures) results from a belief that students learn some material better from visual media. Although changes in technology and popular beliefs about how people learn have fueled the growth in visual instructional materials, the scientific basis for adopting a more vigorous visual approach to teaching is more limited. Even though there is a large literature on new instructional technologies, much of it is anecdotal and not accompanied by empirical justifications of effectiveness. However, a considerable amount of research does exist, stretching back to early work with film, television, and static visual materials. It is important for new work to profit from this accumulated research on the effectiveness and practical benefits of instruction with video and film. Accordingly, a review of this literature will benefit researchers and developers of instruction that use existing and new video technologies.

INSTRUCTIONAL ISSUES

The literature on instructional technology reveals a number of recurrent issues concerning video-based instruction. These generally concern whether television can be used effectively for learning, what features of this medium make learning easier or harder, and what specific techniques improve learning from video-based instruction. Although achievement is a prominent concern, a considerable amount of information has also emerged with regard to acceptance, media perceptions, fidelity, costs, practical usage techniques, and ways to compensate for liabilities of these media. The literature provides a number of lessons learned for more common educational forms like televised lectures or preproduced programs, and it reveals how they are used in classrooms, between distant classrooms, and by students studying alone via correspondence or by computer. Concern or optimism has variously motivated research on whether these forms of education might, under some circumstances, be worse than, equal to, or better than some traditional forms of education.

One realm of concern has been that several characteristics of television might result in some loss in the quality of instruction. Learning might suffer as a result of distancing students from live and interactive classroom experiences or from television's inherent limitations of being transient and limited in view and resolution. That television is typically experienced in the home as a medium of entertainment might also foster similar passive viewing that is inappropriate to educational purposes requiring greater mental effort. Some of these concerns with the linear and passive viewing experience have been addressed in research on teaching techniques and technologies that attempt to promote interactivity. Such endeavors have allowed two-way communication between students and instructors, allowed students to control programs, and combined video with the interactive features of computer-based instruction.

Video-based media are also thought to have several benefits that may offset their liabilities. Video has the capability to convey more forms of information than less enriched media such as radio, text, and drawings. This capability allows students to learn through both verbal and visual means, to view actual objects and realistic scenes, to see sequences in motion, and to view perspectives that are difficult or impossible to observe in real life. The possibility that these representational capabilities could be used to improve learning has been an aspiration of research attempting to mitigate criticisms that video media merely convey instruction that could be delivered in alternative ways. These potential benefits are reflected in popular claims for visual-based forms of presentations in meeting and in instruction (cf. Friedman, 1993). These claims hold that understanding and learning are variously enhanced by bringing together a wide range of media forms that can present the viewer with simplified or concrete information as well as realistic and high-fidelity information. Such claims may be accompanied by arguments that confuse the instructional methods affecting learning with other practical effects or with the medium or technology itself. The recent emphasis on "multimedia" technology is clearly founded on the assumption that rapid access to large amounts of information, illustrated with visuals and incorporating animation, motion video, and digital speech will either enhance the attractiveness of the material or possibly enhance learning.

Video-based media also offer efficient, practical, or convenient ways to deliver instruction so that much of their value lies in a context broader than direct effects on achievement. They offer the potential to serve large numbers of people, to reach those who are widely dispersed in remote areas, and to provide educational opportunities that might be otherwise unavailable. Efficiency benefits of video may also be derived from using instruction that has been previously prepared. For example, it may be used in content areas outside the expertise of local teachers, to standardize instructional quality that can vary among instructors, to maintain quality when trainers are technical specialists that rotate periodically, to offer surrogates for experiences that are otherwise difficult to achieve or are dangerous, and to offer a reusable form of instruction that may be conveniently used when desired. New kinds of costs may result from using technology to supplement or replace traditional forms of instruction. Economic studies of this practical issue may offer some guidance as to how these media could be made affordable for educational audiences whose size does not approach the scale found in commercial mass communication.

SCOPE OF THE REVIEW

Our primary objective has been to present a review of the research literature on the use of dynamic video media in instruction. To the extent that the current literature allows, we attempted to identify significant variables that affect student learning or that bear on other practical issues associated with video-based education. We have found this information useful as background material in conducting subsequent research and in instructional development efforts concerned with learning from video-based media.

The literature on the use of video, television, and graphic visuals in instruction is extensive. We started our review by searching three computerized databases that index the literature on psychology, education, and government-sponsored research: PsycLIT from the American Psychological Association, ERIC from the Educational Resources Information Center, and NTIS from the National Technical Information Service. Illustrative estimates of the extensiveness of the literature may be seen in the results of a search of the ERIC database for the 22 years between 1966 and 1991. Approximately 4,700 references were found for the word *video* alone. Approximately 8,400 references existed for the combination of *educational or instructional <and> TV or television*. Approximately 14,000 references resulted from a search for the combination of *video or TV or television <and> learn(ing) or train(ing) or education(al)*. Many of these articles are not reviewed here because they are expository discussions on uses of video in education or they argue for the use of video-based instruction in various settings.

The studies of greatest interest to this review were those that employed empirical or experimental research methods, illuminated the benefits and liabilities of video, or contributed to the understanding of video from a cognitive science point of view. Early research often involved comparisons of media as if the technologies themselves were important to learning. Subsequent critical perspectives have questioned whether media are only vehicles for conveying teaching methods that are the primary source of instructional effectiveness (Clark, 1983). These conflicting perspectives increase the value of studies that have explored the unique characteristics of a medium (e.g., motion) or attempted to understand the variables operating within a medium as a way of explaining differences between media. The observation that teaching methods are significant variables in the effectiveness of media led us to include general education topics that are not specific to video. The topics reviewed vary somewhat in their level of detail. In some areas, a previous reviewer had cogently drawn the important conclusions. In other areas, no previous review existed and it was necessary to collect and review studies in detail to arrive at a conclusion. Finally, although a greater value was placed on reviewing studies of adult learners, a significant body of the educational literature concerned children.[1] These findings were included when they supported generalizations relevant to the review.

An examination of video-based learning necessarily encompasses a number of other areas of research. The significant body of research with film was considered to have effects that were basically similar to those with video. Both of these areas are often characterized as forms of visual learning. Visual learning can also include other experiences, such as the use of photographs and graphic illustrations, dynamic live presentations, and forms of communication applicable to many media that convey abstract ideas, concepts, or relationships through symbolic representation or dramatization. However, video-based instruction involves more than just visual learning; it also involves spoken and written language and other auditory information. These forms of communication are combined in video so that a wide range of different types of information can be conveyed. Thus, video-based learning encompasses many other media and techniques that may also be conveyed by video in ways characteristic of this medium. We have incorporated brief reviews of a number of other research findings that are not video-based because of their assumed relevance when used in video-based learning. These areas concern other presentation forms such as the relation of text and graphics in static materials like books, human factors engineering, and computer-based instruction em-

---

[1]Many of these topics concern the association of television viewing with global socialization processes or where learning is incidental to recreational viewing for entertainment (J. L. Singer, 1980; D. G. Singer, 1983; Singer & Singer, 1983). These include concerns with broadcast television depicting unrealistic role models or inappropriate stereotypes, modeling of the violence and aggression depicted, developing critical viewing skills, displacing reading and studying, and the positive impact of programs like *Sesame Street* on children's school-readiness skills (Hornik, 1981; Murphy, 1991; U.S. Department of Health and Human Services, 1982a, 1982b). These topics on learning from broadcast television are more peripheral to the present focus on the more explicit educational uses of video in older individuals.

ploying video and animated graphics. A contrast with educational video practices is provided by examining studies on learning from broadcast news. Other areas, such as professional video production techniques, are relevant to all forms of video presentations, but do not focus specifically on education and learning. These additional topics bear on the way visual media interact with other presentation forms, particularly in dynamic visual media such as film and video, where visual images, sound, and text are presented simultaneously.

The ensuing chapters are organized according to the following topics. Chapter 2 reviews several forms of educational television in terms of effectiveness, acceptance, and usage characteristics. Cost–benefit analyses are included at this point because they are largely derived from studies of educational television. Chapters 3 and 4 review related topics on several attributes thought to be leading characteristics of video. These include the value of combining several forms of visual and verbal-auditory information, the value of motion and animation, and a discussion of realism relevant to both of these topics. Chapter 5 reviews that portion of the computer-based instruction literature that involves the use of video and briefly discusses the role of interactivity in its effectiveness. Chapters 6 and 7 review various video production techniques—those employed by video professionals and those that are applicable to education. Although the topics in these two chapters overlap, we attempted to distinguish the information on the basis of its origins in professional "tradecraft" as opposed to educational research. Chapters 8, 9, and 10 examine additional theoretical perspectives on media and learning: the relationship between media perceptions and ease of learning, the concept of media symbol systems, and critical perspectives on learning from media. The final chapter presents a discussion that brings together those useful generalizations resulting from the review.

2 Forms of Educational Television

This chapter discusses general reviews of the effectiveness of instructional television, videotaped instruction, distance learning systems, and the economics of television-centered systems. Some of the questions originally addressed by this research concerned the equivalence of instructional television and face-to-face instruction (W. H. Allen, 1971), whether any differential effectiveness could form a basis for selecting media (Campeau, 1974), and finally whether the live and interactive nature of face-to-face instruction could be approximated in some distance education applications (U.S. Office of Technology Assessment, 1989; Whittington, 1987). In brief, the general result of this work indicates that educational television can be as effective as conventional instruction, that selection among equally effective media focuses attention on costs and the importance of the teaching techniques used within any media, and that fidelity and accompanying support issues are important concerns in distance education.

REVIEWS OF THE EFFECTIVENESS OF EDUCATIONAL TELEVISION

Numerous analytical reviews of hundreds of studies have been conducted, and many other reviews of the reviews have been written, which reference several types of unpublished research (W. H. Allen, 1960; Campeau, 1967, 1974; Chu & Schramm, 1967, 1975; Cohen, Ebeling, & Kulik, 1981; Dubin & Hedley, 1969; Finn, 1953; Jamison, Suppes, & Wells, 1974; Lumsdaine & May, 1965; Reid & MacLennan, 1967; Saettler, 1968; Schramm, 1962, 1977; Stickell, 1963; Texas Higher Education Coordinating Board, 1986; U.S. Office of Technology Assessment, 1989; Whittington, 1987; Zigerell, 1991).

Three general areas may be noted in these reviews: achievement, attitudes, and potentially effective techniques used within the medium.

Achievement and Educational Television

Student Achievement

Finn (1953) conducted one of the earliest reviews. His review is now of general historical interest because it was conducted during the transition period when the availability of television sets was becoming more widespread. His review reflects the impact of this new technology and the social and educational concerns that subsequently became the topics of additional research.

W. H. Allen (1971) reviewed historical trends in educational media research. He noted that there had been repetitive cycles of "evaluative" comparisons, first with film, then with television. He observed that the reason for these evaluative comparisons was that "the educational establishment demanded proof of the effectiveness of the innovative techniques, and the baseline for comparison was clearly the current teaching practices" (p. 6). Thus, an original concern with educational television was that it should not be worse than conventional face-to-face instructional lectures. As a result, many of the early studies of instructional television were evaluations of conventional "talking-head" lectures that were televised.

Perhaps the best known systematic study was conducted by Chu and Schramm (1967), who examined 207 studies involving 421 separate comparisons. No statistically significant differences in achievement were found in 308 studies (73%), 63 studies (15%) found television instruction to be superior, and 50 found conventional instruction better (12%). Similar results were also obtained between comparisons of conventional and televised instruction when the studies were separated by the type of subject matter taught. The two methods also produced similar results when elementary, secondary, college, and adult grade levels were compared, although televised instruction appeared slightly more effective with the younger students. An update of this study was published by Chu and Schramm (1975); the 1967 study was itself an update of an earlier compilation by Schramm (1962). Schramm's 1962 study reviewed 393 comparisons and found 255 (65%) with no difference, 83 (21%) with significant differences in favor of televised teaching, and 55 (14%) with significant differences in favor of conventional teaching.

As part of a review of several media, Campeau (1967) also reviewed studies on film and television. Although she did not present a "head count" of study outcomes, our rough count of 58 studies or comparisons (excluding long-term retention) in her paper showed no difference in 42 cases (72%), TV or film better in 10 cases (17%), and TV or film worse in 6 cases (10%). Campeau (1974) subsequently reviewed only recent adult studies and found few meeting her stringent selection criteria.

Several other similar investigations are discussed in these studies and by subsequent reviewers (Chu & Schramm, 1967, 1975; Jamison, Suppes,

& Wells, 1974; Schramm, 1977; Texas Higher Education Coordinating Board, 1986; U.S. Office of Technology Assessment, 1989; Whittington, 1987). Two of the more frequently discussed reviews were conducted by Stickell (1963) and Dubin and Hedley (1969).

Stickell (1963; taken from Schramm, 1977) examined 250 comparisons of televised and classroom instruction according to whether they could be interpreted in terms of a series of scientific acceptability criteria. Of only 10 studies that were fully interpretable, none found significant differences. Of 23 partially interpretable studies, only three found significant differences, all in favor of instructional television. Of the remaining 217 studies, only 59 found significant differences, and these were divided about equally in favoring either televised or conventional instruction.

Dubin and Hedley (1969) reviewed 381 studies in which college-level classes taught in the conventional face-to-face manner were compared with experimental classes taught by television. Of 191 comparisons, 89 favored conventional methods and 102 favored instructional television, but few of these involved significant differences. In a more selective analysis of 42 studies judged comparable on several criteria, one-way televised instruction produced the same amount of learning as did live instruction using lectures or some additional combination of discussion or demonstration. Some early studies of two-way television also noted in this review were found to be less effective than live instruction; this outcome was interpreted to result from the use of complicated apparatus. As discussed later, more recent studies of video teletraining report little difference between these conditions, but these studies do caution that similar implementation details can be a problem (e.g., audio quality).

Cohen et al. (1981) conducted a meta-analysis of 74 experiments comparing a variety of visual teaching strategies, including films, multimedia, closed-circuit TV, educational TV, and studies on observation/feedback. Meta-analysis is a refinement of previous review approaches where the number of significant study outcomes were counted (viz., "box score tally" or "head count" approach). Meta-analysis additionally provides an estimate of how large an experimental effect was obtained. Meta-analysis techniques aggregate many study findings by converting each finding to an *effect size* in standardized units (by dividing the mean difference between control and treatment groups by the standard deviation of the groups or just that of the control group).

Cohen et al. (1981) found a small average effect size of .15 standard deviation units in the 65 studies that examined student achievement. This is equivalent to a percentile gain of 6 points from the 50th percentile to the 56th percentile for visual-based instruction students, or an average examination score percentage gain of 1.5% from 66.9% for conventional classes to 68.4% for visual-based instruction classes. The overall effect size of .15 reported by Cohen et al. is small compared to studies of computer-based instruction, which are two to three times as large (in the range of .26 to

.42), or studies of interactive video, which are three to four times as large (.5 to .69; see chap. 5 on interactive video). In terms of conventional counts with these 65 studies, the direction of the difference was in favor of visual-based instruction in 37 studies and in favor of conventional instruction in 28 studies. Only 17 of the 65 studies reported significant differences (26%), with 13 favoring visual-based instruction and 4 favoring conventional instruction. The 74% of studies that found no significant difference was comparable to the findings of other reviews, such as 80% in Stickell (1963), and 76% in Chu and Schramm (1967). Cohen et al. also found later studies were somewhat more likely to yield larger effect sizes. In terms of just those 17 studies reporting significant differences, they found 76% in favor of visual-based instruction, whereas Stickell (1963) found only 54% and Chu and Schramm (1967) found only 44%.

When broken down by type of visual-based instruction, almost half of the studies examined by Cohen et al. (1981) used closed-circuit TV. Similar effect sizes were obtained among the categories of instruction: .09 for educational TV; .13 for closed-circuit TV, still projection, and film; and .20 for multimedia. The largest effect size obtained was .41 for five studies using video for feedback, which was noted to be a potential area for future research, such as in teacher education (see chap. 4). Cohen et al. (1981) also found students were equally likely to complete visual-based and conventional classes and their attitudes toward them were very similar.

There is agreement among the conclusions from these reviews and the less well-known reviews they in turn reviewed. The reviews found a pattern of little difference in effectiveness between televised and conventional classroom instruction. With the exception of the newer meta-analysis evaluation techniques employed in the study of Cohen et al. (1981), the comparative reviews of educational television dwindled after the comprehensive study of Chu and Schramm (1967, 1975). The original question that prompted these reviews was answered by finding that educational television techniques resulted in student achievement that was no worse than that of the conventional classroom. Although there are exceptions, many of these studies used what might be characterized as essentially talking-head approaches in which conventional lectures were televised. Some research has continued on the issue, but the focus has been on better controlled evaluations or on newer mixed media or distance education approaches.

Ellis and Mathis (1985) provided a recent example of a controlled comparison of a televised and live instructor that again found no difference. They examined performance in introductory level college courses taught by live lectures or via television in a study addressing the control of methodological problems. They identified 11 previous studies that had problems with random assignment or self-selected subjects or that used studio lectures involving somewhat different presentation styles or more elaborate visual aids than did typical classroom lectures. In their study, students were randomly assigned to adjoining classrooms so that they received lecture instruction at the same time. The instructor delivered the lectures in one classroom and the other classroom received the lectures on television. Additionally, students were rotated between the two classrooms after several lectures and an exam so that all students experienced both treatment conditions. Test performance was equivalent under the two conditions and class attendance was unaffected by the mode of instruction. Thus, this study addressed several methodological concerns and yielded the same conclusion as that reached in many previous studies.

Other Guidance from Early Reviews

Several reviewers extended the scope of their review beyond the comparison of different media to an examination of the effectiveness of achievement-related techniques used within television or film media (W. H. Allen, 1957, 1960; Campeau, 1967; Chu & Schramm, 1967, 1975; Lumsdaine & May, 1965). We briefly highlight some of the techniques that were considered promising at the time of these reviews and other issues that are now of historical interest (several of these techniques are also examined in chap. 7). Interpretations of these usage techniques in these reviews foreshadowed the idea, developed in later critiques (Clark, 1983), that differences between media may be less important than the teaching methods used within a medium. Thus, Chu and Schramm (1975) noted that many of the techniques examined were by no means unique to television, and, as Schramm (1977) commented, "learning seems to be affected more by what is delivered than by the delivery system" (p. 273). Chu and Schramm (1967, 1975) noted that instructional television was rarely used to carry the "whole weight" of instruction. Rather, they observed that, where used effectively, it was interwoven into an integrated teaching–learning system in the context of other learning activities. They discerned a usage pattern in which teaching done best by television was provided that way, and other teaching done better by face-to-face teaching or supervision was provided in that way.

One theme in the early studies with film and television reflected an interest in ways to enhance achievement by inducing student participation. These studies often used experimental interventions that can now be seen as less relevant to linear fixed-paced presentations than to later interactive technologies begun in studies of programmed learning and that subsequently evolved into computer-based instruction techniques (W. H. Allen, 1957; Lumsdaine, 1961; Lumsdaine & May, 1965). In the reviews of film and television studies by Campeau (1967) and W. H. Allen (1960), techniques beneficial to learning included the repetition of viewings, using relevant teacher introductions, and generally positive effects resulting from techniques encouraging student participation. The effect of student participation was qualified by the specificity of questions asked in that they only affected later tests of just that information and by the finding that inducing active or covert student responses depends on the extent to which correct knowledge was gained as a consequence. These conclusions echoed earlier ones of W. H. Allen (1957) on the positive effects of participation, inducing learner responses, and knowledge of results. Inserted questions were judged to have little effect by Chu and Schramm (1967, 1975), but this remains consistent to the extent that it refers to linear presentations not interrupted in some interactive fashion.

Chu and Schramm (1967, 1975) derived 60 numbered conclusions as a consequence of their review. Some of these conclusions pertained to guidance for classroom usage and others related to production techniques. Their review on repeating the viewing of films or televised lessons indicated a benefit of no more than half that of the first viewing, with subsequent viewings yielding diminishing returns. They indicated that a teacher directed follow-up may be more effective than a second viewing and that the usefulness of additional viewings needs to be weighed against the added time required for the repetition. Rest pauses were noted to be beneficial in long presentations, but using a television program to begin or to end a daily lesson was of no consequence. As with presentations that proceed too quickly to allow comprehension, the distraction created by taking notes during viewing was noted to interfere with learning if time for it is not provided during the presentation.

A number of the Chu and Schramm conclusions pertained to viewing conditions. Viewing conditions involving peripheral viewing angles or long distances were judged to be of consequence only when accurate perception of the images was important to learning. Likewise, they concluded that noise could reduce the effectiveness of learning from film and television to the extent that it competes with learning presented in the auditory medium (e.g., ambient classroom or projector noise). Subject to these qualifications, they concluded that the size of the viewing group has little effect and that television can be used effectively to teach college classes as large as 100 or more students. They concluded that learning is little affected by using larger screens or by color versus black-and-white television, although such enhancements are more preferred by students. Their conclusions on the effects of color, screen size and motion were similar. These attributes were seen as being selectively beneficial when they are specifically relevant to some types of learning, such as when color, larger images in close-ups, or motion offered relevant discriminations.

At the time of the Chu and Schramm review, the base of available research left them unable to reach firm conclusions on many topics. For example, they ventured tentative conclusions that dramatization, humor, eye contact, inserted questions, and animation were probably not effective. They left these as open questions along with various issues related to many other production techniques and presentation formats (see chap. 6 and 7).

Attitudes and Educational Television

Evaluations of student attitudes were often subsidiary portions of many studies concerned with student achievement, and several of the reviews mentioned here summarized these findings. As with concerns that students might achieve less with televised than with traditional instruction, concerns with attitudes focused on potentially lowered acceptability. A similar pattern of concern still persists in later studies of distance education and its technical fidelity. Teacher attitudes revolve around their perceptions of the usefulness of instructional television and barriers or difficulties that it presents. Among students, the relevant factors are the extent of personal contact with the instructor and the quality of instruction or the extent to which they can learn from instructional television. In reviewing the findings of other studies concerned with comparisons of conventional and televised instruction, Jamison et al. (1974) offered a conclusion representative of the pattern observed in this period of research: "A significant fraction of teachers and students share initially negative attitudes toward [instructional television, but] these negative attitudes tend to lessen, but not necessarily disappear, with time" (p. 38). Overall, they concluded that "the incidence of unfavorable attitudes tends to diminish as institutions gain experience with the medium. After such experience a majority of students have neutral or favorable attitudes toward ITV" (p. 56).

Chu and Schramm (1967, 1975) drew several conclusions on attitudes toward instructional television in their comprehensive review. They concluded that attitudes toward instructional television were generally favorable among both teachers and students, but tended to be more favorable in elementary schools than in secondary schools or colleges. Administrators appeared to have more favorable attitudes than did teachers. They did not find attitudes to be consistently associated with teaching different types of academic subjects. Students at the college level tended to prefer small discussion classes over television classes, but preferred television classes over large lecture classes. Voluntary home students of televised college classes tended to be more favorable toward learning by television than were students taking these same televised courses in the classroom. Off-campus students valued an otherwise unavailable opportunity for education and the convenience of not having to travel to school. Favorable student responses to instructional television indicated a perception of better prepared presentations or better prepared teachers, which has also been a recurrent observation of teachers in preparing for such courses. Although learning was not impaired by instructional television, Chu and Schramm (1967, 1975) concluded that students are generally more satisfied with personal teacher–student contact. Unfavorable responses to instructional television included concerns with the presentation proceeding without the ability to ask questions or participate in discussions when desired and in not having personal contact with, or getting help from, the teacher. Finally, it appeared to Chu and Schramm that liking instructional television was not always correlated with learning from it.

Dubin and Hedley (1969) also reviewed attitudes among studies at the college level. They found attitudes to be more positive after experience with instructional television than before. About one half to two thirds of the students reported favorable attitudes after exposure to instructional television. When asked to choose between conventional instruction and instructional television, it was estimated that less than one third of the students would opt for instructional television. However, this figure rose to over one half if the conventional instruction was to be in the form of a large lecture course. Faculty attitudes summarized over several studies indicated that about one half of them were favorable toward TV courses, about one fourth were neutral, and about one fifth were unfavorable. They were somewhat less favorable toward teaching such a course (about one third unfavorable) and even less favorable toward doing so on a regular basis (a little less than one half unfavorable). Faculty members were least favorable toward their children attending university TV courses (59%–75% unfavorable) but those with TV teaching experience were more favorable (13%–15% unfavorable).

In the more recent meta-analysis of Cohen et al. (1981), attitudes were not found to differ in comparisons of conventional and televised instruction. They found little difference in 16 comparisons of attitudes toward instructional television (an effect size of –.06) and little difference in six comparisons of attitudes toward the subject matter (an effect size of –.18). At the same time Cohen et al. (1981) published their analysis, Simonson, Thies, and Burch (1979) and Simonson (1980) also abstracted a large number of studies on media and attitudes, but without offering conclusions with regard to effectiveness.

EXTENSIONS OF TELEVISION-CENTERED EDUCATION

Extensions of television-centered education reflect the wide availability of video technologies and continuing interests in using them to expand the forms of education. These include variants of interactive television, uses of videotapes, and forms of correspondence or distance study where students are separated from teachers. The variety in these systems is reflected both in terms of their educational uses and in terms of implementation details and costs of the transmission delivery mechanisms.

Delivery transmission mechanisms are essentially over-the-air transmissions, cable distribution, and copy technologies (Maher, 1982). Variants of these include local closed-circuit TV distribution, cable TV, high-speed land lines, microwave, satellite, low-power local broadcasts, and wide area broadcasts possibly in conjunction with some form of public broadcasting communication network. Delivery could be at a prearranged transmission time or at a desired time with copy technologies such as videotapes.

Many television-centered delivery systems should be considered mixed systems because distinct types are often used in combination (Educational Policy Research Center, 1976; Maher, 1982; U.S. Office of Technology Assessment, 1989). This mix reduces the clarity of distinguishing individual media characteristics, and many implementations appear to yield essentially similar presentations from an educational perspective. Thus, little difference may be experienced between many preproduced or live broadcasts, tapes of them, or other similar audio–visual transmission schemes. However, the linear viewing experience may be altered by attempts to increase face-to-face fidelity and interactivity, such as when receiving students can talk back over a system, or when they control a tape by interrupting it to rewind for reviews and for note taking. Video teletraining forms of distance education attempt to extend the live two-way communication between teacher and students to students at distant sites. More traditional forms of distance education involve correspondence and may involve minimal interaction and utilize additional media such as broadcasts and tapes as supplements to texts. Another experimental form beyond the scope of this review is computer-mediated communication and messaging used as part of a mixed educational system (Mason & Kaye, 1989; S. Wells, 1990).

These extensions of television-centered education have not been accompanied by large head counts of significant study outcomes as was the case with the reviews of the earlier literature on educational television. This is due, in part, to practical acceptance, the mixed variety in the media systems, and the evolving and often experimental nature of some systems. Finally, some characteristics of these technologies yield experiences that are difficult to quantify because they involve convenience, access, travel, control, and practical issues.

Telecourses

A telecourse is a learning system that consists of preproduced televised instructional programs integrated with printed supplementary materials such as syllabus outlines, study guides, textbooks, and tests (Texas Higher Education Coordinating Board, 1986; Whittington, 1987; Zigerell, 1986, 1991). Telecourses are generally preproduced transmissions, although similar mixed system variants include videotapes distributed instead of transmissions, first-time live broadcasts that can be taped, and arrangements where tapes are made available in lieu of retransmissions. Telecourses additionally involve a managing and support staff at the disseminating institution and require students to have common media equipment such as a videotape player or a television set to receive broadcasts.[1] In some telecourses, students can phone or meet with instructors or course support staff. The most frequently offered whole courses are in foreign languages, followed by mathematics and sciences, and then humanities (U.S. Office of Technology Assessment, 1989, pp. 31–32). Not all telecourse distance education endeavors have been successful for various reasons related to transmission costs, access, adequate student loads, or numbers of courses to attract students (a historical review of telecourses and their developers is given in Zigerell, 1979, 1991).

The primary attraction of telecourses for students is convenience. Telecourses are attractive to students at remote locations for whom travel is an obstacle, those who must accommodate regular employment, and those needing flexibility in personal scheduling. The attraction of telecourses for institutions is that they can extend courses to more students, some of whom might not otherwise obtain the instruction, and the potential that sufficient student volume will warrant the costs of transmission, distribution, and administration relative to those for conventional on-campus methods. Based on a survey, Zigerell (1986) provided a profile of the telecourse student in community colleges where part-time enrollments are common. A substantial number were drawn from the regular student body and wanted to earn additional credits at their convenience or with less travel. Most students had not taken telecourses before (65%), were enrolled in on-campus courses (63%), were females (68%), and over one half had children. About 60% carried fewer than 10 semester units and about one half worked at least 40 hours a week. In citing reasons for selecting the telecourse, 41% reported work conflicts, 12% leisure time conflicts, and only 17% reported that they preferred receiving the instruction at home.

The Texas Higher Education Coordinating Board (1986) reviewed various preproduced educational programs based on documents from other colleges or producer evaluations reporting various forms of data. They found four evaluations that specifically reported that student achievement was no worse than that found with conventional on-campus courses. The remaining sources relied on other data such as questionnaires to judge that the quality of education did not suffer with this technique. The Texas review also examined grade distributions at Texas community colleges offering telecourses and found them to be comparable to conventional on-campus courses. However, withdrawal percentages were higher in telecourses than in conventional classes and were higher in urban areas.

[1]It would be difficult to enter any home in America and not find at least one television set (Jackson-Beeck, 1977; U.S. Department of Health and Human Services, 1982a). The Electronic Industries Association (EIA) estimates that almost one third of the homes in the United States currently have color TVs with stereo sound, about one sixth have camcorders, and three fourths have a videocassette recorder (VCR) (Wickstrom, 1992). Similarly, the Nielsen organization reports that of 93.1 million U.S households, 98% have color TV, 36% have two sets, 77% own a VCR, 62% have basic cable, and 28% have pay cable ("Vital stats," 1993). Total average daily viewing is reported to be 6.7 hours (3.7 for men, 4.4 for women, and 2.7 for teens).

It was suggested that higher attrition rates were related to the characteristics of students in community colleges with "open-door" admission policies because withdrawal rates did not appear to differ in a university setting. Students may eventually transfer to traditional on-campus courses after starting in distance education courses. The Texas review noted an analysis of California community college students that showed 86% of those transferring to 4-year institutions subsequently earned satisfactory grade point averages (GPAs).

Higher dropout rates have been noted in distance education and in telecourses (Cookson, 1990; Crane, 1984; Dille & Mezack, 1991; Duby & Giltrow, 1978; O. Peters, 1992; Texas Higher Education Coordinating Board, 1986; R. A. Wells, 1990; Woodley & Parlett, 1983). Student success appears to be generally related to being able to pursue learning independently and to conflicts with work and family life circumstances that are characteristic of students who are more likely to participate in distance education. Increased support is a commonly suggested response to student dropout, such as through educational counseling, performance monitoring, and rapid turnaround in evaluating assignments. Student reasons for dropping out most frequently cite job stress, restrictions on private life and family responsibilities, time available to study, and course length. Demographic characteristics of students at risk suggest that dropping out is more likely among males, younger students, and those with higher course loads, lower educational qualifications, and fewer prior course credits. Dille and Mezack (1991) identified several biographical, belief, and learning style predictors of attrition in community college telecourses. Their findings suggested that success in telecourses is related to an ability to pursue studies independently, as is required more in distance education. Compared to successful students, unsuccessful students who withdrew or received less than a grade of C were younger, less often currently married, and had fewer prior credit hours and lower GPAs. The unsuccessful students held beliefs more in the direction of external events controlling outcomes, whereas successful students were more internally controlled in perceiving events as resulting from their own behavior and had learning styles better suited to independent learning.

The British Open University makes substantial use of a mix of media for most of its courses and provides several experiences with off-campus education using television broadcasts and integrated supplementary materials such as audio and videocassettes (Bates, 1987; S. Brown, 1983; S. Brown, Nathenson, & Kirkup, 1982; Grundin, 1983). This 65,000-student educational system was designed as an alternative in which academic admission requirements are nonexistent, substantial numbers of students are employed, and the majority are part time students in a single course requiring about 10 hours study a week (Kaye, 1973; Laidlaw & Layard, 1974; Lumsden & Ritchie, 1975; Rumble, 1987). Various forms of printed correspondence materials form the core of the courses, accompanied by television and radio broadcasts, video and audiotapes, periodic correspondence on assignments by mail, and tutorial sessions at study centers. An estimated 20% of the instruction is delivered by television (Zigerell, 1979), and about 5% of a student's total study time is occupied by the combination of TV, radio, and audiotapes (Grundin, 1983). Between 1974 and 1982, the average student viewing rate for a broadcast ranged from about 50% to 70% (S. Brown, 1983; Grundin, 1983, 1985). Student ratings of helpfulness are highest for text materials and for circumstances involving direct face-to-face contact, followed by tape packages, which were rated slightly more helpful than the TV broadcasts, and then by radio broadcasts, which received the lowest rating (Grundin, 1983). Surveys related by Bates (1988) suggest that those watching the most programs also tend to be those with higher grades, and borderline students tend to rate TV as being most helpful.

Experience with the evolution of media combinations at the British Open University has suggested three factors that influence student use and response to televised programs. These are access in terms of convenient viewing times, the extent of control over a transient medium, and the extent of integration of televised and printed course materials. These factors are illustrated in the following by a pattern of findings from a series of reports (Bates, 1987; S. Brown, 1983; S. Brown et al., 1982).

In response to an increasing number of courses competing for broadcast time, a number of British Open University repeat broadcasts were reduced to single broadcasts. These were supplemented by videocassettes that were loaned to students on demand as replacements for a second repeat broadcast of a lesson (S. Brown, 1983). Providing the videos either as supplements for poor broadcast times or as substitutes for repeat broadcasts increased the accessibility of the programs and also improved the control characteristics and perceived helpfulness. Use of loaned videocassettes of broadcasts increased viewing rates over first-time transmissions 11% compared to the 8% associated with repeat broadcasts. About 12% of the students sought the loans, and they tended to view them more than once, about 1.7 times on average. Student descriptions of the way they used cassettes indicated they were employed interactively because they frequently interrupted the tapes to review, clarify, or take notes on lecture points. Note taking was 14% higher during tapes than broadcasts. A third of the students interrupted the tapes on the first viewing, and on subsequent viewings only a third watched the tape through continuously.

Experience with the integration of visual and printed course material indicated that students place value on printed material documenting the aims and objectives of a program prior to the broadcast, points to look for during the broadcast, and postbroadcast notes summarizing the main points covered. Postbroadcast print material was important because delivery by a transient medium not under student control sometimes did not allow them to remember points for note taking or to have a permanent record for review. Text was seen as ultimately more accessible than the transient speech and visuals of television because it was a permanent form readily and repeatedly accessible for students to study. In this regard, cassettes and printed texts were similar in terms of students having full control over working through the packages whenever they wished, doing so at their own pace, and being able to interrupt and review them when desired. It has been suggested that student videotapes should be designed to exploit their control characteristics by using segments, clear stopping points, indexing, and integrating them with other media activities (Bates, 1988).

In summary, broadcast media are comparatively inflexible from the learner's point of view because fixed broadcast times limit their access. Tapes allow learners to control the transient and fixed pace nature of the medium. Integrated visual and printed materials are particularly important for documenting programs in accessible texts and notes that can be reviewed.

Tutored Videotape Instruction

Gibbons, Kincheloe, and Down (1977) reported on the effectiveness of a hybrid telecourse technique known as Tutored Videotape Instruction (TVI). The TVI technique attempts to respond to the educational needs of the students by combining the positive features of lectures with those of small-group discussions. TVI makes use of unrehearsed, unedited videotapes of regular classes viewed by small groups of 3 to 10 students who are assisted by paraprofessional tutors. The tape is frequently stopped when more discussion is needed so that the class members manage the lecture themselves to make the instruction respond to their individual needs. These discussions are in addition to those already recorded on the tape from the live classroom.

Gibbons et al. (1977) reported a series of TVI studies with engineering courses at Stanford University. The performance of on-campus students who could ask questions in the live classroom was compared to that of off-campus students who were Hewlett-Packard employees at remote sites. The off-campus students were either at a local Bay Area site receiving live instructional television with a talk-back capability or were at a more distant remote TVI site where they received tapes of the lectures by mail. This program also employed an integrated approach in the sense that attention was given to selecting interested tutors, the performance of the remote site industrial students was monitored, and these students completed the same homework and exams as on-campus students and had it scored by the same teaching assistants who graded on-campus and regular TV students. Several comparisons using both on-campus and off-campus TVI students over 3 years of program operation indicated that the TVI technique was at least as effective as either classroom instruction or instruction by live TV with an audio talk-back capability.

H. R. Stone (1990) reported similar data from the University of Massachusetts for remote-site engineering students that used a variation of the TVI technique. The number of remote-site students in this program fell to around three or less and the course sessions were often conducted without the aid of a tutor. Similar grade point averages were found for groups of on-campus and off-campus engineering degree students, both performing slightly better than off-campus nondegree students.

Interactive Television and Video Teletraining

Interactive television is another extension of televised lecture techniques used for distance education. Sometimes referred to as video teletraining, this form of instruction is transmitted by satellite over wide areas, by microwave in smaller regions, or by land lines. Video teletraining is an educational application derived from teleconferencing, a technology initially developed for conducting small-group televised conferences with interactive two-way communication. As with conferences, real-time interaction with remote sites is of particular interest to a variety of educational, industrial, and military organizations that need to train students who are widely dispersed geographically (Bailey, Sheppe, Hodak, Kruger, & Smith, 1989; Pugh, Parchman, & Simpson, 1991, 1992; Simpson, Pugh, & Parchman, 1990, 1991a, 1991b, 1992, 1993; R. A. Wells, 1990).

Contemporary video teletraining networks surveyed by Pugh et al. (1991, 1992) have successfully employed a wide variety of network architectures using various combinations of one-way or two-way links involving video, audio, and graphic transmissions. Numerous technical features of these emerging systems can potentially affect users, such as the rate of transmitting compressed video; whether synchronous participation is possible; the ability of the student to see, hear, or communicate with the site originating instruction; and the ability of the instructor to do the same with distant students.

Video teletraining systems deliver instruction to students at one or more remote sites by televising an instructor who may or may not be in a classroom with students at the originating site. A typical video teletraining system uses two-way audio and then either one-way video of the instructor or two-way video that allows remote students to be seen. The two-way audio can be synchronous and live by using microphones, or might simply involve a telephone call-in link for remote-site students. Displays of instructional materials may be sent to remote sites by cameras televising conventional uses of writing boards and transparencies, or by using an emerging array of electronic teleconferencing technologies to transmit graphics or to show materials placed on a camera copy stand. Remote sites may have a facilitator to maintain a classroom, operate equipment, distribute and collect materials, or score tests.

In contrast to one-way transmission of instruction where students can neither ask questions of nor receive answers from an instructor, the primary concern in these endeavors has been to approximate the interactivity of the live classroom. Issues concerning the success of such efforts often revolve around (a) how well remote-site students perform compared to students with a live instructor at the central site or in traditional classes, (b) how well the systems are accepted by instructors and students, and (c) how the costs of the technology can be offset by the ways the systems are used. As discussed later, the major cost benefits of video teletraining systems appear to be seen in circumstances where travel, per diem, or duplicated instructor costs are avoided by usage that is intense enough to offset the costs of the technology (Chute, Balthazar, & Poston, 1988, 1990; Rupinski, 1991; Rupinski & Stoloff, 1990; Simpson et al., 1990, 1991a, 1991b, 1993).

The emerging pattern of effectiveness with student performance has been primarily obtained with lecture-based courses delivered on a range of teletraining systems that differ in numerous implementation details. The general conclusion from this evolving field is that remote-site students perform equivalently or show only a small decrement compared to students at live transmitting sites or in comparison to traditional classrooms (Barnard, 1992–1993; Beare, 1989; Chute et al., 1988, 1990; Pirrong & Lathen, 1990; Ritchie & Newby, 1989; Rupinski & Stoloff, 1990; Silvernail & Johnson, 1990; Simpson et al., 1990, 1991a, 1991b, 1992, 1993; Stoloff, 1991; U.S. Office of Technology Assessment, 1989; Whittington, 1987).

One of a series of controlled experiments by Simpson et al. (1991b, 1993) is notable because it compared live and teletraining instruction with several audio and video transmission modes within the same study. A traditional live classroom was only 2% better than the combination of several teletraining groups, which differed only by 1% between the remote and originating sites. An advantage of less than 2% was found for students with fully interactive two-way audio plus two-way video over students with two-way audio plus only one-way video. In a second study, quiz performance for a live classroom was about 5% better than classrooms using only one-way audio and video, with remote- and originating-site students differing by less than 1%. In other experiments by Simpson et al. (1990, 1991a, 1992), similar small differences in performance were found between remote and originating site students (0.5% and 3.4%) and between those with one- and two-way video (1.5%). Remote-site student grades averaged about 2% lower than did originating site students with a two-way video and audio satellite system used for operational Navy training (Rupinski & Stoloff, 1990; Stoloff, 1991). Other studies have reported virtually no decrement for video teletraining students (Chute et al., 1988, 1990; Pirrong & Lathen, 1990; Ritchie & Newby, 1989; Silvernail & Johnson, 1990). Beare (1989)

EXTENSIONS OF TELEVISION-CENTERED EDUCATION 21

found no differences in grades between students receiving instruction by one-way video and two-way audio and those receiving instruction by a variety of methods involving conventional lectures, lectures with videotapes for review, and independent study with audio or videotapes.

Increasing the degree of fidelity or interactivity of video teletraining to that with live instruction generally increases effectiveness and satisfaction. The conditions most critical to success appear to be video allowing students to watch the instructor and two-way audio between them, with video showing students to the instructor possibly being more of a monitoring convenience (Simpson et al., 1991b, 1993). Effectiveness may decline when the load on an instructor becomes too great, such as with an increased number of students and sites (Rupinski & Stoloff, 1990). Student preferences for a traditional live classroom may be lessened to the extent that higher fidelity conditions can be created at remote sites. Implementation details such as the clarity of images shown and the quality of the audio can cause negative comments (Barker & Platten, 1988; Beare, 1989; Hansford & Baker, 1990; Rupinski & Stoloff, 1990; Simpson et al., 1990, 1991a, 1991b, 1993; Stoloff, 1991). Audio difficulties also include transmission of extraneous classroom noise, conversations, and difficult to use audio apparatus. Audio problems were responsible for an initial report that live instruction was better than two-way television in an early study (Dubin & Hedley, 1969), but later implementations have been more sensitive to reducing audio problems. Stoloff (1991) found increases in student and instructor satisfaction as such problems were addressed in a maturing system. Remote students also became more indifferent to the differences between video teletraining and traditional methods of instruction, although instructors still tended to favor traditional methods.

Courses delivered by video teletraining may involve special considerations regarding instructor behaviors and the design of instruction and classrooms (Simpson, 1993). The live interactive nature of teletraining requires that instructors encourage the participation of remote-site students and attend to their needs to obtain help and resolve questions. As with any television system, materials and demonstrations to be shown electronically need to be well designed and presented in a manner so that they can be seen well by all. The configuration of a classroom should provide for optimal student viewing of the instruction and other participants. Classrooms should be arranged to create an environment more like a classroom than a TV studio by avoiding a clutter of equipment or barriers between the instructor and students. The design of the teletraining system interface should make the technology transparent to users and under their control. In general, to the extent that a teletraining system mimics a live classroom, instructors and students can behave in ways they are already familiar with from traditional classrooms.

Finally, the capabilities of two-way video and audio raise the possibly of extending the range of course content beyond traditional lectures to content that challenges a noninteractive medium. New possibilities include highly interactive small-group processes and role playing between remote sites. Others would involve interactive demonstrations of training aids, hands-on laboratories, and the value of remote presence in performing collaborative tasks with shared views of objects (e.g., Gaver, Sellen, Heath, & Luff, 1993; Simpson et al., 1992).

Supplementary Classroom Use of Videotapes and Films

A continuing increase in the availability of instructional videotapes and their characteristic manageability by classroom teachers has made this technology particularly attractive. Videotape players are readily available in virtually all educational settings at this point in time. In 1977, one third of all schools had one or more VCRs; this rose to three fourths in 1983 and then rose to roughly 90% by 1988 when over half had more than one VCR (Glenn & Carrier, 1989; Herx, 1986; U.S. Office of Technology Assessment, 1989, p. 38). Reider (1984, 1987a, 1987b) characterized the now common use of videotapes in classrooms as a "quiet technological revolution." The VCR has taken a place alongside the overhead projector and has superseded previously successful classroom technologies such as the filmstrip and 16mm film. Schramm (1977) characterized such "little media" as being those over which classroom teachers have a maximum amount of control. Compared to films, tapes are more easily reproduced, have lower media costs, and are more easily distributed and retained locally compared to previous systems depending on requests from a central library. In addition to these more traditional educational uses, videotapes have recently appeared both as a new method of distributing advertising and as instructional introductions provided with commercial products.

The attractiveness of these media is attributed to their offering an accessible technology under the direct control of the classroom teacher (Chu & Schramm, 1975; Reider, 1984, 1987a; Schramm, 1977). The control involves the ability of the teacher to preview a film or tape, to introduce it at any time that it is optimal to do so, to stop it at will for discussion, and to rerun it for review at any time. This control is not possible with live broadcasts unless they have been taped for replay at the convenience of the teacher. These control features allow teachers the opportunity to use several very effective introduction and follow-up techniques commonly recommended for classroom use of films, filmstrips, or videotapes (W. H. Allen, 1960; Campeau, 1967; Chu & Schramm, 1975). Research on these techniques has shown that teacher introductions and class preparation can increase learning compared to when these introductions are omitted. Important preparatory features include identifying difficult portions of the content to appear, listing points to look for, presenting brief descriptive stories of the content, and providing simple motivational statements or warnings that the content could be tested. Teacher-directed reviews and summaries following the film have also been found to be about as effective as introductions and, in some cases, were more effective than a second showing of the film. A combination of teacher introductions with a follow-up that includes class participation in discussions is recommended to maximize the benefit of these techniques.

Several studies provide estimates of the relative usage of visually based instructional media, in particular how often films and tapes are used and who uses them. Overhead transparencies are probably the most universal visual medium in all types of settings because they are easily used and most organizations can produce them (Radtke & Ulozas, 1991; Seidman, 1986; Smeltzer, 1988). Films and videotapes are commonly available in preproduced form and tapes have come to replace films. Although most organizations can present videotapes for instruction, far fewer can locally produce instructional tapes with a sophistication that exceeds using a camcorder to record general events.

Relative media selection and utilization patterns are reflected in several studies of public school teachers in the elementary, middle, and high school grades. A 1972 nationwide study indicated that classroom teachers are the most important element in selecting films for classroom use (Breen & Ary, 1972). The percentages for those responsible for selecting films were given in categories that allowed respondents to choose more than one category: teachers (55%), principals (46%), librarians (40%), audio–visual coordinators (32%), and teacher committees (23%). Film rentals (73%) exceeded purchases (48%), and only 13% reported having a stated policy for the evaluation and selection of films. In a 1986 media utilization survey, Seidman (1986) found the most frequent visual-based materials used were paper-based pictures, overhead transparencies, and filmstrips. Only 10% to 15% never used these traditional media, compared to 34% who never used motion pictures and 52% who never used videotapes. Combining films and videotapes, about four tenths of the teachers never used them, about one tenth used them on a weekly basis, about one fifth on a monthly basis, and about one fourth used them a few times a year. In a slightly earlier survey, C. B. Smith and Ingersoll (1984) found that school teachers used prerecorded videotapes on a weekly basis about 10% of the time, about 40% reported never using them, and a little less than one half reported that they were at least moderately available. Compared to videotapes, approximately twice as much usage and availability was reported for audio–visual kits consisting of filmstrips, audiotapes, and other related materials.

Smeltzer (1988) studied media utilization among community college instructors and found that about one fourth of them used either films or videotapes once a year, about one third used them once a month, and about one third never used them. By comparison, about one fifth never used overhead transparencies, but over one half used them on a daily or weekly basis, and another one fourth on a monthly basis. This study also suggested that use of films and videotapes tended to be correlated with a student-oriented teaching strategy, but not with a content-oriented teaching strategy. A survey of 135 Navy schools conducted in the early 1980s reflects usage for a similar age group in a technical training environment (Wetzel, Van Kekerix, & Wulfeck, 1987a). This study found that 58% of the schools used either film or video in their courses and that this usage occupied about 5% of the course time.

A generalization often suggested in these various studies is that when media are used, they tend to be less complex media such as transparencies, or at the lower grades, bulletin boards and pictures (Descy, 1992; Seidman, 1986). Additionally, it appears that there may be a slightly greater use of some visually based materials in the lower grades in comparison to the higher grades, although the overall relative pattern of media usage over the grades tends to be similar. This corresponds with the more positive attitudes that teachers in lower grades have toward educational television (Chu & Schramm, 1975). Although videotapes have come to replace films, relatively slow changes over time might be expected in the overall pattern of media choices or in the amount of total classroom time they occupy.

Despite these generalizations, a recent study by Descy (1992) suggested an increase in the use of media previously regarded as being more complex. Among first-year elementary teachers, he found that 68% of his teachers used videotapes at least few times a month. Only about 5% of these teachers never used videotapes, compared to about half of those in the studies from the mid-1980s (cf., Seidman, 1986; C. B. Smith & Ingersoll, 1984). Similarly, about three fourths of these teachers reported that students used computers at least once a week, compared to around one fifth in the mid-1980s. Descy (1992) attributed some of this increased use of media previously thought to be more complex to these technologies having become "household appliances." This is suggested by the report of nearly half of his teachers that they used computers themselves at least once a week. Similarly, the presence of VCRs in three fourths of American homes also suggests a increased familiarity with videotape media ("Vital stats," 1993; Wickstrom, 1992). Even among children as young as 4 to 6, for example, Krendl, Clark, Dawson, and Troiano (1993) found that three fourths knew about starting a tape, one half knew about skipping over parts of a tape, and one half could actually perform the task of inserting a tape correctly.

Other Practical Characteristics

Several often-discussed practical benefits of television-centered education are not easily expressed in terms of either achievement or costs. These benefits are generally related to convenience, control, access, standardization, quality, or other efficiency reasons.

Several of these benefits were already mentioned in connection with the use and acceptance of tapes in classrooms and by telecourse students. The same theme emerged in both instances with regard to the inconvenience of fixed broadcast times and the transient one-time learning experience of television, and both revealed preferences for viewing programs when desired and for control over the pace of programs with tapes. From a different perspective, a by-product of the schedule imposed by broadcasts or from mailings may be that telecourse students are provided a means to pace their studies (Zigerell, 1991).

Instructional television, tapes, or films potentially offer a standardization in the quality of instruction over many sites by minimizing differences in the quality among instructors. Extreme examples are in developing countries with few or poorly qualified teachers or in remote areas with such small populations that qualified teachers are in short supply (Educational Policy Research Center, 1976; Hawkridge 1987; Hosie, 1985; Jamison, Klees, & Wells, 1978). A common instance in rural areas concerns the breadth of course offerings possible by small teaching staffs who may not have qualifications to provide some specialized courses (Barker, 1985). Thus, importing preprepared presentations offers some equalization of opportunities between large and small schools, assists teachers in fields where they may not be prepared, or allows inexperienced teachers an opportunity to watch expert teaching in their own fields (Schramm, 1977; U.S. Office of Technology Assessment, 1989). Standardizing instructional quality may also be of particular relevance in situations where instructors are drawn on a rotating basis from technical specialties that do not include some background in teaching methods.

Although some of these instances of the benefits of standardization are from specialized contexts, the reasoning can be applied generally to all of education. As Chu and Schramm (1975) observed, instructional television "can share a good teacher with a very large number of classes, rather than one" (p. 100). They also indicated that favorable student responses to instructional television reflect a perception of better prepared presentations or better prepared teachers, which coincides with the experiences of teachers preparing for such courses. For example, a Miami University study reported that the average preparation time for 1 hour of conventional university instruction (1.7 hours) was about three times greater with closed circuit courses (5.3 hours) and was five to six times greater with open circuit television courses (9.6 hours; Dubin & Hedley, 1969; S. Wells, 1976). Although it has not been quantified, duplicated teacher preparation efforts might be reduced by using prepared video material, although the time for previewing and developing introductory and follow-up activities would still be required.

Several benefits of television, tapes, or films are also cited with regard to the quality of the educational experience and the opportunities they offer (S. Brown et al., 1982; Schramm, 1977; Zigerell, 1991). Schramm (1977) noted that these media "can introduce demonstrations otherwise impossible in the classroom, take the student to a part of the world he or she could not otherwise experience, bring into the classroom a distinguished visitor or a teacher with special expertise [and] offer a change of pace from the routine of everyday teaching" (p. 194). Similarly, S. Brown et al. (1982) noted that "there are many pedagogical functions which would be difficult to achieve without the help of audio–visual media [and] the difficulties and costs of providing these functions live are so great that audio–visual media are the only feasible alternatives" (p. 219). They emphasize the idea that media can be substitutes for many live experiences. For example, audio–video media can provide students with a kind of substitute field trip by taking them to places where they could not go, present eminent speakers they could not hear otherwise, and show technically complex or hidden processes that could not be easily created or repeated in laboratory demonstrations.

Another realm of beneficial substitute experiences provided by video is where danger and safety are involved. In instances such as these, costs may not be easily determined except in an analytic or catastrophic sense. In addition to providing a dangerous experience in a distant safe way, destructive processes can be captured on video so they only need to be performed once. An example of these would be an interactive videodisc application used in place of chemistry laboratory equipment that is too delicate or expensive for actual student use. In this instance, students would be allowed to experience experiments that are too hazardous or proceed too quickly or slowly for the students to run themselves (S. G. Smith, Jones, & Waugh, 1986). Similar reasoning is not uncommon as a rationale for many training simulators (Hays & Singer, 1989).

Zigerell (1991) echoed many of these general quality benefits in his historical review of the evolution of telecourse endeavors and their associated program formats or production techniques. He observed the evolution of two realms of programming that have educational value to different audiences. One is the more expensive, broadly educational program of interest to general TV broadcast audiences. Examples are highly visual, general documentary style programs or public broadcasting programs that provide intellectually respectable alternatives to programs on commercial channels. This general style of educational television can be distinguished from more professor-centered courses that appeal to formal students who are credit oriented. The better programs of this type are not so much TV programs as enhanced or simulated classroom lectures that attempt to go beyond straight lectures by exploiting some alternatives offered by the medium. So long as they are relevant to an educational goal, these alternatives involve a mix of formats that are preferred by students. This mix of formats in either realm of programming includes interviews, guest expertise, on-location films, film inserts, simulations, or even occasional drama, which together complement the curriculum with concrete or interesting experiences. Zigerell also touched on a theme we develop later. In achieving a polished professional production to reduce the dullness of monotonous talking-head lectures, the use of irrelevant material more appropriate to entertainment or the overuse of slick techniques used for their own sakes may go beyond what is needed for student interest or learning.

ECONOMICS OF TELEVISION-CENTERED EDUCATION

The comparable educational effectiveness of television-centered and conventional instruction leaves decisions among media to be based on other criteria such as system costs and convenience (Jamison, Klees, & Wells, 1976, 1978). The literature on costs includes more formal economic studies primarily concerned with the cost structure of mass education, and ones providing some generalizations about costs of different media and transmission methods.

Cost Analysis

Methods

Cost–benefit and cost-effectiveness studies use comparative methods that differ primarily in the outcome evaluated (H. M. Levin, 1988). Cost–benefit or efficiency studies assess outcomes in terms of their comparative monetary values, comparing costs to available resources or income or to the costs of alternative educational systems. Cost-effectiveness studies assess outcomes in educational terms, by comparing the costs of obtaining a given amount of achievement. Both rely on adequate descriptive data from cost accounting and budget reports and on predictive methods for analyzing and estimating costs (Wilkinson, 1982).

Although there is no shortage of methods available for performing cost analyses of benefits or effectiveness, several factors reduce the value of prior cost studies for providing clear-cut prospective guidance (Carnoy & Levin, 1975; Maher, 1982). The comparability between studies is often reduced because individual studies reflect highly specific features of an implementation. Comparability is additionally reduced by incomplete or unsystematically collected basic data lacking in sufficient detail, changes in costs over time, varying predictive assumptions possibly involving underestimates, and obscuring compensations from other sources such as subsidies or common overhead and facilities. As a consequence, it is not uncommon for such costs to be reported in terms of ranges and for practical guidance on media selection costs to be reduced to general terms such as high, medium, or low (e.g., W. H. Allen, 1967; Chu & Schramm, 1975; Schramm, 1977).

Cost Categories and Terminology

Costs are owed to many sources, which are in turn affected as a function of a number of other system variables. Costs can be for personnel such as faculty, support staff and general administration, facilities, supplies, equipment, maintenance, replacements, instructional development, and access charges such as cable leases and air time. These costs in turn vary in terms of system variables such as the number of sites, students, teachers, hours of instruction, and lifetime factors related to length of use and temporal changes in costs.

There are numerous ways to summarize, categorize, and subdivide these costs (Bates, 1987; Haeghen, 1981; Head & Buchanan, 1981; Jamison et al., 1976, 1978; Jamison & Klees, 1975; Kiesling, 1979; Mace, 1982; Maher, 1982; McCabe, 1979; Van Der Drift, 1980). One common division is between relatively fixed *initial* costs for purchases or development and *recurrent* or ongoing yearly costs. Costs are also commonly characterized as *fixed* or *variable* costs when they are viewed in terms of the extent to which they change as a function of the amount usage.

Initial costs have a useful lifetime beyond their purchase; for example, start-up capital costs for equipment and facilities at either the central production site or the local delivery sites. Costs for the development and production of instruction are also initial costs when they are reused in subsequent distributions; for example, telecourses that are recorded and subsequently broadcast or distributed on tape. Initial costs can vary considerably between different media; for example, in terms of the transmission equipment involved or the magnitude of a production that could range from a simple televised talking-head lecture to a high-quality television production. Initial production costs differ little whether they are subsequently delivered by live television or are delivered by tape. These costs are fixed in the sense that their usage by many or just a few students does not alter the initial cost outlays for capital equipment, facilities, or productions subsequently reused.

Costs are recurrent when they are ongoing expenditures related to operating an instructional system. Costs that reoccur on a yearly basis are related to delivery, transmission, distribution, maintenance, expansion, and salaries. When operation of a system extends over time, recurrent yearly costs are the source of most expenditures and can exceed initial expenditures. Some recurrent costs may also be fixed, such as those for services unrelated to the amount of usage (e.g., leased lines). Costs are variable when they reflect changes in usage and demand. Variable costs are primarily instructional delivery costs that change with the number of students and hours of instruction, which in turn affect the number of sites, channels, instructors, courses, and videotapes. Recurrent costs can include additional capital equipment when the size of an operation changes.

Personnel salaries are a significant source of variable costs. They increase much more with the number of students in traditional face-to-face instruction than in television-centered systems using fewer instructors for more students. Changes in costs over time characteristically show that personnel costs are most subject to increase whereas the costs for equivalent equipment purchased at a later time tend to decline.

Finally, these cost categories may be interpreted over some lifetime of a media system, with a primary concern being the extent to which high usage supports the system. Actual recurrent costs during a year may be averaged with or without the initial fixed costs. Resources for initial fixed costs must be found for expenditure early in a project. Their relative long-term impact is reduced over the total life cycle of a system to the extent that greater subsequent usage reduces the average cost. The economy of scale reflected in terms relative to the number of students is variously expressed as the cost per student, cost per student per course, or cost per student per hour of instruction. The comparability of such averages between studies is often limited. This is because they may reflect different implementations of units and course length between institutions, differences in what cost items have been included, and the use of differing schemes applied to groups of school systems such as redistributions of broadcasts or tapes. Maher (1982) collected such averages from many studies but found such wide variability that he was unable to reach conclusions about the actual costs of delivery systems.

Representative System Costs and Characteristics

These conceptions of media cost structures allow several generalizations from the literature on educational media and technology. Some of the more notable cost relations concern the importance of an economy of scale based on usage and demand, the magnitude of fixed capital and development costs, the high cost of operation with larger interactive media, the high cost of personnel, and the interchange of personnel and system costs when a mass education technology is employed (Bates, 1987; Kiesling, 1979; Mace, 1982; Maher, 1982; Rumble, 1982, 1987).

Basic Cost Relations in Mass Education

The cost structure of technologically based learning systems for mass or distance education involves relatively large fixed costs and relatively lower variable costs in contrast to conventional learning systems that involve higher variable costs relative to fixed costs (Jamison et al., 1976; Laidlaw & Layard, 1974; Mace, 1982; Rumble, 1982, 1987; Wagner, 1972, 1977). The relationship of relatively smaller variable than fixed costs for distance education produces a lower average cost as the number of students rises compared to conventional systems in which more students lead to larger variable costs. In effect, the advantage of distance education lies in substituting capital for labor or in converting variable direct instruction costs to fixed costs. That is, fixed costs unrelated to the number of students in the form of a multimedia publishing enterprise centralizing delivery and production of teaching materials are substituted for the variable costs of conventional education where staff and student numbers are closely related. The greater decline in marginal costs of each extra student for distance education relative to conventional systems depends on large numbers of students to achieve the benefit relative to the inherent capital, production, and transmission or distribution costs.

Cost Comparisons of Distance and Conventional Education

On the whole, the economic studies of distance education indicate that its per student costs are comparable with or less than the per student costs of conventional campus-based colleges. Costs per graduate tend to be less favorable because many distance education populations are often less degree oriented than conventional education populations. A few representative instances cited here offer conclusions in terms of relative savings and reveal considerable variability in costs. Although not all such endeavors have been successful, the general cost analysis relations discussed earlier play in the success of such systems (additional examples are provided in case studies given in Educational Policy Research Center, 1976; Jamison & Klees, 1975; Jamison et al., 1976, 1978; Rumble, 1982, 1987; Zigerell, 1979).

McCabe (1979) contrasted the mix of cost categories of traditional education with those for television-centered or telecourse distance education. His estimates were given in relative terms within each type of education for community colleges and they are generally similar to figures from other studies. With traditional instruction, he estimated institutional support costs to be about 50% and the remainder to be direct instruction costs, consisting of 5% for instructional materials and 45% for instructional personnel salaries. Thus, in traditional instruction, 90% of the direct instruction costs were for salaries. With television-centered distance education the relative structure of delivery costs is altered. The institutional support figure drops from 50% to 35%, and salary costs drop from 45% to the range of 15% to 35%. Relative increases in costs are seen in the cost structure for instructional materials acquisition and modification, which rise to 15% to 20%, and new delivery system costs are incurred in the range of 5% to 15%. Thus, when students are off campus, institutional support costs are relatively less, salaries of personnel involved in direct delivery of instruction are less, and an increase is seen in new system, materials, and development costs. As a rule of thumb, McCabe estimated that television-centered per student per course costs are roughly 40% of those of a traditional course.

Kiesling (1979) performed an economic cost analysis of the University of Mid-America, which provides televised courses for which participating institutions accept credit. The capital costs directly related to instruction for this open university were found to be much larger than for traditional higher education institutions in Indiana, which had much higher teaching-related personnel costs. He concluded that for large undergraduate lecture courses, final per student costs for open universities would cost no more than traditional instruction and would most likely effect cost savings relative to traditional instruction of approximately 20% to 30%.

A series of cost studies of the British Open University included comparisons to conventional campus-based universities (Bates, 1987; Laidlaw & Layard, 1974; Lumsden & Ritchie, 1975; Mace, 1978; Rumble, 1987; Wagner, 1972, 1977). Roughly one tenth of the costs are for a central faculty, one fifth for central administration, one fifth for broadcasting-related functions, one tenth for correspondence, and from one fifth to one third for functions related to face-to-face contact with students and administration at study centers. Televised instruction accounts for roughly 13% to 16% of the annual budget (S. Brown, 1983; S. Brown et al., 1982). Although numerous differences in the functions performed by the two systems have been noted, the general finding has been that the Open University is less costly because of the higher ratio of fixed to variable costs compared to traditional instruction. The cost reduction arises through lower direct contact with students brought about by the mass distribution of the instruction of a smaller centralized teaching staff. Compared to conventional campus-based universities, Open University per student costs were estimated to be about one third (or from one fourth to one half depending on the adjustment) and unit costs per graduate to be about one half (Wagner, 1972, 1977). Variable costs were substantially below those of conventional universities, and within the Open University variable costs appear to be about one third that of fixed costs (Laidlaw & Layard, 1974; Lumsden & Ritchie, 1975; Wagner, 1972, 1977). Although larger enrollments should result in lower costs in such a system, reductions in average costs were mitigated when the number of smaller specialized courses were increased to offer greater student choice (Wagner, 1977).

The variability observed in the benefits of distance education is highlighted by a study of the University of the Air of Japan (UAJ) in which it was compared to several types of traditional institutions (Muta & Sakamoto, 1989). Costs for salaries at UAJ were lower than those at national, public, and private conventional universities. UAJ salaries were about one third of the delivery costs, compared to about three fourths for these conventional universities. The cost per student at UAJ was two fifths, one half, and three fourths that of the three types of conventional universities. Although the UAJ per student cost was lower, the cost per graduate was not lower than those for conventional universities because of the wider range of student goals found in a distance education population.

A number of case studies of distance education programs in developing countries do not generally offer a comparison with existing conventional programs (Jamison & Klees, 1975; Jamison et al., 1976, 1978; Rumble, 1982). Several case studies used instructional radio, which was judged to be about one fifth the cost of instructional television. For instructional radio, higher reported costs per student were achieved with several thousand students and lower costs were achieved with several hundred thousand students. For instructional television, the costs were about three to five times as expensive as those for instructional radio, with the lower figures being associated with nearly a million students in a reasonably compact geographical area. Jamison and Klees (1975) concluded that "the heavily front-loaded costs and rear-loaded utilization of technology projects results in a requirement that projects last 10–20 years to allow unit costs to fall to a reasonable level" (p. 375).

Rumble (1982) offered observations on the number of students needed to operate distance education universities. He concluded that they begin to reap the economies of scale beyond about 35,000 to 40,000 students and are on par with conventional universities as they approach 20,000 students. He commented that they are probably not cost efficient below 10,000 although they may still be justifiable on noneconomic grounds. These magnitudes should not be confused with the smaller numbers required for more local applications, such as using telecourses in conjunction with a conventional institution's regular courses.

Costs for comparable alternative methods are often examined in terms of a "break-even" point. This is the point at which the cost of a method for a given number of students matches the income available (Mace, 1982; Maher, 1982). Zigerell (1986) offered a practical suggestion for determining this point in the absence of large cost analyses. He suggested a quick break-even point calculation of dividing the sum of the course acquisition and support costs by the average student cost for an equivalent conventional classroom course as an estimate of how many students must be enrolled in a telecourse for it to be equivalently cost beneficial. He observed that additional students can be served at a marginal cost once this break-even point has been reached.

The cost advantages of mass or distance education can be undermined by several factors. These are either increases in variable costs related to the number of students or costs that add to existing costs (Jamison et al., 1978; McCabe, 1979; Rumble, 1982, 1987; Wilkinson, 1982). In systems where a wider range of courses is desired for more advanced students, such specialized courses often drive up costs as a consequence of the smaller enrollments. Similarly, variable costs directly related to the number of students drive costs up. Examples of re-introducing cost elements that vary directly with the number of students include costs for tutors and counselors, or media costs related to distributions to individual students. Compared to media designed as replacements, media provided as supplements to conventional instruction can also increase costs. Thus, supplementing the efforts of a classroom teacher by adding media results in additive costs unless some change is made in the student–teacher ratio. Adding such media may be driven by other noncost benefits and their costs vary with the selectivity of the application. To the extent that media such as television-centered systems involve redesign or replacement of classroom instruction, the cost benefits will be greater than when added to unchanged existing cost elements.

Sharing relationships within and between organizations are frequently a consideration in distance education and television-centered systems. This is particularly true for smaller operations, because sharing enables costs to be borne by many (Bates, 1987; Educational Policy Research Center, 1976; Maher, 1982; Zigerell, 1979, 1986, 1991). Whether a technological infrastructure already exists within an organization for other purposes or can be shared between organizations can have an important effect on costs, that is, because new additions then become marginal costs on an already established system. Such structures or sharing can enable organizations to participate by reducing large capital investments for equipment, facilities, and communications network access, as well as provide relationships with consortiums or public broadcasting organizations. Finally, it has been repeatedly noted that successful endeavors depend on high-level support within an implementing organization.

Production and Delivery Costs and Characteristics

Television-centered media differ substantially in costs for development and delivery. The ability to initially opt for a medium can be affected by its costs for development, production, equipment, and personnel. These are generally large initial fixed costs required to enable subsequent delivery and distribution. Whereas fixed costs are generally not related to the amount of subsequent usage, costs for delivery and distribution involve variable costs that are affected by the number of student usages. Decisions implied by these cost relations may be altered when they are additionally considered in terms of the relative advantages and disadvantages of a delivery system in the context of a specific implementation.

Bates (1987) summarized production cost experiences within the context of the British Open University relative to conventional face-to-face lectures. He estimated that rough fixed production costs for televised lectures are two to five times as costly, print-based materials are 2 to 10 times as costly, and high-quality TV programs are 20 to 50 times as costly. Although production costs are fixed, in that they do not vary with the number of students, expected usage still needs to be considered in initiating production. Where available, it is generally more economical to buy materials and services than to produce them inhouse unless warranted by sufficient volume. He estimated that it was not economical to produce higher quality television unless a course could average at least 500 students a year, or at least 3,000 or more in total. The costs of maintaining an existing course also need to be considered, which Wagner (1977) estimated to be about one tenth the cost of developing a new course. Bates noted that the variable costs for delivering TV broadcasts are minimal compared to such variable costs as dubbing and mailing materials, which can become expensive because they vary directly with the number of students and programs. Wagner (1975) found that unit costs decline with increasing numbers of students in a nontutored videotape instruction program where tapes of classes were distributed to college students at remote industrial locations. The economic liability of increasing the number of sites was shown to be offset to the extent that new students were added.

Acquisitions of preproduced programs are the common alternative to producing programs for many schools. When the costs of such programs are high, purchases on a per use basis are a means of accommodating smaller budgets. Films are more expensive than tapes and many distributors of educational 16mm films have transferred them to videotape, with the costs dropping at least by half (Herx, 1986; Reider, 1985). The higher cost of films previously led to the creation of centralized film libraries shared by schools, but the lower cost of tapes has made it possible for local schools to conveniently maintain their own libraries. Herx (1986) indicated that it has become very common for schools using instructional television to deliver programs with videotape recordings instead of direct off-air broadcasts. Reider (1985, 1987b) described a large videotape program in Baltimore County where purchases of 16mm films were discontinued in favor of videotapes. The program was enabled by outfitting the average school with about seven VCRs. Taped programs were initially purchased with duplication rights. The bottleneck created by duplicating tapes and the associated costs eventually led the district to simply make quantity purchases of original copies from distributors.

As with production costs, there are also large differences between different delivery or transmissions methods in terms of both their costs and associated advantages. One comparative evaluation of instructional television costs illustrates some of the basic patterns (Educational Policy Research Center, 1976; another earlier example of this approach is reviewed in Schramm, 1977). This study made a set of estimates comparing transmission methods for a very large system assumed to consist of 1,400 schools. Microwave, satellite, and cable methods were a little more than twice as costly as public television broadcasts. An extreme use of tapes to deliver public television broadcasts by routinely copying and mailing them was estimated to be nearly five times as costly as broadcasts. However, these costs of a purely taped system would be substantially reduced if tapes were subsequently reused by sharing and could be reduced by half if mixed with a cable system. Whereas over-the-air broadcasting requires only a standard television set for reception, satellite and microwave techniques were noted for their high initial capital costs and their need to be intensively used to be cost beneficial. Cable was deemed a less costly choice than these to the extent that a system was available in an area. Cable offers greater channel capacity than receiving broadcasts and involves smaller capital outlays, although its costs can depend on the details of local cost arrangements.

Local closed circuit TV within a college could be considered to represent a low end of delivery system costs. This type of system may be quite affordable, with a break-even point for usage ranging from 200 to 350 students for large lecture classes (Schramm, 1977). At the high end, different modes of satellite transmission for interactive television can involve major differences in costs (Bailey et al., 1989; Simpson et al., 1991b, 1993). Systems using full two-way transmissions of video and audio were noted to be significantly more costly than one-way video systems where audio talk-back can be more economically accomplished by using regular phone lines. More recent high-speed land-line technologies now provide a long-distance alternative to satellites for a limited number of sites.

In comparing delivery or transmission methods, cost differences can be mitigated when they are also considered along with their relative strengths and weaknesses in a specific implementation (Educational Policy Research Center, 1976; Maher, 1982). For example, broadcasting was seen as a good choice for high-density population areas, satellite delivery was seen as effective with remote populations distributed over large areas, cable was seen as good for multichannel distribution when a cable system was in place, and videotape was noted to offer scheduling flexibility and variety in program choice. Over-the-air transmissions were noted to have the liability of being direct-delivery technologies where materials must be used at the time of transmission and therefore have scheduling problems and lack of local choice. Although videotapes require physical distribution, which can involve costs that vary with the number of sites, they offer greater flexibility and may be less expensive when shared or when an initial small investment is desired. Maher (1982) observed that open broadcasting, videotape, and satellites have become inherently mixed-mode delivery systems used in combination. For example, transmissions can include tapes combined with live teacher presentations, or broadcast telecourses may be taped for later use so that students have the opportunity to review programs or to view programs missed during the broadcast schedule.

One concern with the higher cost media used in open universities is that their budgetary role is proportionately greater than the role they represent in terms of students' total study time (Rumble, 1987). Several studies at the British Open University have explored cost trade-offs among combinations of various media such as broadcasts, repeat broadcasts, mailed materials, and audio. S. Brown (1983) and Grundin (1983) reported on a videotape loan program in which tapes were provided on demand as replacements for a second repeat broadcast of a lesson. Lending videotapes increased program viewings by 11% over single transmissions, compared to the 8% achieved through repeat broadcasts. Costs were reduced by 60% to 70% in substituting tapes for the repeat broadcasts because fewer people watched repeat broadcasts or borrowed the videotapes. S. Brown (1983) estimated a potentially cost-beneficial strategy in which both broadcasts would be replaced with tapes for low-volume courses, tapes could be used instead of repeat broadcasts for medium-volume courses, and two broadcasts alone could be used for high-volume courses. The costs of dubbing and mailing videotapes were estimated to be significant enough with medium-size courses that they could exceed single transmission costs if all students received all tapes.

Grundin (1983) compared the cost benefits of broadcast TV with radio broadcasts and "audio–vision" packages consisting of a combination of audiotape and printed visual materials. The cost differences among these are substantial, with a 25-minute program being 10 times more costly to produce for TV than for radio (Laidlaw & Layard, 1974). The relative distribution costs within the production center were about 90% for television and video compared to 10% for radio and audiotapes (Grundin, 1983). Considering these media in terms of student helpfulness ratings showed that the tape packages were rated slightly more helpful than the TV broadcasts and the radio broadcasts were rated as the least helpful. Listening rates for audiotapes were 34% higher than for the radio broadcasts. The higher listening rates of tapes and the lower helpfulness ratings of broadcasts were interpreted to reflect the greater personal control characteristics offered by the tapes. Mailing audiotapes was estimated to be cheaper than radio broadcasts as long as there were not more than 1,500 students per course, and about three fourths of the courses had volumes below this point. Production and distribution costs for the audio–vision packages were from one fourth to one half as costly as broadcast TV. Because students spent more time using the tapes, the cost per student medium contact hour indicated TV was five times as expensive as the audio–vision packages.

Costs related to travel and per diem are additional costs unique to some forms of education involving remote or widely dispersed locations. In the case of instructors and military and industrial students, costs are incurred when they are not working or are traveling long distances. Student costs are often not prominent in studies of general education where the focus is on the costs to an educational institution. In addition, costs may not even be calculable with some rural students in the sense that they might not even attempt to receive training because access is prohibited by long-distance travel. Several interactive television studies provide examples of considering travel, per diem, and personnel costs in rural areas or for organizations with widely dispersed personnel. Rule, DeWulf, and Stowitschek (1988) reported on an interactive television project that provided in-service teacher training in a rural area. They found the costs of travel and staff time to be reduced in comparison to estimates of providing similar training by traveling to the remote sites. Simpson et al. (1990, 1991a) compared estimated travel and per diem costs for Navy instructors and students with the costs for a two-way land-line video teletraining system between San Diego and San Francisco. This system configuration was estimated to be more costly than sending an instructor to the remote site, and both were less costly than having students travel to an instructor.

Rupinski and Stoloff (1990) reported on the costs of an East Coast Navy satellite video teletraining system using both two-way video and audio. They found that the operating budget for the system during a 6-month period was less than the costs that would have been incurred for travel and per diem of students. They also found shorter courses to yield greater savings because they permitted more personnel to use the system over a given period of time.

Stoloff (1991) made a more detailed cost analysis of potentially enlarging the Navy system to other sites including the West Coast. The potential training courses identified were shorter specialized fleet type training courses where about 15 to 20 students would temporarily be away from their duty station. The break-even point for an expanded system was estimated to occur during the third year of the assumed 5-year life cycle. An initial full implementation of the system was shown to be less costly than incremental expansion of sites because averted travel and per diem costs were realized at a later time. Although equipment purchases involved greater initial costs, leasing was found to be more costly overall. Although leasing offered flexibility in making later technical changes to the system, including additional purchase costs still provided a substantial margin of benefit over leasing. Relative to conventional training costs, increasing the number of projected sites yielded greater savings for the satellite system than for exporting instructors to the sites. Within limits of classroom size, increased savings resulting from increasing the number of students was suggested to be achieved better by increasing class size in preference to adding additional sites. Stoloff offered general rules of thumb indicating that adding a new site should be supported by a demand of at least 400 students a year, and adding additional classrooms to an existing site should be supported by at least 200 students. Consistent with other studies (Educational Policy Research Center, 1976), uneven demand at sites for particular courses of varying lengths was noted for potentially producing inefficiencies in scheduling that could result in excess capacity.

The television-centered and distance education literature offers a few findings relevant to organizations who employ students with regard to widely dispersed sites, travel, and videotapes (S. Brown 1983; Grundin 1983; Rumble, 1987; Rupinski & Stoloff, 1990; Stoloff, 1991). First, the distance education studies indicate that providing specialized courses in areas where there are relatively few students is not generally cost efficient (Rumble, 1987). Second, students are generally relocated to a centralized school site when they must attend lengthy courses. However, when training is for shorter periods away from a home site, then significant student travel and per diem costs are a concern (Rupinski & Stoloff, 1990; Simpson et al., 1990, 1991a, 1991b, 1993; Stoloff, 1991). Such costs can potentially be avoided by using transmission systems such as satellites that can span widely dispersed areas, so long as they are used intensely. Examples of intense usage could include tight scheduling of teletraining classrooms or using them for high-volume courses that are short and occur frequently. Intense usage and avoiding travel and per diem costs make the costs of such a system more feasible for specialized courses given intermittently. Finally, this literature suggests that, although videotapes may be costly when provided to large numbers of people, they may be cost efficient when provided to a smaller total number of students (S. Brown 1983; Grundin 1983; Rumble, 1987). The total benefit varies with the magnitude of the initial fixed costs for producing taped programs, would be less when these costs must be borne by only a small number of students in a specialized course, and would be relatively greater to the extent that tapes are used as an alternative delivery medium for a subset of a larger population or are reused by many students at a site. The ability to view tapes when desired is an additional benefit when broadcast scheduling conflicts with other work-related events.

Cost-Effectiveness

In general, the pattern of equivalent educational efficacy revealed in the reviews of educational television leaves the selection of media to cost, access, control, and convenience factors. As noted by Bates (1987), "It is much easier to discriminate between media on the basis of access or cost, than it is on teaching effectiveness" (p. 10). Formal cost-effectiveness studies are rare (studies of the cost of obtaining an amount of achievement). This is primarily because care must be taken to observe achievement in systematic and comparable ways and reliable costs associated with those same conditions must be available. An illustration of weighting educational outcomes and costs is provided by H. M. Levin (1988) with other than video media (see also Fletcher, Hawley, & Piele, 1990). Estimated costs for a period of time were divided by estimated educational achievement for the same period of time yielding an estimate of cost per unit of achievement (e.g., estimated annual cost to obtain an additional month of student achievement per year of instruction). Such a measure can then be compared between different media, methods, or changes in their quantity. This method was used to illustrate that peer tutoring was more cost-effective than computer-assisted instruction, which in turn was more cost-effective than adult tutoring, longer school days, and smaller class sizes.

In reviewing studies of interactive videodisc instruction, Fletcher (1990) identified 13 instances within the studies where it was possible to obtain a cost ratio. The ratio was calculated by dividing the costs of an experimental treatment by the costs of a control treatment. All of the ratios were less than one, indicating lower costs for the interactive videodisc instruction than for conventional instruction. Many of these were training studies involving a comparison with the use of actual equipment; fewer were comparisons with traditional instruction. The studies did differ in what costs were considered, with five cost ratios being only for initial investment, four for operating and support costs, and four for some combination of the two. Although Fletcher found interactive videodisc instruction less costly and more effective in terms of achievement, the studies did not employ cost-effectiveness methods that varied the costs of inputs in conjunction with effectiveness outputs.

Few studies have done such true cost-effectiveness analyses of costs and educational outcomes in the same study. Several studies reported here dealt with effectiveness and costs separately and then combined them verbally, rather than combining them in terms of cost per an educational outcome. H. M. Levin (1988) and Fletcher (1990) cautioned that data should be drawn from the same comparative study to ensure that the same cost and effectiveness models have been used. They also indicate that combining meta-analysis effectiveness results with cost data from separate sources may not be appropriate. What seems more common in the literature is an acknowledgment of the idea of cost-effectiveness and an attempt to arrive at a more informed judgment or opinion by rationally using perceived effectiveness and estimated costs from separate sources (Mace, 1978). An example of this from the Open University reports argued that television broadcasts were less cost-effective than other media such as audiotapes with visuals because these audio–vision packages were both less costly and received higher student ratings (Grundin, 1983; Mace, 1978). Likewise, Fletcher (1990) found videodisc instruction to be both effective and cost beneficial, but judging it cost-effective is only a reasoned extension because the data were not obtained from the same studies to allow expression of the costs per unit of achievement.

3 Processing Visual and Verbal Information

This chapter reviews learning studies in which visual information was combined with verbal information in either auditory or textual form. Dynamic video presentations are particularly characterized by the combination of visual and auditory information in close temporal sequence. The primary focus of this chapter is on how those two sources of information affect comprehension in dynamic presentations. The first part of this chapter examines this focus under three subtopics: educational studies on combining visual and verbal material, studies of visual and verbal information in news broadcasts, and studies that bear on the interrelation of comprehension and attention. The final part of this chapter briefly reviews the literature on the use of static visual illustrations in text in terms of several generalizations relating to the use of visuals in video presentations.

PROCESSING VISUAL AND VERBAL INFORMATION IN DYNAMIC PRESENTATIONS

Visual and auditory information are used in typical educational video presentations in a multiple media format that requires the viewer to watch still or dynamic visuals and listen to narration and other sounds. Thus, television comprehension would be defined in terms of the ability to process parallel audio and visual information channels and to integrate their information semantically (D. R. Anderson & Lorch, 1983). Optimizing this bisensory presentation to enhance the delivery of these symbolic forms of information involves careful selection of the sensory mix so that learners are not overloaded with information (Hanson, 1989). This is particularly important in transient presentations over which learners have little control, and may be even more of a concern in commercial broadcasts characterized by a fast pace (Singer & Singer, 1983; J. C. Wright et al., 1984).

Comparing Components of Visual-Verbal Presentations

The general question addressed in the studies reviewed in the following was whether learning outcomes are affected by the concurrent presentation of visual and verbal information in video or film. This was typically accomplished by comparing the combination of these sources of information with their separate components. Other approaches varied the order of presenting the components, varied the amount of redundancy or competition between the components, or assessed the extent to which learning from these sources of information was affected by learner characteristics such as age and visual/spatial capabilities.

Order of Visual and Verbal Presentations

Three studies illustrate that learning is affected by the order in which visual and verbal information is presented. An early study by Gropper (1966) taught physical science concepts to eighth graders with nonoverlapping text or visual movie segments. These segments were presented in either order by serially intermixing them or by presenting them as entire visual or textual segments. The nature of the concepts being taught allowed them to be presented visually or by text employing technical language augmenting the concepts. Test scores increased more when the visual material preceded the text than when the text preceded the visuals—either in segments on the same topic or as entire segments. The visual–text presentation sequence also resulted in shorter study times. Students of below-average ability also profited most from the visual information. A subset of students in the study who passively watched the visual presentation performed poorer than those who made active responses predicting physical outcomes of demonstrations. Visually presented information appeared to benefit performance on either visual or verbal tests, whereas verbally presented information was primarily beneficial for the verbal tests. For the materials used in this study, visuals appeared to offer a more readily encoded and explicit form of instruction.

Baggett and Ehrenfeucht (1983) systematically varied the order in which visual and two forms of verbal information were presented to college students. A narrated biology film (full audio–visual) was compared with several components of information from the film—the motion film given visually with no sound (silent visual-only), or verbal information from the film in either a written textual form or in the form of audio-only narration. Each of these two verbal forms of information was presented before or after the silent visual-only motion film. Presenting the text version prior to the visual-only silent film, or in the reverse order, yielded a level of recall that was similar to that with the full audio–visual version of the film. Recall was affected by the order in which the audio-only narration and visual-only silent film versions were presented and both were worse than the full audio–visual film. Performance was most impaired when the audio-only narration was given before the visual-only silent film was seen. Thus, compared to the simultaneously presented audio and visual information in the film, there was no advantage to sequential presentation of text and visual information even though it could be studied twice as long. However, when information is presented by audio, there is a disadvantage to having it precede the viewing of visual information—it is better to hear a narrative after seeing visual information. The authors suggested that auditory verbal information is not as readily retrieved or associated with visuals as is textual verbal information, which may be processed relatively more like visual information. Taken together, these results suggest that there is little competition for resources when visual and auditory information are presented simultaneously.

Baggett (1984) varied the temporal order of presenting audio and visual information within a filmed presentation, in contrast to the previously mentioned studies where order was varied with larger blocks of information. College students were presented audio narration and visual information at the same time or were given these presentations 7, 14, or 21 seconds before or after one another. The audio narration presented the names and uses of the parts of a mechanical device shown in the visuals. The length of the delay between visual and auditory presentations was a significant factor in recalling the names on either an immediate or 7-day delayed test. Performance was found to be best when the visual and auditory information were presented simultaneously and when the visual information preceded the auditory information by 7 seconds. Those conditions presenting the audio before the visuals produced the worst performance, declining as more time elapsed between the audio narration and the visuals. Overall, as more time elapsed between the audio and visuals, recall was reduced more when the audio narration preceded the visuals than when the visuals preceded the narration. The findings with this task suggest that the visual information was of relatively greater importance for comprehension than was the auditory information supporting and elaborating it.

Equivalence of Content

Comparisons between visual and verbal presentations may require judgment or intuition in attempting to render their content equivalent (Baggett, 1989b; Friedman, 1993). Many of the studies reported in the following sections attempted to take account of this stimulus equivalence problem in one way or another. Two studies particularly focused on how the equivalence of the two types of information can be empirically derived to better assure that the same concepts are available from either source.

Baggett (1979) developed structurally equivalent visual and auditory versions of a film in order to assess the semantic information carried by these sources. She experimentally derived a structurally equivalent audio version of the short story given in the film *The Red Balloon*, which contained no dialogue. College students wrote summaries of the episodes from the story after viewing or hearing the story, either immediately or 7 days later. Summaries written immediately after the presentation were found to be structurally similar for either visual or auditory conditions. However, the visual content was more memorable because recall after 7 days deteriorated more for the listeners than for those viewing the film. Baggett and Ehrenfeucht (1982) also developed an empirically equivalent narrated audio version of the narrative movie story *The Unicorn in the Garden*. Using a model yielding estimates of the information encoded, they concluded that the movie or narration versions were encoded equally well by college students, but that the movie was encoded better than narration by junior high school children.

Audio–Visual Comparisons Using Children's Stories

The studies in this section all include some comparison that involves a combination of visual and verbal information, typically between audio–visual and audio presentations. These studies were also primarily with children and used stories or segments from children's television. These comparisons are relevant to the question of whether multiple sources of information enhance learning or possibly compete with one another. These studies also show a congruence between the kinds of information presented and tested in the sense that visual and verbal measures reveal details of their source of presentation.

Nugent (1982) compared several components of video presentations and generally found better retention for stories presented via the combination of visual and auditory information than those presented via a single information source. In one experiment, redundant information was presented by either video, audio, or text shown in the video. Fourth, fifth, and sixth graders were either presented each of these alone, two of them combined, or all three presented together. Test performance generally increased as more channels of information were added, and visual information combined with either of the other inputs maximized learning. In a second experiment, narrative and video were constructed to be relevant to one another, but not redundant. Video, audio, or audio–video presentations were given to fourth and fifth graders who were then tested by questions on the visual or narrative information. On visual information questions, the video and audio–video presentations led to better performance than the audio narration presentation. On narrative information questions, the audio and audio–video presentations led to better performance than the video presentation. In other words, combined audio–video presentations led to performance on either visual or verbal information that was as good as that with audio-only or visual-only presentations. Thus, visuals did not interfere with learning the narrative information, and the audio presentations did not interfere with learning visual information. Taken together, these experiments indicated that visual, audio, and textual channels containing the same information allowed learning from each, but learning was maximized by combining pictures with text or audio. When less redundant information was given so that some information was more specific to a channel, visual and audio information did not interfere with one another.

Pezdek and Hartman (1983) presented televised segments to young children by either audio, video, or a combination of the audio and visual tracks. The content in the segments shown contained information that had been conveyed primarily in the audio, in the visuals, or involved some coordinated relationship between both audio and visual information. Similar performance was found with audio–visual and audio presentations when audio information was tested, and both exceeded the visual presentation. Similar performance was found with audio–visual and visual presentations when visual information was tested, and both exceeded the audio presentation. This pattern was also found when the content involved relations between audio and video information. Thus, the level of comprehension found with the audio–visual presentations was closely approximated by either audio or visual track presentations when the tests targeted the same respective audio or visual information. In other words, segments containing primarily audio information did not have to be viewed, and segments containing primarily visual information did not have to be heard.

Hayes and Kelly (1984) tested the memory for the temporal order of events in video presentations that had been edited so that some sequences were given only with audio, with visuals, or with both audio and visuals. Temporal order was remembered best with the audio–visual presentation, followed by the visual presentation, and then the audio presentation. The audio–visual and visual presentations were not significantly different, but were both significantly better than the audio presentation. For the very young children in this study, visual information appeared to contribute more to the interrelation of televised sequences than did auditory information.

Pezdek, Lehrer, and Simon (1984) compared the performance of third- and sixth-grade school children who were given a story by audio-only narration, by an animated audio–visual video, or by having them read an illustrated version of the story. Similar performance was obtained when the story was presented either by television or text and performance with both of these was better than with the audio presentation.

Pezdek and Stevens (1984) presented 5-year-olds with segments of *Sesame Street* that had a video track, an audio track, the two tracks combined normally, or mismatched audio and video segments. The audio–video mismatch condition was found to reduce memory for audio information more than it did for memory of the visual information. Memory for the audio information was similar in the congruent audio–video match condition and in the audio-only condition. Thus, audio information may be more sensitive than video information to an incongruent mismatch, but video information does not interfere with processing audio information in simultaneous audio–video presentations typical of television programs. The results also suggest that video material appears to be more salient and memorable than audio material.

Meringoff (1980) gave grade-school children either an audio–video version of a story or one that was read from an illustrated book. The audio–video group remembered more story actions and drew inferences that were based more on the visual information. Those who were read the story recalled more story vocabulary and made more extrastory inferences based on general knowledge or personal experiences.

Beagles-Roos and Gat (1983) found that 6- to 10-year-old children differed in the kinds of information they learned from stories that were given by audio narration or by an audio–visual television presentation. Television viewers were better at recalling details from the stories, in remembering the order of events, and in making correct inferences about the behavior of story characters. Those who only heard the audio version were better able to recognize expressive language from the story, but their greater use of the verbal source of information for inferences was accompanied by the use of knowledge unrelated to that explicitly presented in the story. They concluded that children listening to the audio version processed the verbal information more deeply and used prior information to fill in details and make sense of the story. By contrast, the television viewers were able to process both audio and visual material as a whole, which produced fewer areas of ambiguity that required inferences beyond observed behavior.

Hayes, Kelly, and Mandel (1986) found that different kinds of information are retained from audio-only or audio–visual television presentations. Preschool children differed from college students when they retold stories given by these media. Children who listened to the audio-only version made more comprehension errors than did those who watched the audio–visual televised version, whereas adults' performance did not differ between the two presentations. The poorer performance of the children in the audio-only condition reflected primarily that information that was more central to the story. Those who listened to the audio-only version retold stories that included more dialogue and sound effects, but they also included more erroneous information and distorted details. Retention by those in the televised group reflected more visual action sequences. These findings were interpreted by the authors to mean that children hearing a narrative may be more likely to arrive at incorrect notions about a story's content than those whose comprehension is guided by video features.

Gibbons, Anderson, Smith, Field, and Fischer (1986) also presented very brief stories to 4- and 7-year-olds by either audio narration or audio–visual depictions of the actions of dolls. Both versions contained utterances of the characters, but the audio version described actions via narration, whereas the audio–visual version depicted the actions. Younger children recalled more following audio–visual presentations than audio presentations, whereas older children's recall differed little between the presentations. Actions were more salient because they were retained more often than utterances, particularly for the younger children. During recall, relevant inferences were the most common elaboration exceeding what was contained in the story, and these were more frequent for the audio–visual than the audio conditions.

Gaining Access to Audio–Visual Information

Two studies are notable in assessing viewer interest in receiving either audio or video information. Participants in both studies actively made responses in order to gain access to audio or video information.

A study by Rolandelli, Wright, Huston, and Eakins (1991) suggested the salience of visual information for young children watching cartoons. They gradually degraded the quality of the audio, video, or both audio and video and measured how quickly children acted to restore the quality to normal. Latencies to restore the quality to normal were systematically affected by the three degrade conditions, which were also found to have received equal amounts of visual attention (looking). Audio–video degrades were restored quicker than visual degrades, which were in turn restored faster than were audio degrades. Latency to restore either video or audio–video degrades was faster when they were looking at the screen than when they were not looking, but latency to restore audio degrades did not differ between looking and not looking. These results suggest that dual modality presentations maximize children's attention. An ancillary finding emerged from a second study by these authors in which they used a manipulation similar to the studies given in the previous section. A narrated video was found to increase auditory, visual, and inferential comprehension more than a nonnarrated video.

Somewhat different results were obtained in an earlier study by Ksobiech (1976). University students either saw video segments and made responses to maintain the presence of the audio or they heard the audio and made responses to maintain the video. Students receiving presentations for the purpose of an "examination" uniformly made more responses to maintain the audio (given continuous video) than they did to maintain the video (given continuous audio). This demand for maintaining the audio more than the video was substantially reduced or eliminated when the presentations were given for the purpose of "enjoyment." Visually oriented lecture material received somewhat more responses than did verbally oriented lecture material, but the responses to these types of material depended on the purpose of the presentation. A greater demand for the audio over the video was shown for the verbally oriented lecture material than for the visually oriented lecture material. These results differ from

Rolandelli et al. (1991), even when the most comparable conditions between them are considered. The Rolandelli et al. (1991) study showed quicker responses to restore video than audio, whereas Ksobiech found little difference in the demand for either audio or video among the visually oriented enjoyment conditions. Because Ksobiech used university students with material from a government course, the Rolandelli et al. finding suggests that the salience of visual information is related to their having used young children who viewed a cartoon for enjoyment.

Relationships With Skills and Abilities

Fewer studies than might be expected have related individual differences in ability to learning from video. Many of the studies throughout our review report general relationships between learning and individual differences in ability. Many of these relationships involved instructional conditions that W. H. Allen (1975) characterized as performing a compensatory function of greater aid to lower or middle-ability individuals. However, many of these findings result from implementing an instructional strategy that is conveyed in video in ways that are not particularly different from other media (e.g., structuring content, emphasizing relevant points, or encouraging participation and providing feedback). The studies given in the following relate individual differences in ability more specifically to video or film, and generally share a common emphasis on visually related content.

Two studies by Pezdek and her associates suggest that television comprehension is related to visual/spatial abilities, and that the general cognitive processes involved in reading and television comprehension come to overlap with increasing age (Pezdek et al., 1984; Pezdek, Simon, Stoeckert, & Kiely, 1987). In one study with junior and senior high school students, a positive relationship was found between comprehension of television news stories and reading comprehension of text versions of the same stories (Pezdek et al., 1987). The news items had visuals that were a dynamic part of the story shown. In contrast to these young adults, television and reading comprehension were not related with third- and sixth-grade school children, although reading and listening to audio narration were related (Pezdek et al., 1984). The positive relationship found with young adults was attributed to their having developed overlapping cognitive skills that were general to both reading and television comprehension (Pezdek et al., 1987). Younger viewers may show little relationship between television and text comprehension because they have not yet developed the more automatic decoding processes used in reading, skills that are little used in television comprehension. They are also possibly less familiar with some syntactic conventions of television.

In addition to the general comprehension processes suggested by the findings with young adults, Pezdek et al. (1987) also found television comprehension to be related to some more specific visual/spatial abilities. In a second study, the television comprehension scores obtained for the high school students in their first study were used to select those with high and low scores. These students were then given two tasks, a visual/spatial ability test in which paper folding had to be visualized and a picture–sentence verification task allowing spatial or verbal strategies to be inferred. Those individuals who performed poorly on the previous television comprehension test scored lower on visual/spatial ability and were more likely to use a verbally based strategy. Those who performed well on the television comprehension test scored higher on visual/spatial ability and were more likely to use an imagery-based strategy.

Koran, Snow, and McDonald (1971) provided teacher trainees with instruction on a classroom analytic questioning technique that they subsequently performed. The instruction involved modeling the skill and was presented either by a video portrayal or by a written transcript. Video modeling led to better performance on several measures. A complex set of findings was obtained when these performance measures were predicted from a host of previously collected ability measures. A test of memory for details in filmed scenes was positively related to better performance with the video modeling instruction, but unrelated to performance with written modeling. A hidden figures test was negatively related to performance following video modeling, but was positively related to performance following the written modeling instruction. Thus, ability in film memory was a positive benefit in learning from related video-based instruction. The interpretation of the relationships found with the hidden figures test was more tentative. It apparently involved a perceptual–analytic ability related to general fluid intelligence that was a better basis for learning from written material, particularly for those low in film memory.

Several experiments conducted by Salomon (1974, 1979; Salomon & Cohen, 1977) also reveal relationships between performance on tests related to visual ability and performance on learning tasks presented by video or slides. These experiments employed various pretest measures of visual ability that involved noticing or picking out details, recalling details, identifying missing items or gaps in visuals, and relating partial visuals to whole images. The relationship between performance and these ability or aptitude measures varied somewhat as a function of the kind of experimental treatment employed. However, the general pattern of results in the experiments showed that these visual ability measures were related to learning performance as measured by visually oriented posttests involving multiple-choice items, ordering, and recall of details.

Swann and Miller (1982) found a small effect on the memory for details of a video interview as a consequence of individual differences on a pretest of the vividness of imagery. For high visualizers, memory for the interview was improved by an audio–video presentation compared to an audio-only presentation. Low visualizers did not benefit from seeing the audio–video presentation.

Gibson (1947) compared three methods for teaching an aerial gunnery aiming technique to young men in World War II: a 15-minute sound animated training film, an illustrated training manual read for 30 minutes, and a 30-minute lecture using 19 slides from the booklet. Learning measured by a multiple-choice test showed that the filmed instruction was superior to the other two relatively similar methods even after 2 months. The relative benefit of these training methods was compared among students from the highest and lowest 30% of the overall course achievement distribution. Although good students performed best overall, the poorer students showed a greater relative gain with the film compared to the other two instructional methods. Gibson examined those test items differentiating the media and suggested that they were ones reflecting dynamic concepts, changing events, covarying relations, and providing a vicarious action experience. Thus, the generality of Gibson's positive findings with the film method might be qualified by observing that it was particularly congruent with instructional content that also involved highly spatial and dynamic material.

Relationships between individual differences and visually oriented material are also revealed in additional research covered under topics discussed later. The section examining the use of static illustrations in text reveals that individuals lower in general ability or prior knowledge generally receive a relatively greater benefit from illustrations so long as they are not too complex. Relationships with visual/spatial abilities and visually related content were also found in two studies examined later. Chute (1980) used color and monochrome presentations and found an instance where color was detrimental to those of lower spatial aptitude because it was apparently irrelevant to learning shapes. Blake (1977) used motion and animation to show chess moves and found that they were of benefit to individuals with low visual ability.

The effect of motion was also examined in a series of studies that assessed individual differences in general ability. An assortment of relatively conventional instructional film content was used in comparisons between a variety of motion and still films that were narrated in various ways or were silent (W. H. Allen, Cooney, & Weintraub, 1968; W. H. Allen, Daehling, Russell, & Nielsen, 1970; W. H. Allen & Weintraub, 1968). Individual differences were not particularly pronounced in those instances where these film modes affected performance. There was little relationship between learning from the various film conditions and general measures of the grade-school children's ability. With the exception of a beneficial effect of motion with content that involved serial ordering, the pattern of these findings support the idea that different presentation modes have little effect when used with very general kinds of instructional content. Thus, it would appear that the potential benefits of motion presentations in film or video, and any potential relationships with ability, depend on the use of content that is also dynamic, sequential, or visually oriented.

W. H. Allen (1975) reviewed these and a number of other earlier studies of individual differences in general ability with respect to a host of media. He observed an inconsistent pattern of instances where a medium led to proportionately better performance for either high- or low-ability individuals. He was led to the conclusion that "there is no easy answer to the problem of selecting the optimum presentation mode for a particular ability group" (p. 165). He suggested that an important consideration with regard to who might benefit from various media is whether a task calls upon an ability and whether the level of difficulty of the task exceeds these capabilities or supplements them. For example, those of higher ability might benefit and those of lower ability might be disadvantaged by fixed-paced, multichannel pictorial motion presentations that are perceptually complex and information laden. However, reducing the pace and information load could potentially be of more benefit to lower ability individuals when the presentation provides an explicit and concrete source of information that supplements their processing abilities.

Discussion of Components of Visual and Verbal Presentations

The studies reviewed generally support the idea of a benefit to simultaneous verbal and visual information when they are carefully matched. Combining visual and verbal information in video presentations generally leads to either equal or better learning compared to when these sources are given alone. These were typically comparisons of audio and audio–visual presentations. Studies varying the order of presenting visual and verbal information suggest the primacy of visual information and the need to carefully match the two sources of information. Learning is best when they are presented simultaneously or when the visuals precede the narration by up to 7 seconds. Presenting narration in advance of visuals appears to be detrimental.

Visual and verbal information each contribute to learning when tests are designed to measure the information unique to the source of their presentation. Thus, information from visual sources is reflected in tests tapping visual information and verbally presented information is reflected in verbal measures. The different kinds of information given in each source are difficult to compare directly, and attempts to equate their content may to some extent reduce the difference between the two. However, more detailed measures of what is learned tend to reflect the different kinds of information given in visual and audio presentations. Information from video is seen in the recall of visual and action details, whereas information from the audio is seen in the retention of various audio and linguistic details that tend to be accompanied by additional verbal embellishments.

Based on studies like these, Kozma (1991) concluded that "people can construct a mental representation of the semantic meaning of a story from either audio or visual information alone, but it appears that when presented together each source provides additional, complementary information that retains some of the characteristics of the symbol system of origin" (p. 192).

The finding that combined visual and audio information leads to better or equal learning in video presentations is generally interpreted to mean that these sources do not compete for processing resources. When a conflict exists, information in the audio may be more susceptible than that in the visuals, such as in the Pezdek and Stevens (1984) study where an audio–video mismatch reduced memory for information in the audio more than in the video. The studies reviewed here were characteristically typical of normal viewing conditions where audio and video did not conflict. This focus is more applicable to conventional classroom education than several other more theoretical lines of research (Dwyer, 1978; Hartman, 1961). Thus, simultaneously presenting different channels of unrelated or contradictory information with nonmeaningful materials in atypical learning tasks is a research focus distinct from facilitating student learning with coordinated visual and verbal information designed to complement one another. The studies reviewed here were also not particularly directed at theoretical inferences about basic mechanisms such as whether pictures and words are processed by single or dual input mechanisms and subsequently stored in single or multiple representational memory codes (Baggett, 1979; Clark & Salomon, 1986; Pavio, 1971). These issues remain to be resolved or reformulated, with preferred proposals being that information is either stored in the verbal or visual modality in which it is presented, or in a single conceptual memory storage model resulting from dual modality input processing.

A few studies found relationships between abilities and learning from visual presentations when the information being learned was also visually based. However, the bulk of the other findings were with children. These findings generally pertained to age-related individual differences and suggested a somewhat greater salience of visual information for younger children. Pezdek and colleagues (Pezdek, Lehrer, & Simon, 1984; Pezdek et al., 1987) suggested that the general cognitive processes involved in reading and television comprehension appear to come to overlap as learners develop skills with age. Children are still developing verbal skills so that more linguistically abstract verbal content is less comprehensible and there may be a greater reliance on visual information. Rolandelli (1989) observed that the visual modality may appear to be more effective for young children because it provides them with more concrete information. This would seem to be consistent with the general tendencies to remember more action-related content and to include more extrastory content in recalling information presented in narration than in visuals. Adults have more well-developed processing skills for both visual and verbal information that enable them to extract more information from the transient presentations typically encountered with television. The fast pace used in many commercial television programs may also hinder cognitive processing when viewers have less well-developed learning strategies (Singer & Singer, 1983). However, comprehension can be improved when programs employ a slower pace and greater continuity (J. C. Wright et al., 1984).

Learning from Television News Broadcasts

A number of studies have investigated the relationship between visual and verbal information in the context of television news broadcasts. Many of the more controlled laboratory studies of learning from news broadcasts have used news items for other purposes as a source of research stimuli. News clips are brief and easily arranged in controlled sequences, and a number of studies have used these items to evaluate the relative contribution of video and auditory information. Fewer studies have done so in naturalistic settings in order to assess incidental learning. Several general characteristics of news broadcasts are noted as a preliminary to examining these studies.

News broadcasts are one of the primary exceptions to the perception that adult television viewing is for entertainment purposes. Studies of home viewers generally show memory for news items to be poor. Viewer attention to television news is generally correlated with increased knowledge of news events (Chaffee & Schleuder, 1986). Although some data suggest that viewers watch the news for information (Berry, Gunter, & Clifford, 1981; Graber, 1990), a segment of viewers appear to watch regularly with little intent of being informed on current events (W. R. Neuman, 1976).

W. R. Neuman (1976) phoned households after the completion of the network news without the residents having prior knowledge that they would be questioned. Half of those viewers who had watched all or part of the newscast could remember no news stories even when prompted or quizzed for details. Their reported motivation for watching the news indicated that 12% watched to relax, 51% were casual viewers, and 17% watched to keep informed. Neuman found that, without prompting, viewers who watch to "keep informed" could only recall about 7% of the approximately 20 news stories per broadcast, or an average of 1½ news stories. Casual viewers recalled about 6% and viewers who watched "to relax" recalled less than 4%. Overall recall increased an additional 20% when viewers were prompted with a list of the headlines from the newscast. Katz, Adoni, and Parness (1977) also called viewers after news broadcasts and found 28% reported that they were attending to the news and 21% could not recall one news item. Stauffer, Frost, and Rybolt (1983) found attention to news programs was somewhat greater among viewers who had previously been phoned and asked to watch their favorite news program. Of an average of 13.3 news items from different network news programs, those who had been asked to watch recalled an average of 3.0 items, whereas others who had not been asked to watch recalled 1.9 items.

Typical television news stories are presented in such a way that comprehension is often difficult (Berry, Gunter, & Clifford, 1981; Graber, 1990; Gunter, 1980). The verbal stories are short, making it difficult to convey much information, to provide explanations, or to establish a context. Learning is also constrainted by the short duration of the visuals, the large number of visuals, and the number of visuals that represent stereotypes that are not related to verbal content.

Graber (1990) illustrated a number of these features in an analysis of one week of network news broadcasts on political topics. About half of the visuals were found to enhance what was being said, whereas the remaining half were categorized as presenting either irrelevant or redundant information in a routine or stereotypical way. Excluding shots of reporters, the most frequently used visual in 70% of the stories was a close-up of an identified person. She also found 33% of all stories were presented in less than 1 minute, and 79% in less than 3 minutes. When stories from the Public Broadcasting System (PBS) were excluded, three quarters of the stories had visual scenes that were less than 20 seconds long, and between a third and a half of the stories were heavily illustrated with more than 10 visuals. Salomon (1983) found that university students perceived news broadcasts to require more mental effort to understand than news in print, an exception to the general perception of television being easier to learn from than print.

Taken together, these observations suggest that the continuous stream of information featuring short items that change frequently challenges the ability of viewers to comprehend the news. The low recall in home viewers may partially be explained by the combination of this presentation format, their often being engaged in other activities while viewing, and the wide range of content that can fall outside of personal interests. Those aspects of a television news broadcast that do deal with topics about which viewers already have some knowledge tend to be remembered better (Findahl & Hoijer, 1985), as are personally relevant stories given in an audio-only radio broadcast format (Schneider & Laurion, 1993). Viewers are also more likely to recall information from summary statements and from violent stories, and less likely to recall information from similar topics grouped together (Berry et al., 1981; Furnham & Gunter, 1987; Graber, 1990; Gunter, Berry, & Clifford, 1981; Son, Reese, & Davie, 1987). Interestingingly, one study found that intervening commercial interruptions do not appear to affect retention of information from regular broadcast television programming (Cavanaugh, 1984), although another suggests that some reorienting attention is apparently devoted following an interrupting program segment (Geiger & Reeves, 1993).

Visual and Verbal Information in News Broadcasts

The studies given in this section specifically investigated the relationship between audio and video information presented in television news broadcasts. These generally show that memory for information from the news is positively affected to the degree that the auditory and visual information meaningfully correspond, but may be disrupted when they are deliberately made incongruent. Isolating the effects of visual and verbal information appears to have been somewhat more fruitful in those more carefully controlled studies discussed earlier in this chapter. A more inconsistent pattern of results is shown in the studies of news broadcasts, possibly because of the difficulty in controlling the many variables present with these materials (Berry et al., 1981) and ill-defined terminology (Hanson, 1992). One concern with these materials is whether the visuals really supply information central to comprehension of the story. For example, generic pictures or clip-art may be weakly related to a story, and some types of content may be inherently difficult to depict when they involve abstract ideas (e.g., economics or the failure of a bank).

Graber (1990) presented news stories by both audio and video or by audio alone. Subjects seeing an audio–video version recalled a higher proportion of visual themes than verbal themes. They were also less likely to add extraneous embellishments in recall than those only hearing the audio version. The most widely recalled verbal themes were capsule summary statements, and the most commonly recalled visuals involved depictions of people. When asked what contribution the visuals provided to the stories, the most common responses of those seeing the audio–video version cited realism (34%), clarification (16%), and emotion (13%). In a field study by Katz et al. (1977), adults were asked to watch the evening news normally or listen without watching the screen in their normal home setting. Viewers recalled slightly more news items than those who listened and did not watch the screen, but this difference was not significant. However, being able to watch the news did significantly increase recall for items that the authors considered intrinsically less interesting to the viewers, whereas no effect was found on items judged as more important. Longer news stories were found to increase recall, and stories at least 2 minutes long were remembered more often when viewed than when they were only heard.

Gunter (1980) compared the recall of three types of very short news items given by both audio and video or by audio alone with the screen covered. The three types of news items were: a talking-head on-screen narrator with no visuals, film clips with an off-screen narrator, or stills with an off-screen narrator. Recall of the three types of items did not differ when given by audio alone, but the film clips and stills resulted in better recall than the talking-head items when given by audio–video. The audio–

video presentation yielded better recall than the audio-only presentation for film clips and stills, but only the film clips were significant. The audio presentation produced better performance than the audio–video presentation with the talking-head news items. Thus, audio–video presentations with visuals other than the narrator appeared to be beneficial, whereas seeing the narrator in the otherwise nonvisual talking-head presentation apparently interfered with learning.

A subsequent series of studies by Gunter and Furnham compared retention from reading a printed script with that from audio–video and audio-only presentations of several kinds of televised materials studied in the context of a number of other variables (see summary in Furnham, Gunter, & Green, 1990). These studies uniformly found that recall was better with print than with audio–video and audio-only presentations. However, these studies reveal an inconsistent pattern where either audio–video or audio-only presentations produced equal retention, or one or the other was better than the other. Of four studies on news items, two found audio-only better and two found no difference. Audio–video was found better than audio-only in four other studies using commercials, political party broadcasts, a magazine program, and a program on information technology (Furnham et al., 1990, Study 1).

Son et al. (1987) found better retention for news stories with well-synchronized narration and pictures compared to when the same content was altered to disrupt the synchrony of the narration and pictures. They also found the addition of a "recap" of the main point of a news item benefits retention. Findahl (1971) found higher retention rates when still images were combined with a highly redundant narrative message. This presentation was better than when the stills had a low correspondence to the narrative, or when the narrative was given by either audio alone or by a pictured speaker without stills. Because visual information was in the form of either a person talking or a still visual image, these conditions minimized the competition for processing resources by allowing viewers to focus on the auditory message. Findahl's use of a recognition measure might account for the absence of the effect shown by Gunter (1980) where recall showed an on-screen narrator to produce poorer performance than audio alone. More equivocal results were reported by Brosius (1989), who found adding still photos to the news only increased recall of the general topic covered but not more detailed information. He also found illustrations that fit the news story were recognized but not recalled better than illustrations that did not fit the news story, and slight benefits of increasing the redundancy of the audio narrative on recall of detailed information.

Two other seemingly conflicting studies varied the degree to which narration and accompanying visual images corresponded (Drew & Grimes, 1987; Grimes, 1990). Higher correspondence between narration and visuals produced better memory than when they had a lower but still related correspondence for some measures but not others. In the Drew and Grimes

(1987) study, the benefit of higher correspondence was found for story comprehension and memory for audio information, but not memory for visual information. It was hypothesized that visual information was not benefited by the highly redundant condition because attention shifted to the auditory channel either to avoid distraction or because this channel typically carries the most information in the news. In the Grimes (1990) study, the benefit of higher correspondence between narration and visuals was found for recognition of visuals but not facts. When visuals were made to be incongruent with the narration, fact recognition was impaired whereas visual recognition was increased. The earlier study by Pezdek and Stevens (1984) also found reduced memory for audio information in an audio–video mismatch condition. However, Grimes's finding of increased visual recognition seems to suggest the mismatch led to some preference for viewing the visuals.

Finally, two studies of individual differences reported findings relevant to processing visual and verbal information in the news. As noted previously, Pezdek et al. (1987) found those who were better at comprehending news items also performed better on visual/spatial tasks. Stine, Wingfield, and Myers (1990) found that older adults did not benefit from watching the video portion of news broadcasts. Elderly adults performed similarly whether they listened, listened while watching video, or listened while reading the narration. Younger college-age viewers recalled more from listening accompanied by video than when they listened only, and performed even better when listening while reading the narration. Thus, audio–visual presentations typical of television enhanced recall over listening to narration, but the addition of visual information benefited younger and not elderly viewers. A number of other studies have found correlations between memory for the news and age, education, and verbal skills (Cavanaugh, 1983, 1984; Findahl, 1971; Hill, Crook, Zadek, Sheikh, & Yesavage, 1989; Stauffer et al., 1983; Stine et al., 1990). Typically, performance increases with age until early adulthood, then remains relatively constant with increasing age until the late 60s, at which point performance decreases among the elderly. Performance is usually better for those with higher verbal skills or more education at all ages including the elderly.

Discussion of Learning from News Broadcasts

Learning from television news is generally low in home viewers who appear to monitor news programs with a low level of engagement. Learning is made more difficult by the large number of short visuals that must be processed, many of which are generic or weakly related to the story line. Television news broadcasts might be characterized as violating cuing, pacing, and redundancy principles that have been found to be effective in educational television. A number of variables have been shown to have small effects on learning, but no collective combination of formats have been particularly noted to increase learning uniformly (Berry et al., 1981; Brosius, 1989; Graber, 1990). Typical generalizations about what is remembered from the news stress several factors: the extent to which the visual information is relevant to the verbal story line, the extent to which memory load is affected by the pacing and density of information, the extent to which viewers attend to news content, and the extent of individual interest in particular news content.

The more controlled studies in the earlier part of this chapter allow the conclusion that audio–video presentations are at least as good or better than audio presentations. The somewhat inconsistent findings in studies of news broadcasts leave conclusions in this area more tentative and qualified. Memory for information from the news appears to be positively affected to the degree that the auditory and visual information meaningfully correspond, may or may not be beneficial when they are redundant, and may be disrupted when they are made incongruent. These qualifications reflect the general characteristics of news items where visual and verbal material is communicated in a very different context and form than found in educational settings.

Attention and Comprehension

A theoretical framework has emerged from studies attempting to understand the relation between attention and comprehension in television viewing (D. R. Anderson & Lorch, 1983; Collins, 1982; Huston & Wright, 1983; Kozma, 1991). This line of research questioned the extent to which program content controls a viewer's attention or results from the viewer's own active processing of the content. There appear to be several generalizable themes from this research, despite it having been conducted with children in incidental learning circumstances. One important aspect of this work is the characterization of viewing as being strategic. Viewers appear to strategically monitor programs and actively determine the processing resources devoted to extracting information. A second aspect of this work is that it serves to qualify the importance of formal features that are the basis for many professional production techniques. A topic related to the active aspect of viewing appears later in the discussion of the mental effort viewers invest as a consequence of their goals, purposes, and media perceptions (chap. 8).

Observations of children watching television indicate that attention is discontinuous and periodic (D. R. Anderson & Lorch, 1983; Huston & Wright, 1983). They often look toward and then away from the stream of information on the screen, particularly while engaging in alternative activities. Features of the medium that determine attention and that are distinct from program content are termed *formal features* because they can be employed across different themes and messages (Huston & Wright,

1983). Formal features are visual or auditory techniques and events such as the level of action, pace, zooms, perspective changes, unusual sounds, and so forth. It has been found that viewer attention is gained and maintained by such attributes as auditory changes, women's and children's voices, peculiar voices, sound effects, laughing and applause, camera cuts, and women characters. Some attributes that inhibit attention are extended zooms and pans, animals, still pictures, and male voices. Many of these are auditory attributes that serve to cue visual attention because they are associated with and predict content shown on the screen. Some of these cues relate to sensory appeal and entertainment value, and others serve as markers analogous to punctuation. As markers, they signal breaks in content and transitions among scenes or between programs and commercials. Because viewers engage in other activities while watching television, the auditory attributes and those from peripheral vision often provoke shifts in attention between these activities and viewing. The importance of audio lies in the fact that viewers can always hear a program, but may not always see the screen except peripherally. These observations suggest that viewing involves some continual monitoring at varying levels and that certain cues serve to recapture attention. D. R. Anderson and Lorch (1983) additionally observed a dynamic tension between attention shifts and an "inertial" tendency for viewing or nonviewing to persist across changes in content as a response to the unpredictable nature of the presentation.

D. R. Anderson and Lorch (1983) contrasted two views relating attention and comprehension in television viewing. They collectively characterized older popular views as a *reactive* theory and more recent cognitive views as an *active* theory. The reactive theory characterizes the viewer as being controlled by the television set, whereas the active theory puts visual attention under active viewer control where it is deployed in the service of efforts to understand the program.

The reactive theory reflects popular opinions characterizing the viewer as a passive recipient that is acted on by television (e.g., J. L. Singer, 1980). That the viewer's reactions are controlled by manipulating the superficial characteristics of the medium seems to justify typical professional production techniques. Thus, television is seen as having the ability to capture and sustain the viewer's attention by the manipulation of "formal features" such as visual complexity, movement, cuts, pans, zooms, and sound effects. Once the viewer's attention has been captured, comprehension and retention are assumed to follow automatically without any special incentive to do so.

Whereas formal features are the focus with the reactive theory, the active theory shifts the emphasis toward what the viewers do overtly and covertly while watching. The active theory emphasizes the effects of both formal features and those features of the content that are comprehensible. The active viewer theory assumes that the viewer plays a critical role by monitoring, filtering, and processing the presentation to construct expectations about what information will occur. Rather than being passive recipients of information and images, viewers monitor the presentation within the context of what they already know about the content and the specific purposes to which that content will be applied. Within this perspective, the production techniques used in a video presentation will be effective to the extent that they advance the viewer's purposes. Younger viewers would generally be seen as being more reactive to the formal features of television than older viewers whose attention becomes more voluntary and strategic.

It is generally proposed that visual attention is guided by the comprehensibility or meaningfulness of the presentation (D. R. Anderson & Lorch, 1983; Huston & Wright, 1983; Rolandelli, 1989). D. R. Anderson and Lorch (1983) proposed a time sharing of visual attention between television and the attraction of alternative activities that may be ongoing during viewing. When attention is directed at an alternative activity, the viewer uses informative cues to guide attention to television during these periods of viewing inattention. Viewers monitor the presentation for cues that may indicate the presence of interesting content by listening to the audio and through peripheral vision or occasional glances at the screen. Shifts between low-level monitoring and more focused visual attention result from changes in perceptually salient program features partly because prior experience with these noncontent features predict important content within the programs. Attention is maintained by the need to resolve "questions" suggested by samples of information that grow out of the individual's experience and interests. Attention would lag to the extent that the presentation involves routine, predictable, or difficult content. Using concepts similar to Schank and Abelson (1977), routine information would quickly fill in the "slots" of a prototypical knowledge "schema" or "script" derived from prior experience with the medium, and unfamiliar or difficult content would have no prior schema.

D. R. Anderson and Lorch (1983) reviewed several lines of evidence supporting the idea that viewers attend selectively on the basis of their perceptions of the comprehensibility of the content. The effects that changes in comprehensibility have on attention support the idea that television is more than a passive experience and involves active processing of the content. For example, greater attention was found for dialogue with an immediate referent than for referents that were more removed and less immediately concrete. Recall was also little affected by changing attention to alternative activities by manipulating the presence or absence of toys. Comprehensibility also affected attention in experiments where formal features were maintained and program comprehensibility was perverted by distorting either the auditory or visual track of programs. Various manipulations altered the normal sequence of the visuals but not the auditory track, or used a normal visual track with either the utterances of the auditory track reversed or given in the Greek language. Less visual attention was given to randomly edited segments than normal segments, and even less was given to backward or foreign dialogue. This ranking corresponded to separate adult ratings of the comprehensibility of these conditions. Anderson and Lorch argued that these links to comprehension support an active theory because the perceptually salient formal cues were not effective in capturing attention when the comprehensibility of the content was reduced.

The D. R. Anderson and Lorch (1983) view leans heavily toward comprehension affecting attention. That is, the causal emphasis of the reactive theory is from attention to comprehension whereas the causal emphasis of the active theory is from comprehension to attention. However, Huston and Wright (1983) observed that the correlation of attention and comprehension involves a more interactive relation between the two. They contended that the apparent paradox that one must attend in order to comprehend can be interpreted in terms of a *sampling* explanation similar to the time sharing idea of D. R. Anderson and Lorch (1983). Thus, brief attending from time to time offers the opportunity to evaluate the appeal of that sample and provides the basis for decisions to continue attending based on predictions about what continued attention would yield. They view comprehension as affecting attention in an inverted U-shaped function. In this proposed relationship, content that is either very simple or very difficult to comprehend maintains attention poorly, whereas attention is better maintained by content of intermediate difficulty. Thus, comprehension may be achieved very quickly with simple content, which further attention will do little to increase, and attention will fail to promote comprehension with content that is too difficult for the viewer. Within the intermediate region of difficulty, attention is necessary but not sufficient for comprehension. That is, attention provides an opportunity for comprehension to occur. Thus, formal features can bring about increases in attention if they predict something interesting to the viewer and comprehension results when the viewer invests some mental effort in processing the content.

Rolandelli et al. (1991) subsequently provided some evidence suggestive of auditory attention being used to monitor programs for important visual content and to process information semantically. Looking served as an index of visual attention, and auditory attention was indexed by responses to restore a gradually degraded quality of the audio to normal. Videos were shown that had music and sound effects, but differed in whether or not narration had been added to the program. Auditory attention was unaffected by narration and did not depend on looking, although narration understandably benefited an auditory comprehension test. In contrast, the addition of audio narration increased both visual attention and visual comprehension test performance. Auditory and visual attention were uncorrelated without the narration, but they became correlated when the video was narrated.

In summary, the generalizable framework derived from this work is the conception of a "window of cognitive engagement" (Kozma, 1991). Perceptual features not only elicit and maintain attention, they also serve as an aid in the selection of content to be further processed. Attentional monitoring initially provides samples of information that vary in comprehensibility. These samples can predict future content of interest and lead to the subsequent deployment of continued attention and the processing of comprehensible information. Production techniques for instruction must therefore go beyond the level of attracting attention by additionally attempting to convey comprehensible information.

PROCESSING VISUAL AND VERBAL INFORMATION IN STATIC MATERIALS

Although the main emphasis of our review is on dynamic video media, several findings with static materials are relevant. The following discussion is primarily concerned with the role of different kinds of visual illustrations used in conjunction with text. Although this method of learning is, on the surface, less complex than with dynamic presentations, a large research literature attests to the complexity of the way textual material interacts with pictures, graphs, and diagrams. For example, early researchers were unable to clearly determine if illustrated text was beneficial or if it possibly overloaded learners (Holliday, 1973; M. V. Moore & Nawrocki, 1978; Samuels, 1970). The more recent consensus is that pictures can have a positive effect on prose learning when they provide a meaningful supplement to text information (Alesandrini, 1984; Levie & Lentz, 1982; Peeck, 1987; Pressley, 1977; Pressley & Miller 1987; Schallert, 1980).

Generalizations Relevant to Video

The extensive literature on static visual and verbal information provides several generalizations relevant to video presentations that have not been as fully explored within videos. These are applicable to the extent that similar principles operate within videos or to the extent that video merely serves as a medium conveying information in a similar way. The relevant generalizations are summarized here prior to illustrating them in the remainder of this section with examples from pertinent research or reviewers (W. H. Allen, 1975; Dwyer, 1978; Levie, 1987; Mayer, 1989a; Peeck, 1987; Royer & Cable, 1976; Schallert, 1980; Stone & Glock, 1981; Winn, 1987b).

First, studies of illustrated text are relevant to video presentations in the sense that they both use complementary alternative sources of information. In this literature, supplementing text with illustrations may benefit learning when the illustrations represent text-relevant information, elaborate on it, or illustrate information central to the text. Second, visuals offer the opportunity to depict spatial-structural relationships in the text and to convey more concrete representations when textual material is abstract or difficult to comprehend or to express verbally. Additionally, there may be an optimal level of detail in illustrations that aid learners in extracting relevant information. Third, visuals can be beneficial when they provide an initial organizational aid or aid in forming a schema or a mental model of how things work that might otherwise have to be constructed by the learner from the text. Finally, illustrations may offer some benefits to learners with lesser skills, abilities, or prior knowledge. Although much of this research concerns representational pictures, the range of visuals that have been studied extends to diagrams that mimic objects or schematicize them, and to graphs and charts that present abstract representations.

The general framework in which learning from illustrated text is viewed involves an incremental acquisition of information, which is a function of how much information can be held in working memory while advancing through instruction that requires these two sources of information to be coordinated. This process is in turn facilitated by the amount of prior knowledge about a domain or about graphics conventions, and is affected by how the information has been organized and coordinated in the presentation (Friedman, 1993; Hegarty, Carpenter, & Just, 1991). Although readers of text and viewers of video must both integrate information from visual and verbal sources, these forms of learning differ in an important way. Readers can adjust their own pace of information acquisition and can recover from comprehension failures by rereading text to clarify points in the text, but viewers of typical videos are constrained by the fixed pace of the transient presentation (Kozma, 1991).

Studies of Illustrated Text

Dwyer's Studies and Visual Detail

A well-known series of visual instruction studies by Dwyer (1972, 1978) exemplified the benefit of using illustrations to depict spatial-structural relations. These studies provide a large number of findings with a consistent set of materials. Dwyer devised an instructional unit on the human heart using a standard text accompanied by as many as eight versions of the visuals and four types of tests. The visuals were simple line drawings, detailed shaded drawings, photographs of a heart model, or photographs of actual hearts and were prepared in color or black-and-white versions. The tests were a drawing test, a test to identify parts of the heart, a terminology test, and a comprehension test on heart functions. A general pattern in these studies was that different types of tests differentially reflected the kinds of information given in the instructional presentations. Thus, simple line drawing presentations were effective with the drawing and identification tests, detailed shaded drawing for the identification test, and an oral presentation was more effective with terminology and comprehension tests. Over a number of studies, the simple line drawing presentations emerged as being more effective than the more complex visuals, with the photographs and models of the heart being the least effective in complementing the verbal instruction.

Dwyer's studies support the general conclusion that visuals emphasizing the relevant critical details are most effective and that arbitrarily adding visual realism does not increase learning. Fully realistic illustrations and photographs of models and actual hearts were not as effective as drawings designed to emphasize the important spatial-structural features of the heart. Dwyer's studies also indicated that the amount of time allowed to process information in visuals can affect how much information is extracted, with lesser detail making less demands when time is constrained. Too much realistic detail increases the difficulty of extracting relevant features and this difficulty is exacerbated when study time is limited, giving less detailed visuals an advantage. This general relation would apply to transient presentations like those on television where the pace of information is fixed. Some of Dwyer's findings also suggest that simpler visuals reduce the difference among students from different levels of ability. Students of lower ability may be overloaded by increases in visual detail that can still be processed well by those with higher abilities (Dwyer, 1978; Parkhurst & Dwyer 1983).

Dwyer's (1972) research used a consistent set of materials to demonstrate that an optimum level of visual detail appropriate to an instructional objective may benefit comprehension. Other researchers have used different materials and settings in studies that are relevant to this relationship (Borg & Schuller, 1979; Gorman, 1973; Haring & Fry, 1979; M. V. Moore, Nawrocki, & Simutis, 1979). Borg and Schuller (1979) simplified the graphics used in U.S. Army individualized lessons that involved a combination of visual (filmstrip) and oral (tape cassette) information. A self-paced lesson on a tank-mounted machine gun used 113 visuals, 70 of which were considered to be complex. The detail in these visuals was modified so that only 16 complex visuals remained and the instruction was not improved in other ways. The simplifications included removing superfluous foliage, mountains and trees, hands shown on the equipment, details of uniforms, and the use of some sketches in lieu of scale drawings. Students learning from these two versions did not differ in their performance. The authors suggested that use of simplified visuals would therefore reduce lesson development costs significantly. The absence of an effect could probably be interpreted in two ways: The efforts devoted to creating realistic graphics are ineffective in enhancing performance and do not support a realism theory, or simplifying the graphics did not improve performance as might be expected from Dwyer's work. The authors conceded that the original and simplified drawings probably differed less than did the extremes of Dwyer's visuals.

Gorman (1973) presented simple and complex illustrations showing architectural principles to fifth- and ninth-grade students and college juniors. After viewing pictorial examples and nonexamples, students were required to identify correct test examples. No performance differences were found between simple and complex illustrations for any of the grade levels. M. V. Moore et al. (1979) varied the sophistication of the graphics used in three versions of a computer-based lesson on the mechanics of hearing given to Army personnel. One version used simplified block diagrams and two others used more realistic detailed line drawings either with or without animation. The more realistic graphics contained only enough detail for visualization of the important physiological components. Lesson completion time and factual posttest performance did not differ in comparing simple and complex illustrations or animation. Haring and Fry (1979) presented fourth- and sixth-grade students with a textual story that was accompanied by text-redundant pictures depicting different levels of detail. They presented the story for learning by itself or accompanied by pictures that depicted either the main ideas (agents and actions) or both the main ideas and nonessential descriptive details. Compared to the text-only story, both stories with pictures facilitated recall, but only for the main ideas. The stories illustrated with added details did not enhance or impair recall relative to the stories depicting only the main ideas.

These further studies on detail in illustrations indicate that additional pictorial detail does not usually benefit learning. This pattern agrees with Dwyer's (1972, 1978) findings, but his studies also suggest that learning may be better with minimal detail or hindered by greater realistic detail. This difference may reflect factors Dwyer himself identified with regard to test measures and training methods. Thus, the detriment of visual detail may be greater when time is constrained with fixed-paced instruction, less potent when ample time is allowed to extract information in self-paced instruction, and better revealed with tests sensitive to visual rather than verbal information. Basic laboratory studies more clearly illustrate the detrimental effects of visual detail and placing constraints on visual processing. Thus, recognition memory for pictures decreases as the exposure time is limited and decreases the likelihood of noticing details (Loftus & Bell, 1975). Likewise, the speed of detecting an object in a photograph is faster for a coherent than a jumbled scene (Biederman, Glass, & Stacy, 1973). Hegarty et al. (1991) also observed that more complex diagrams lead to more visual inspections than less complex ones during the reading of an illustrated text on how a pulley works. Low-ability individuals inspected the diagram more than high-ability individuals over all levels of complexity.

Meta-Analyses and Kinds of Visuals

Systematic empirical evidence for the effect of illustrations in text was provided by a meta-analysis of a large number of studies conducted by Levie and Lentz (1982). They examined studies conducted with subjects from grade school through college that involved pictures and drawings that were representational (i.e., they represented what things look like as opposed to other forms like maps or diagrams). They concluded that reading illustrated text was superior to unillustrated text, and they estimated that subjects learned about one third more from reading illustrated text. In 23 studies involving 46 comparisons, 85% of the comparisons were significant, and the average effect size favoring illustrated text was .55, an increase of half a standard deviation. A smaller group of 10 studies involving 16 comparisons offered information on learning material that was not illustrated. In nearly all of these comparisons, the presence of illustrations did not help or hinder learning other content that was not illustrated. Levie and Lentz (1982) also performed a meta-analysis in which they computed effect sizes for 96 of Dwyer's studies that compared text alone to text with illustrations. In 41 comparisons, 36 showed some advantage to illustrated text. The effect size was influenced by the degree to which the tests measured visual information. The drawing and identification tests emphasizing pictorial information generated the largest effect, whereas text comprehension test results showed a very small effect size.

Based on their review and meta-analysis, Levie and Lentz (1982) derived a number of concluding guidelines on combining text and illustrations that are summarized in the following list. Combining these media generally has positive effects when the illustrations are congruent with and directly relevant to the text passage being studied.

1. Learning from text will be aided by relevant illustrations.
2. Learning from text that students are required to read is not facilitated by unrelated illustrations.
3. Learning from illustrated portions of a text will have little or no effect on learning from portions of the same text that are not illustrated.
4. Illustrations may function best in aiding long-term retention.
5. Illustrations may function as substitutes for words.
6. Textual prompting or references to pictured information may aid the reader in extracting relevant information from complex illustrations.
7. Readers prefer illustrated text over nonillustrated text even when they do not extract information from the illustrations.
8. Poor readers may benefit more than good readers from illustrations that are not too complex.

The Levie and Lentz meta-analysis findings indicate that learning from text is facilitated by illustrations, but this facilitation seems to be circumscribed to information in the text that is actually depicted in the illustrations. It is less clear what kinds of information may profit most from illustrations or what forms of illustrations are most beneficial (Peeck, 1987). Several categorizations of the types or purposes of visuals have been offered, but these vary somewhat among authors (the discussion of realism at the end of chap. 4 presents some related categorizations by Friedman, 1993, and Salomon, 1979).

Levin, Anglin, and Carney (1987) classified the purpose of pictures in conducting another meta-analysis of the "pictures in prose" research. Their analysis of pictures excluded graphs and diagrams and most of the studies involved immediate retention. They found that learning is aided by pictures that are relevant to the text and that the purpose of a picture strongly influenced effect size. They distinguished among five functions of pictures: decoration (text irrelevant), representation (showing actors and objects to reinforce the narrative), organization (summarizing distinctive features or procedures), interpretation (clarify abstract concepts), and transformation (creating a memorable mnemonic). Text-irrelevant decorative pictures did not aid remembering and had a slight negative effect. Positive effect sizes of approximately three quarters of a standard deviation were found for the more commonly occurring types of pictures used as illustrations (representation, organization, and interpretation functions). An effect size nearly twice this large was found for the small number of comparisons involving transformation illustrations.

Alesandrini (1984) distinguished among three broader categories of visuals termed representational, analogical, or arbitrary. His analytical review suggests that all three types are beneficial within their respective realm of application. Representational visuals physically resemble a thing or concept. Analogical visuals show something else but imply a similarity, such as with abstract concepts. Arbitrary visuals such as graphs, charts, diagrams, and flow charts are highly schematized visuals that may not look like what they represent, but are logically or conceptually related to what they represent. Compared to representational pictures more commonly used in educational materials, these latter forms may make greater processing demands on learners because they involve lesser physical similarity to their referents.

Winn (1987b, 1989) more extensively reviewed the research on charts, graphs, and diagrams, the bulk of which concerns diagrams in science-related educational materials. He observed that these studies are less focused on understanding graphic properties than on how learners with weaker skills appear to derive benefit from them. He defined charts and graphs in terms of their expressing relationships among continuous or categorical variables often involving numeric values (also see Hartley,

1992; Wainer, 1992). Diagrams describe whole conceptual processes and structures that are often at levels of greater complexity. Winn (1987b) noted that these graphic forms fall in the center of the continuum between pictures and words, sharing the attribute of abstraction with words and the meaningful use of spatial layout with pictures. These forms have the advantage of efficiently summarizing information in ways that provide an explicit and simplified view of complex relationships. The use of space is central to the way these forms convey information, primarily by the way elements are grouped, ordered, and sequenced. However, the idea that graphics are self-explanatory becomes less tenable with forms like diagrams, charts, and graphs. Prior knowledge may be required to understand the potentially more complex content or the symbolic conventions employed in these graphic forms. These forms require some understanding of conventions such as action lines, the meaning of symbols, knowledge that axis values generally increase to the top and right in graphs, and knowledge that diagrams use left-to-right or top-to-bottom sequences. According to Winn, the potential compensation offered by diagrams depends on whether the learner can process the information given, has knowledge of their conventions, is directed to inspect them, and whether the text gives supporting explanations. For complex explanations, adding a diagram to text may offer an advantage over an elaborated verbal explanation, and an explained diagram would be more effective than an unexplained diagram (Guri-Rosenblit, 1988).

Other Functions of Illustrations

One often noted general function of illustrations and diagrams is that they provide an alternative source of complementary information to that given in a text. This function is illustrated in various ways, first by a study with pictures and then by several studies using diagrams. Rohwer and Harris (1975) conducted a study to examine the effects of presenting the same information orally, by text, or by still visuals. These three conditions were presented separately, in paired combinations, or all three simultaneously. Fourth-graders were required to distinguish between two examples of each concept (cars, monkeys, or tribes), based on single and combined media presentations. In general, combining pictures with either oral or print versions tended to be better than combining these two verbal forms. This reveals a complementary benefit of the pictures, which were by themselves less effective than either of the verbal forms. Another important finding of this study concerned the comparison of students from two schools whose students differed in their socioeconomic status (SES). The low-SES students benefited from combined media conditions, particularly the oral plus pictures combination, whereas the combinations of media tended to be of much less benefit to high-SES students. Thus, a lowest common denominator approach suggested by these findings would be to use a combination of media that would benefit those with the most to gain without affecting or causing a detriment to those with more skills.

Several studies with illustrations and diagrams also reveal ways in which text is supplemented by these alternative sources of information. Diagrams can serve several purposes: aiding the formation of a representation of the text information, acting as a memory aid for information that has already been read, and providing new information not given in the text (Hegarty & Just, 1989; Hegarty et al., 1991). For example, Stone and Glock (1981) suggested that having information in text and illustrations provides a reader with an opportunity to clarify information from alternative sources. They found that adding illustrations to text resulted in fewer assembly errors on the orientation of parts with an assembly task, suggesting that the illustrations offered an alternative source of spatial information not provided by the text. Similarly, the pattern of results in a study by Booher (1975) suggested that in learning to operate equipment, textual information was relied on for gaining information on procedural steps, whereas visual information was used in locating objects.

Observations of eye fixations during learning reveal patterns in the way learners consult visuals as an alternative source of information to that given in the text. Stone and Glock (1981) observed two basic patterns in their study of college-age readers of illustrated assembly instructions. That these readers typically examined an illustration for a second or two prior to reading the text was interpreted in terms of using the picture to evoke an initial schema of the situation. During reading, they periodically referred back to the illustration about 17% of the time, appearing to be comparing the content of the text and illustration. More casual observations by Rusted and Coltheart (1979) suggested poor readers were more prone to move their eyes frequently from a passage to the picture, apparently checking features in the pictures as they read.

Hegarty and colleagues made a more detailed examination of eye fixations by giving college students a display that combined text and a diagram of a mechanical pulley (Hegarty & Just, 1989; Hegarty et al., 1991). They examined where in the text learners chose to inspect the diagram and at which portions of the diagram they looked. They found that most eye fixations pertained to encoding new information or integrating previous information. Processing information from the diagrams appeared to follow attempts to extract information from the text. They observed that diagram inspections were related to linguistic boundaries in the text, which implied that the diagram was consulted to verify the textual material. A little more than one third of the visual inspections were on diagrammatic referents related to the last sentence read, about one half were on referents related to information in previous sentences at that point, and about one tenth were related to portions of the diagram that had not been mentioned in the text up to that point. Initial "formation" inspections related to the last sentence read increased with the amount of information that the text contained about the configuration of the pulley. More of these kind of diagram inspections occurred when reading a longer text with descriptions referring to spatial locations and connections of the pulley system than when reading a shorter text that did not include this configuration information.

Over all types of inspections, individuals with lower mechanical ability inspected the diagram longer when reading the longer text with the configuration information than when they read the shorter text without this information. Higher ability individuals spent less time inspecting the diagram with the longer descriptive text than they did with the shorter text, even though it referred to the diagram less. Thus, individuals with lower mechanical ability appeared to use the diagrams to aid in forming a representation of the configuration when the text included references to this information. Higher ability individuals could apparently extract more information from the descriptive text and consulted the diagrams more when the text did not include all the relevant information.

Another common explanation of the value of illustrations is that they offer a means to provide concrete examples of abstract concepts. A simple example with children was provided by Dixon and Saltz (1977), who found pictures or words were about equally effective for teaching functional concepts (e.g., the concept of a container), whereas pictures were better for teaching visually oriented concepts (e.g., pointed or round things). A related finding was seen in the previously discussed study by Gropper (1966) that used abstract physical science concepts that could be represented either visually or verbally. The value of the visual presentation was shown by its positive effect on both visual and verbal tests, whereas the verbal presentation primarily benefited just the verbal test. A study by P. J. Moore and Skinner (1985) found performance on more difficult kinds of questions involving inferences to be facilitated by illustrations when the passages they accompanied were more abstract.

A study by Royer and Cable (1976) illustrated that difficult to comprehend abstract information can be made easier to learn by providing concrete information in visual or verbal forms. Using materials on heat flow and electrical conductivity, they presented college students with one of several initial passages prior to a second passage that was abstract. Compared to when the first passage was abstract or unrelated, learning of the second abstract passage was facilitated by the transfer of ideas from first passages that used pictures, appropriate analogies, or physical references. Thus, abstract information can be made easier to learn by a more concrete context created verbally or visually. These alternative ways of increasing the concreteness of the abstract material tend to confirm a general relationship that is typically given as an attribute of visuals.

Understanding "systems" of knowledge that are complex and abstract can involve students constructing their own representation or "mental model" of the functional relations within these knowledge systems. The process of developing a mental model may be made more efficient by presenting students diagrams when the model and diagram share similar spatial properties (Winn, 1987b). Diagrams can aid in forming a mental model of how a system works by summarizing key information that might otherwise have to be constructed by the learner from text.

Mayer (1989a, 1989b) studied mental models with a variety of scientific texts that were accompanied by diagrams and illustrations designed to aid novice learners in focusing their attention on explanatory information in the texts. His series of studies on how systems work included topics such as brakes, radar, a camera, Ohm's law, programming, nitrogen cycle, and physical density. These texts involved explanations of the workings of these systems and the accompanying visual-verbal diagrams illustrated a conceptual model of the key elements of the textual explanations. Comparisons between those without the conceptual model and those who received the model either before or within the instruction revealed a general pattern over a series of studies. First, presenting a conceptual model increased retention of the concepts and explanatory information. Second, those receiving a model retain less verbatim information or nonexplanatory information, suggesting that the original presentation format is lost due to an active reorganization of information by the learners. Third, presenting conceptual models improved the ability of students to transfer what they had learned to solving new problems. These results indicate that illustrations of a conceptual model can help novice learners to think systematically about scientific material.

In later studies, Mayer and Gallini (1990) varied the extent to which illustrations were explanatory with individuals who had either low or high prior knowledge of a domain. Passages on how brakes, pumps, or generators worked were accompanied by either no illustrations, illustrations that labeled the parts, illustrations that labeled the major action steps, or that used both the parts and steps information in a series of illustrations. The combined parts and steps illustrations consistently improved the performance of the low prior knowledge individuals on conceptual recall and problem-solving tests, but not on nonconceptual or verbatim information tests. This benefit of showing the state of components at various points in the operation of the system was found with high prior knowledge individuals only with conceptual recall in one domain where the material was more complex. The authors' interpretation of these findings emphasized that effective illustrations depend on the appropriateness of text, tests, illustrations, and learners. Thus, the effectiveness of illustrations is dependent on "when the text is potentially understandable, when the value of illustrations is measured in terms of learner understanding, when the illustrations explain, and when the student lacks previous experience" (p. 725).

Individual Differences

Finally, the literature on learning from static graphics and text offers a somewhat better view of the role of individual differences than does the more limited literature with video. A number of the studies cited earlier suggest a pattern where lower prior knowledge or ability students derived the greatest benefit from illustrations. This pattern is also observed by several more systematic reviewers of this literature (Levie & Lentz, 1982; Peeck, 1987; Winn, 1987b, 1989) and by commentators on several media (W. H. Allen, 1975; Kozma, 1991; Salomon, 1979). Levie and Lentz (1982) characterized this as a slight trend for statistical reasons, and it becomes apparent from several analytical reviews that a number of factors determine who will benefit from illustrations (Peeck, 1987; Winn, 1987b, 1989). It is nearly axiomatic in studies involving individual differences that a learning outcome is highly dependent on the particulars of the instructional methods, tasks, and the difficulty of the learning materials used. These dependencies figure heavily in explaining a number of exceptions in which either poorer students derived no benefit or better students derived more benefit.

W. H. Allen (1975) examined several media and derived a family of conditions that facilitate lower and middle-ability learners, which he characterized as compensatory functions. The most efficacious methods for these students were ones compensating for attentional, discriminational, analytical, and mental processing deficiencies. Deterrents to learning were methods that disregarded their ability by placing difficult to meet demands on their capabilities. He found it was much easier to identify instructional methods for lower ability students than it was for higher ability students. He characterized the appropriate methods for higher ability students as being ones that challenged their greater abilities, allowed greater freedom, and maintained their interest. Using the terminology of Salomon (1979), Winn (1989) similarly distinguished instructional techniques that use visuals to "supplant" or compensate for poor skills and those that use the abilities that students possess to best advantage by "activating" them. He noted that the level of difficulty in the materials used is important to understanding when graphics might lead to a greater benefit for lower ability or prior knowledge students or when more benefit might be derived by the better students. The caution associated with increasing graphic support for the lower students is that it may only work well up to the point where the amount of additional information exceeds their processing capabilities. A lowest common denominator approach would balance an attempt to provide aid to lower students with an attempt to avoid hindering higher ability students who might benefit from more complex graphics.

Kozma (1991) also derived several generalizations that emphasize the way visuals are used as an alternative source of information during reading. He observed that readers use pictures initially as an organizational aid, to evoke prior domain knowledge, or possibly to establish a preliminary mental model of the situation. They then use illustrations in a periodic fashion as they read, with those with less domain knowledge being more likely to consult the illustration for clarification. He believed that these findings with text and pictures are parallel to those with video in the sense that "audio may be sufficient for those knowledgeable of a domain, but visual symbol systems supply important situational information for those less knowledgeable" (p. 192).

4 Dynamic Visual Presentations

This chapter reviews the uses and effectiveness of motion in film and video. The studies reviewed include general studies involving motion; studies of motion and procedural learning; studies of modeling movements, feedback, and sports; studies of video feedback in teacher education; and studies of animated graphics. Finally, the role of realism and fidelity is discussed based on the review of the features of motion in this chapter and of pictorial fidelity from the previous chapter.

MOTION ATTRIBUTES AND FUNCTIONS

Motion is widely cited as a unique beneficial feature of video or filmed instruction. Motion is thought to be beneficial primarily because it provides discriminations. Other specific attributes of motion that can be beneficial include its attention value, depicting continuity in sequential temporal-spatial relations, when it is a defining characteristic of a concept to be taught, when a motion itself must be learned, and when it directly represents information that is difficult to describe verbally (W. H. Allen & Weintraub, 1968; Blake, 1977; Gibson, 1947; Gropper, 1968; Hannafin & Phillips, 1987; Hochberg & Brooks, 1978; Jeon & Branson, 1981–1982; Laner, 1954, 1955; M. V. Moore & Nawrocki, 1978; Spangenberg, 1973; Swezey, Perez, & Allen, 1991).

Discrimination information provided by motion may not be easily conveyed in still images. These circumstances include those of discriminating figure from ground, revealing three-dimensional relations, and indicating directionality, speed, and velocity (W. H. Allen & Weintraub, 1968; Blake, 1977; Gropper, 1968; Hochberg & Brooks, 1978; Spangenberg, 1973). Instances of these specific discriminations being critical to learning might be exemplified in procedural learning of assembly and operation sequences. They would also be found when motion conveys defining characteristics of the learning material in spatial and temporal concepts, such as depicting planetary or atomic interaction concepts. Thus, motion can reveal the relation and distinctiveness among objects as they interact, fit and move together, and indicate relevant speed and temporal relations. Motion changes reveal boundaries and directions of movement that static images may not allow when figure-ground discriminations are made difficult by similar physical characteristics such as size, shape, color, texture, and position. Beyond these basic discrimination functions, motion can also be used to draw attention to critical elements of a scene just as with other static cuing devices (Blake, 1977; Dwyer, 1969; Spangenberg, 1973), and it may also serve to maintain interest in a general way simply by providing state changes (Hochberg & Brooks, 1978).

The attribute of continuity given in motion subsumes its discriminability attribute. Continuity conveys a temporal-spatial connectedness between scenes by showing how events sequentially transpire and lead to one another in time. Some types of procedural learning may be conceived in terms of discrete steps, but other types may require a conception of continuity. Continuity would be beneficial when a chained series of steps are dynamically interrelated and need to be viewed sequentially (W. H. Allen & Weintraub, 1968; Gropper, 1968; Spangenberg, 1973). Details revealed by continuity include depicting minute changes not captured by segmented views and showing simultaneous motion of objects in different directions. The time course of events depicted with motion can be compressed or expanded to illustrate information normally occurring too quickly or slowly. Motion can also depict unfamiliar actions with low verbal codability that may not be readily described accurately with words (Spangenberg, 1973). This function may be either with conceptual material that is difficult to convey, when language is a barrier, or when learning an action itself. When learning an action or movement, presenting instruction with motion allows a demonstration to serve as a model for performance, particularly when the activity is unfamiliar to the learner (W. H. Allen & Weintraub, 1968; Gropper, 1968; Spangenberg, 1973). Feedback allows performance to be adjusted or corrected in comparison to a standard. The effectiveness of feedback is increased when a view of one's own behavior is provided, either when dynamically performing a specific motor action or when received after a delay in the form of verbal evaluative feedback. Instruction containing elements such as those described previously may dictate the selection of media capable of depicting motion. Blake (1977) suggested that it may often be difficult to determine ahead of time what aspects of a task are critical to learning, so that decisions by many developers may be based on convenience.

Liabilities of motion are associated with inappropriate uses that create discontinuity or too rapid a pace (W. H. Allen & Weintraub, 1968; Hochberg & Brooks, 1978; Kozma, 1986, 1991). These areas of concern are noted in characterizing commercial programming and as prospective cautions when producing educational presentations. The transient nature of television or motion films can in some implementations lead to a lack of learner control over the rate of presentation when it exceeds the learners' capacity for processing the information (Kozma, 1986, 1991). As with distracting static pictorial details, disruptive effects may also result from discontinuity created by "cutting," rapid scene transitions, and short sequences. Processing of information from newly presented scenes may disrupt ongoing processing of previous scenes and may exceed the capabilities of some learners (Hochberg & Brooks, 1978).

GENERAL STUDIES INVOLVING MOTION

Many of the earliest studies on the effect of motion were comparisons of films with either filmstrips or slides. Reviewers in two different decades failed to find one or the other consistently better than the other (W. H. Allen, 1960; Hoban & Van Ormer, 1950). Hoban and Van Ormer (1950) offered an interpretation of those cases where differences did appear. Differences were possibly due to the slower rate of presentation when filmstrips were found superior and to having shown "interacting events" in the films when they were found superior. W. H. Allen (1960) concluded that slides and filmstrips were about as effective as either silent or sound motion films.

Allen and his associates subsequently conducted a comprehensive series of large studies pertinent to the general effect of motion in instructional films (W. H. Allen, Cooney, & Weintraub, 1968; W. H. Allen & Weintraub, 1968; W. H. Allen et al., 1970). W. H. Allen and Weintraub (1968) studied the effect of motion with a total of 81 different silent instructional presentations given to fifth- and sixth-grade students. The effect of motion on learning was investigated by presenting material via silent motion pictures, sequenced filmstrip still pictures simulating movement, and single slide still pictures showing the principal points of the action. Three different films were used in each of 27 conditions derived from combining these three motion presentation methods, three subject matter areas, and three types of instructional objectives. The three subject matter areas were science, motor skills, and social studies, whereas the three types of objectives covered were knowledge of specific facts, serial ordering, and learning concepts. The students were given objective tests following the given film, which required serial ordering in the case of these objectives. The main finding over all these conditions favored motion presentations; the motion picture mode of visual presentation was superior to the sequenced and still picture modes for about 70% of the comparisons. There were no practical differences between the sequenced and still modes. Content involving serial ordering appeared to benefit the most from the motion picture mode, and concept learning was the least affected.

Subsequent studies by Allen and colleagues (W. H. Allen, Cooney, & Weintraub, 1968; W. H. Allen et al., 1970) indicated that the superiority of motion over still conditions was eliminated when sound was added in the form of spoken verbal information. In the 1968 study, differences in learning between motion pictures and still slides were not found with sixth-grade students over several different types of audio narration. In the 1970 study, fifth- and sixth-grade students received either motion pictures or still pictures, which were in turn either silent or accompanied by verbal narration. The pattern of results over a large number of other comparison conditions and content again suggested that the effect of motion was minimal when accompanied by verbal narration. Silent still presentations tended to yield the worst learning, and sound versions of the motion and still presentations yielded the best learning. The effect of adding sound was more powerful than that of adding motion. That is, the circumstance where (a) sound was added to either motion or still presentations and found to increase learning over silent presentations (particularly for stills) yielded more positive comparisons than the circumstance where (b) motion was added to either silent or sound presentations and found to increase learning over stills. Compared to the earlier W. H. Allen and Weintraub (1968) study, the benefit of motion over stills was less pronounced for the silent conditions. This apparent discrepancy was presumably due to the use of instructional content that was similar to that subset of content found less effective in the earlier study.

Blake (1977) examined the effect of motion in teaching chess moves to subjects who were identified as being high or low in spatial/visual aptitude. Three instructional films were used: a still condition simulated a slide presentation, an arrows condition additionally included animated cuing arrows showing the direction of movement, and a motion picture condition showed the movements in full motion. High spatial aptitude subjects performed similarly over these three presentation modes and they outperformed those with lower aptitude. However, low-aptitude subjects performed better with both the arrows and full-motion presentations, which did not differ from one another. These results were consistent with Blake's hypotheses about detail and fidelity only being effective to the extent that motion cues are relevant to learning. That is, the two forms of motion would provide little benefit for those with sufficient spatial ability, and motion would be beneficial only up to the point where it became critical to learning. Thus, for those with lower ability the benefit of the motion provided no increment over the animated arrows because this added detail was beyond that necessary or critical to learning.

A related study of chess by Frey and Adesman (1976) used sequential slide presentations of the chess moves and found better recall when the sequence showed more meaningful chunks. An elementary concept learning experiment by Houser, Houser, and Van Mondfrans (1970) required subjects to associate a name with geometric shapes that were static or rotated. Motion picture presentations were superior to slide presentations in associating a name to a rotation motion concept compared to associating a name to a static nonmotion concept.

Dwyer (1969) investigated the use of motion to focus student attention on the important aspects of instruction by having a person point out critical elements of the heart in a videotaped slide show. However, conclusions relevant to the effect of motion were reduced by the absence of comparisons between the same materials with and without motion. In a later comparative synthesis of separate experiments, it appeared that some small localized benefit of the pointing was realized relative to an experiment using only static arrows (Dwyer, 1972, 1978).

Taken together, an unreasoned blanket use of motion for general types of content would not seem to offer a particularly more effective technique than some sort of still presentation. This was particularly true among the Allen studies (W. H. Allen & Weintraub, 1968; W. H. Allen, Cooney, & Weintraub, 1968; W. H. Allen et al., 1970) where more factual types of content benefited from motion only when narration was not used. Rather, these findings suggest that the benefit of motion depends on the content and what one is learning. In discussing relevant evidence at the time, W. H. Allen and Weintraub (1968) suggested that motion would be useful when the particular content to be learned involved the characteristics of movement or the movement itself, and when the content is differentiated by cues in the action of the movement. These conditions are particularly characteristic of the procedural learning studies discussed in the next section in which several additional comparisons of motion and still presentations are found. Findings favorable to motion in these procedural studies were reported by Jeon and Branson (1981–1982), Roshal (1949, 1961), Sheffield, Margolius, and Hoehn (1961), and Spangenberg (1973), whereas lesser or no benefits were found by Cornell and Hay (1984), Laner (1954), and Swezey et al. (1991).

STUDIES OF MOTION AND PROCEDURAL LEARNING

In procedural learning, an ordered series of acts, operations, or steps must be carried out by the student in the proper order. Procedures are very frequent instructional objectives in technical training (Wetzel, Van Kekerix, & Wulfeck, 1987b) and can often be highly specific to a piece of equipment, requiring detailed task analysis (Tar, 1986). The wide variety of procedural tasks and associated instructional details affecting learning is suggested by the taxonomy given by Konoske and Ellis (1986): (a) operator tasks, (b) maintenance or repair or assembly tasks, (c) paper-based tasks, and (d) tasks of locating information or objects. The beneficial effects of motion would probably be best realized in the first two categories because more discrimination and continuity information is involved.

A common technique for procedural learning is to present a demonstration by a model, the performance of which can serve as a standard. A classic illustration of a task involving both continuously changing cues and low verbal codability is seen in the learning of knot tying by sailors. Roshal (1949, 1961) found learning of knot tying to be significantly enhanced when shown in motion compared to when shown by stills. Showing the knot being tied from the subjective perspective of the performer was much more effective than a 180° reverse perspective from an observer viewing the performer. Additionally, showing a pair of hands manipulating the rope did not increase learning compared to just showing the movement of the rope. Blake (1977) suggested that depicting the hands was an instance of irrelevant detail in supporting the general observation that it is often difficult to determine what components of a task are critical. Roshal's knot tying task seems to compel the use of motion, illustrating W. H. Allen and Weintraub's (1968) conclusion that depicting motion during learning may be especially beneficial when the content to be learned involves motion. Because many procedures involve learning to do something, motion has been studied by researchers in the context of film or video-based studies notable in their combination of various features of procedural learning, motion and hands-on performance (Baggett, 1989a; Gropper, 1968; Jeon & Branson, 1981–1982; Laner, 1954; Spangenberg, 1973; Swezey, Perez, & Allen, 1988, 1991).

Two early studies on procedural learning demonstrated that practicing during a film can be effective when the learner is allowed enough time to participate without missing relevant information in the film (Ash & Jaspen, 1953; Jaspen, 1950; both as described in Travers, 1967, and in W. H. Allen, 1957, 1960). Naval trainees viewed films that demonstrated the assembly of the breech block of an anti-aircraft gun and either watched passively or actually practiced the assembly during the film. The films also used either a fast or slow rate of development. The slow film was consistently associated with better performance. The audience participation condition involving actual practice was very effective when the film used a slow rate of development, but was slightly detrimental with the fast film. Showing the film twice increased the speed of assembly when practicing during the slow film, but not the fast film. The need to allow adequate practice time during a film demonstrated in these studies was noted by Travers (1967) as an explanation for the failure to find benefits of similar hands-on participation conditions included in the knot tying study by Roshal and a later one by Rimland (1955, as described in Travers, 1967).

Another pair of early studies by Laner (1954, 1955) failed to find benefits associated with motion. In the 1954 study, film and filmstrip presentations were used to present instruction on how to repair a broken window sash. The two methods did not yield overall differences on a performance test, and time to completion was not measured. Although Laner noted performance on some subtasks appeared to be affected by the continuity of motion, he concluded that the adequacy of the presentation methods used was more important than merely the fidelity of the representation. In the 1955 study, instruction on the operation of a trigger mechanism was given by film and compared to instruction given by text and pictures. Presentation mode did not yield significant performance differences, but, as noted by Spangenberg (1973), the relevance to procedural learning was reduced by the fact that the motion condition did not provide a model of the assembly procedure.

Exploded views are commonly used in technical manuals to show the parts of a device. Sheffield et al. (1961) used these views as a starting point for an "implosion" technique in which the parts of a motor appeared to jump into place in the sequence of reassembly. Two groups observed the same training film demonstrating the components and assembly of a servomechanism motor. One of the groups also viewed brief (about 1 minute) reviews that used the implosion technique to show the device being reassembled, piece by piece, through a series of still images of the device at each stage of the task. As the device appeared to reassemble itself, each piece was identified by a narrator. Both groups subsequently practiced assembling the motor two times before taking a final hands-on performance test. The implosion group performed significantly better in terms of the time to complete the task, steps performed correctly, and overall rate of performance on the practice sessions and final test.

Gropper (1968) found actual practice to be superior to videotaped recognition practice. He investigated the mode of student practice and the size of the instructional units given by filmed demonstrations of a procedure involving the assembly of an electric motor. Instruction was delivered by videotaped demonstration to two groups, but their subsequent mode of practice was either hands-on assembly practice or recognition practice in the form of an additional filmed demonstration. Subjects who had practiced assembling the motor made fewer errors and took less time than subjects who had only recognition practice. Over four different unit sizes of how much of the procedure was demonstrated, a steady trend of increasing errors accompanied larger instructional unit sizes. A significant interaction was found where students with below-average ability made more errors with increased demonstration unit size, but students with above-average ability were unaffected by the size of the demonstration unit. Additionally, students engaging in supplementary recognition practice tended to be less affected by the increased demonstration unit size than students who watched only the original demonstration. Gropper concluded that two groups of factors were critical: discriminations and the integration of response sequences in the procedure.

Spangenberg (1973) studied the effect of motion during hands-on practice of a procedural motor skill involving the disassembly of a machine gun. During instruction, the soldiers were cued to perform the disassembly while viewing either a motion videotape or videotaped still sequences using the same soundtrack. Correct performance by the motion group exceeded that of those given the still sequences, and the time to perform the task was less for the motion group. Spangenberg attributed the effect of motion with this task to several factors related to the synthesis of response sequences: providing learners a different internalization of the skill by continuously depicting minute motions, simultaneously depicting motion in different directions, and depicting a desired action involving low verbal codability that could not be readily described with words. Spangenberg also suggested that the importance of these factors should increase to the extent that an activity is unfamiliar to the learner.

Jeon and Branson (1981–1982) trained a procedural motor skill involving basic manipulations of a grenade launcher with different media: a movie with sound, slides with sound, and a printed workbook. With a hands-on performance test, the film group performed better than the slide group, which in turn performed better than the workbook group. The film and slide groups completed the instruction faster than did the workbook group, with the motion film condition requiring three fourths the amount of time taken by the workbook group. A written test yielded no significant difference between groups, which the authors interpreted as being due to a mismatch between the skill taught and the method of testing.

Swezey et al. (1988) summarized a related series of previous studies that showed the importance of hands-on performance in procedural learning. They also reported a new study on electromechanical maintenance involving the removal and replacement of a fuel pump on a diesel engine simulator. Comparisons were made between videotape lecture instruction and computer-based instruction, each with or without opportunities for hands-on practice or using a job performance aid (JPA) consisting of diagrams and step-by-step procedures. Compared to having no JPA, providing the JPA during training reduced both the number of errors and experimenter interjections to provide assistance on both an immediate and delayed hands-on performance test. Time to complete the performance test was significantly reduced for subjects having hands-on experience during training compared to those with no hands-on training on both immediate tests and those repeated after 7 days. Access to the JPA materials had a powerful effect in enhancing performance, even when it was substituted for the other instructional methods. No major differences occurred between computer-based instruction and videotape instructional methods, leading the authors to suggest that JPAs may be a potent alternative method for maintenance tasks.

In a later study with the diesel engine simulator, Swezey et al. (1991) compared a motion videotape and a static 35mm slide–audiotape program as instructional media in combination with several instructional strategies. Over several tasks and measures, they found little benefit of the prior motion instruction compared to the static presentation, although a minor number of comparisons were in favor of motion. The study may be likened to the earlier W. H. Allen and Weintraub (1968) study in the sense that a general effect of motion was studied rather than training in a more specific set of movements or manipulations requiring motion.

Simpson et al. (1992) compared performance on Navy damage control procedures learned in a traditional hands-on laboratory or by a videotaped demonstration without hands-on practice. Both groups subsequently took individual performance tests on three procedures: a watertight door chalk test procedure, assembly of a marine strainer, and assembly of watertight door dogs (latches). The videotape group took from 1 to 3 minutes longer to perform the tasks than did the hands-on laboratory group. The videotape group made a nonsignificant greater number of errors on two of the tasks than did the laboratory group, but made significantly fewer errors on the more difficult door dogs task. The greater errors made by the laboratory group on the door dogs task was attributed to nonassembly steps in the procedure (e.g., lubrication) that were apparently conveyed better in the videotape. Overall, the hands-on laboratory experience yielded a small advantage over the videotape demonstration in terms of speed and accuracy, with the exception of nonassembly steps being better learned from the videotape on one task.

In what might be considered a form of hands-on or procedural learning, Cornell and Hay (1984) assessed incidental route learning of a seven leg route between buildings. Young school children were given a slide presentation, a videotape, or actually walked the route with a guide. When tested in the same medium as trained, the children who actually walked the route performed better than did those with slide or videotape training, both of which resulted in essentially similar performance in terms of errors made. A finding relevant to the issue of realism was that the disruptive effect of tracing the route backwards was not present for the group actually walking, whereas it was prominent in the slide and videotape presentation.

Declarative and procedural knowledge involved in route learning were differentiated in a study of children from 9 through 12 years old by Gale, Golledge, Pellegrino, and Doherty (1990). The children were given five daily exposures to two routes through an unfamiliar suburban neighborhood, either through actual field experience of walking the route or by viewing a videotape simulating the walk. Children viewing the videotape then actually walked the route after they had completed the five daily viewings. The performance of the videotape viewers was substantially below that of the children who actually walked the route for 5 days. However, the videotape viewers performed at a level very similar to that of those walking the route on their first free walk day after having been led through the route on the previous day. Recognition tests of scenes from the walk did not differ between those walking and viewing the video. The authors concluded that seeing the route by either experience led to declarative knowledge "about" the route, whereas "how-to" procedural knowledge was best conveyed by actually performing the task.

A series of studies by Baggett (1989a) and her associates have shown the benefit of combining a video presentation with hands-on practice, the benefit of well-organized video presentations of a procedure, and that some interactive presentation schemes may complicate beneficial effects of practice and organization. She also theorized that motor and practice components stand apart from acquisition of cognitive schemes of the procedures. These studies are characterized by well-elaborated structural analyses of procedural tasks and have recently led to the interesting conception of *visual cohesion* (Baggett, 1989b; Baggett, Ehrenfeucht, & Guzdial, 1989). One expression of visual cohesion was in terms of the number of times a visual element occurred in adjacent frames depicting the sequence of parts to be assembled for an object. This conception is analogous to that developed for verbal materials where text coherence or cohesion are characterized in terms of propositional argument repetition or word repetition (cf. Kintsch & Van Dijk, 1978). Extending ideas on the connectedness of meaningful verbal units to the realm of visual units awaits further development.

Baggett (1987) tested the role of hands-on practice in combination with filmed training with the assembly of a model helicopter kit. The model was built from memory after a training session by six treatment groups tested immediately or by six similar groups tested after a delay of a week. The six treatment conditions consisted of one or two repetitions of either the film or hands-on building practice in the presence of a model, or building followed by the film, or film followed by building. On the immediate test, having engaged in some motoric hands-on practice yielded an advantage. The best performance was found with those who had practiced twice and with those who had practiced once in combination with seeing the film once (in either order). The next best performance resulted from practicing once or seeing the film twice, and the worst performance resulted from seeing the film once. After a delay of a week, the group practicing prior to seeing the film maintained an advantage over the other groups, which performed similarly except for the same poor performance of those seeing the film only once. Thus, the importance of hands-on practice was indicated by the superior initial performance found when the motor component was combined with either a film or a second repetition of practice. Baggett concluded that forming one's own concept via hands-on motoric practice seems to yield a precedence over the visual and linguistic representations resulting from viewing a film. The long-term advantage of having practiced prior to seeing a film also suggests that more lasting concepts result from an ordering where the concept is originally formed on one's own and then subsequently reinforced by viewing the film.

A later study by Baggett (1988) did not find actual practice on an assembly task to be of benefit during interactively controlled video instruction. A postinstruction performance test on assembling an object showed that those who practiced during interactive instruction performed no better than those who had passively watched a videotape. A potential explanation for the finding was that a competition or interference existed between actually practicing assembly and interacting with the computerized instruction. This could not be conclusively confirmed because these two groups did not differ from other subjects who were not allowed to practice during the interactive instruction or who practiced only when the screen was blank. The absence of an effect when practice was simultaneously mixed with interactive audio–visual instruction was tentatively interpreted by distinguishing between the acquisition of motor skills and cognitive understanding. Baggett suggested that the motoric elements of practice remain "outside" the cognitive concept of building the object and possibly do not become integrated with the visual and linguistic information until practice has been more extensive.

Shyu and Brown (1992) also allowed subjects to practice during interactive video instruction on learning a procedure in which a bird (crane) was constructed from paper through a series of folds. A learner control group reviewed the steps of the procedure in any desired order from a program menu. A program control group was only allowed to review the steps in a fixed order, although each step could be reviewed as often as desired while on that step. The learner control group performed the task better on a posttest than did the program control group. However, the superior performance of the learner control group could also be explained by their having spent approximately 40% more time during the instruction.

Baggett and Ehrenfeucht (1988) found the organization of video-based procedural instructions to have a strong effect on learning. They created two narrated films that were empirically based on sequences obtained from subjects who had previously built the object in the presence of a model. One film gave a sequence typical of a majority of these subjects, and the other film gave a valid but atypical sequence based on a minority of the previous subjects. New subjects then built the 80-piece object from memory after watching one of the two videotapes showing its assembly. Viewing the well-structured instructional sequence typical of the majority of previous subjects led to better performance of the procedure than did viewing the atypical minority sequence. The sequences performed by these new subjects indicated that those receiving "minority" instructions evidenced conceptualizations that were more characteristic of the "typical" conceptualization, although significantly less so than those actually viewing the typical instructions.

Baggett et al. (1989) also compared organizational schemes on a graphics system supporting a repair task on a 40-piece assembly kit. The benefits of well-organized sequences were not realized, apparently because interactive system features allowed out of order sequences. Short access routes to relevant frames were interpreted to be important in this configuration. Similarly, Baggett (1989a) found that linguistic access to a system by typing in questions was infrequently used compared to a more direct menu-based touch screen method of seeking information during instruction on assembly and repair.

In summary, the studies of motion and procedural learning reveal a number of instances where motion was beneficial for learning when compared to the use of more static or textual methods. Several instances showed even more powerful benefits to result from the addition of hands-on practice or, in one case, a job performance aid. The procedural learning situations studied were often ones in which selected aspects of the tasks were shown and depicting these in motion was beneficial because it provided additional critical discrimination and continuity information. Many of these tasks also involved lower verbal codability or learning the depicted motion itself. Studies using a wider variety of more general factual content in which critical discriminations play less of a role appear to benefit less from motion, particularly when accompanied by verbal narration.

MODELING MOVEMENTS, FEEDBACK, AND SPORTS

Demonstrations are used in training motor skills because these visual presentations are thought to offer a way of communicating that is more direct than only verbal means. Motion film or video has proven useful as a tool for training various perceptual motor skills in applications that provide a model for performance or feedback during acquisition. These techniques have been used in field studies on sportslike skills or movements to provide a demonstration as a form of mental practice or discrimination training prior to performance, or to provide feedback during or following performance as a kind of corrective guidance. Many of these studies are not well known and are reported in unpublished investigations in the field of physical education (Dukelow, 1979; Rothstein & Arnold, 1976). The wide variety of sportslike skills that have been used include: swimming, gymnastics, wrestling, karate, fencing, jumping, throwing, batting, racquetball, tennis, badminton, volleyball, basketball, archery, bowling, and golf. Three areas of research in learning motor and sportlike skills that are applicable to video presentations include general studies of mental practice, demonstrations, and feedback.

Mentally practicing prior to actually performing a motor skill has been studied in contexts other than with video, but these findings can be mentioned in conjunction with video demonstrations to the extent that both involve symbolic rehearsal. Reviewers have concluded that mental practice prior to performing a skill influences performance somewhat better than no practice at all (Richardson, 1967a, 1967b). Feltz and Landers (1983) conducted a meta-analysis of a large number of studies where the performance of students using mental practice was compared to the performance of controls. They found mental practice to yield a positive overall effect size of .48 or almost half of a standard deviation. The effect sizes were slightly greater for more experienced performers, when mental practice was closer to the time of performance, and for published over unpublished studies. The effect sizes were also related to the type of task performed, with larger effects being obtained for tasks with cognitive elements that could be rehearsed symbolically. Cognitive tasks yielded an effect size of 1.44; motor tasks, .43; and strength tasks, .20. These findings might suggest that video demonstrations and feedback would be beneficial to the extent that they are mediated by more symbolic-cognitive forms of mental practice.

The effectiveness of a demonstration depends on the observer attending selectively to its critical features in order to form a cognitive representation of the skill to be performed (Adams, 1987; W. R. Carroll & Bandura, 1982). Several studies illustrate the use of video for repeated demonstrations given as a form of rehearsal and discrimination training to prepare the student to execute a skill.

Burroughs (1984) studied an instance of discrimination training with filmed simulations on the type and location of baseball pitches. Baseball players who viewed the film improved their ability to identify the location of pitches, but not their recognition of the type of pitch because performance was near a ceiling level. Presentations given in real time or by slow motion did not affect their performance. Haskins (1965) also used filmed visual discrimination training to improve the response time of tennis players to perceive the direction of a tennis return. Gray (1990) gave beginning racquetball players videotaped modeling rehearsal prior to skill tests and found a favorable performance effect on forehand but not backhand shooting compared to those with no modeling. In interpreting backhand shooting as a more difficult skill, the authors suggest that some amount of actual practice for more complex skills may be a limitation of imagery techniques in preparing a mental copy of the skill to execute. In a series of related studies, J. G. Williams (1987a, 1988, 1989a, 1989b) had subjects model an arm action depicted by lights on key joints in a demonstration video display. Accuracy in recognizing the movement as a "darts-style" throwing action and timing performance in modeling the action increased as the displayed velocity approximated the most natural or realistic speed. Masterson (1976) reduced instruction time for a simple psychomotor assembly task with compressed motion pictures and found that a demonstration film can be compressed at least up to a third without significantly affecting task performance.

Some learning can be achieved by observing the critical features of a demonstration in order to form a cognitive representation of the skill to be performed. However, feedback providing knowledge of one's actual performance plays a key role in learning motor skills (Adams, 1987; W. R. Carroll & Bandura, 1982). The conceptual representation of a demonstrated skill can be used as a standard to guide the enactment of the behavior, but knowledge of one's actual performance provides a basis for judging discrepancies that can be used to correct performance. Three techniques for providing learners with knowledge of the results of their performance can be distinguished in shaping movement sequences. Performers can be shown their pattern of responses, this pattern can be shown along with an ideal pattern to be achieved, and this pattern can additionally be supplemented by providing information about the discrepancy between a model and actual performance. A study by Whiting, Bijlard, and den Brinker (1987) illustrates an example of a continuously demonstrated model during performance. They trained a cyclical action consisting of slalom-type ski movement on a ski simulator by providing a videotape of a dynamic model during training. Subjects allowed to view the dynamic model produced more fluent movements than those having no model.

Reviewers of video feedback studies with sports skills note that the pattern of results on the effectiveness of the technique has been somewhat uneven (Dukelow, 1979; Kernodle & Carlton, 1992; Rothstein & Arnold, 1976). Rothstein and Arnold (1976) reviewed more than 50 unpublished master's thesis and doctoral dissertation studies that used videotape replays for learning sports skills. Overall, they found positive effects of videotape feedback on skill learning in 37% of the reviewed studies. By subdividing the studies in terms of several features, a smaller number of studies revealed patterns suggesting several hypotheses on the most effective combination of techniques used with video feedback. Their analysis suggested the hypothesis that video replays are more effective for advanced performers, longer periods of training, and when directed viewing procedures that focus attention on relevant aspects of the skills are employed. Positive effects of the video replay were found for 60% of the studies in which directed viewing was used, whereas 30% of the studies were positive when cues were not provided to the learner. They also noted that advanced learners appeared to derive a greater benefit from video replays than did beginners. This is consistent with the finding that directing attention to the relevant aspect of the video is more effective, because more advanced learners would also be better able to discriminate what is relevant in the video.

Several published studies using attention-directing guidance as part of the video feedback procedure exemplify the pattern suggested by the Rothstein and Arnold (1976) review. Del Rey (1971) directed attention to critical aspects of the fencing lunge and found that speed and form improved more with videotape feedback than when these cues were only read without video feedback. Rikli and Smith (1980) provided instructor feedback comments to all subjects, and found that the addition of video replays was effective for intermediate but not beginning-level tennis players. Likewise, Bunker, Shearer, and Hall (1976) found older, more mature students better able to attend to the relevant features in video feedback while learning to flutter kick. Burkhard, Patterson, and Rapue (1967) provided corrective comments along with filmed feedback to one of two groups of students learning two elementary karate defensive maneuvers.

Only one of the filmed sequences produced significant results, but the trend of the data favored the feedback group. Dukelow (1979) and Kernodle and Carlton (1992) reviewed a number of other studies in which little effect was found and that frequently failed to specify the nature of any guidance provided in conjunction with the video replay.

Two additional studies employed manipulations that more clearly illustrate the importance of receiving information on critical aspects of a task and its effect on subsequent performance (W. R. Carroll & Bandura, 1982; Kernodle & Carlton, 1992). Following the hypothesis of Rothstein and Arnold (1976), Kernodle and Carlton (1992) recently illustrated the importance of both attention-focusing cues and providing specific prospective guidance. Subjects threw a ball with their nondominant hand and were scored for throwing form and the distance thrown. Attention-focusing cues involved telling the subjects where they should focus their attention just prior to viewing a videotape of their performance. Prospective guidance involved seeing the videotape and then receiving directions on how to improve performance on the next throw. The prospective guidance was slightly more effective than cuing in producing gains in throwing form and distance. Both of these techniques were significantly better than merely watching a videotape without cues or guidance, or only receiving a verbal report on the distance thrown.

A study by W. R. Carroll and Bandura (1982) illustrates the value of viewing actions that are not readily observable and the value this information provides after some initial experience in developing a conception of the action. Following a demonstration by a model, subjects reproduced a novel arm movement involving actions that were not fully visible to them. The accuracy of reproducing the actions was enhanced for those who were given video feedback as they performed. The effect of feedback was more pronounced for more complex movements, and its greatest effect was later in learning. Those who were given the feedback only later in learning performed nearly as well as those given feedback throughout and performed better than those given the feedback only early in learning. The subjects also periodically rated the similarity of their actions to the demonstrated model and attempted to arrange a series of pictures of the skill in the correct order. Performance on these measures of the developing conception of the demonstrated actions increased over trials and therefore paralleled the effects that feedback had later in learning. These results suggested that feedback was effective in reducing the discrepancy between conception and action as a consequence of a developing conception of a skill that was not normally visible.

In summary, the general conclusion to be drawn from this collection of studies is that visual-based training providing modeling and feedback can be an effective technique in learning motor skills. The technique offers the opportunity to provide information that can be used in making corrective actions during skill acquisition. These generalizations are subject to some qualifications. More complex skills may require some amount of actual performance for visual monitoring to be effective, and some initial level of skill on the part of the learner may aid in noticing relevant features. It appears that video feedback is more likely to be effective when attention is drawn to critical aspects of the task, either through attention to the display or through prospective guidance offered along with the video replay. This theme of depicting the critical features of a task and focusing the learner's attention on them is similar to that noted earlier with regard to the studies on procedural learning.

VIDEO FEEDBACK IN TEACHER EDUCATION

Video has been proven to be a useful tool in teacher education. It has been successfully used for providing demonstrations and feedback in "microteaching" practice sessions for training teaching skills. Illustrating the benefit of a video demonstration, Koran et al. (1971) found that a model of a teaching skill given by video produced better teaching performance than when given in written form, and both were more effective than no guidance. Illustrating the benefit of feedback, Jensen and Young (1972) had student teachers deliver practice lessons and then view a videotape of their behavior in conjunction with feedback given during an evaluation. A control group received no videotaped feedback. Both groups were evaluated on three occasions during subsequent student teaching in real public school classrooms. The experimental microteaching group received superior ratings on five of six rating scales, with the effect generally increasing during later evaluations.

Several reviewers provide a positive outlook for techniques using videotapes for demonstrations and feedback. The previously discussed meta-analysis by Cohen et al. (1981) examined a small number of studies that involved feedback for teacher training or skill acquisition. They reported these techniques to yield a moderate positive effect size of 0.41 standard deviation units. Frager (1985) and Fuller and Manning (1973) reviewed teacher education studies using videotapes for demonstration and feedback and noted an important feature of the techniques employed. The most effective combination of techniques goes beyond simply viewing the video of one's performance. This form of feedback should also be accompanied by a critique or evaluative feedback provided by others to realize the effectiveness of the technique. Thus, the video replay provides an opportunity for evaluative feedback to be offered, and the combination of these maximizes the benefit. This pattern of results is similar to that shown in the previously discussed sports studies, where guidance during a video replay was also associated with a larger benefit.

Video feedback techniques are also popular in several other areas in addition to teacher training (Fuller & Manning, 1973). An assortment of unpublished papers and talks encountered in our computer literature search were in areas beyond the scope of the present review. Instances where it appeared that a specific skill could be targeted were in training interviewing and counseling skills where audio may in some instances be as good as video (Hosford & Johnson, 1983; Schwab & Harris, 1984), in management training where modeling skills in delivering on-the-job training were enhanced by video feedback (Decker, 1983), and for improving team performance for trauma resuscitations (Hoyt et al., 1988).

STUDIES OF ANIMATED GRAPHICS

Graphic animation is often used within instructional video and film presentations, as well as in the context of computer-based instruction. The effectiveness and common usages of animation are reviewed in the following for both of these visual instruction application areas.

Graphic animation combines graphic illustration with simulated motion to present objects, processes, or concepts. The advantages of graphic illustration in instruction are the ability to control the appearance of a subject; the ability to emphasize the important parts of a subject by removing unnecessary, distracting details; and the ability to visually present subjects and ideas that would be difficult to illustrate in the real world. Animation can also be considered a special case of motion. The advantages of presenting motion in instruction include the abilities to aid discrimination, gain and direct the viewer's attention, depict temporal and spatial changes as a continuous process, and teach movement or the "trajectory" of an object in space. Animation is also related to the concept of realism in pictorial media, insofar as animated graphics use a simplified form of realism to simulate the appearance, movement, functions, and effects of real objects and events. Because animation combines graphic illustration, simplified realism, and motion, many of the concepts associated with those topics discussed elsewhere in this review also apply to the instructional uses of animation.

Uses of Animation in Instruction

Rieber (1990a) identified four common uses for animation in his review of the literature: directing the learner's attention, presenting information, enhancing practice, and increasing a lesson's cosmetic appeal.

Directing Attention

A basic use of animation is to attract or direct the viewer's attention to particular portions of the screen. This use of animation can be applied within an animated graphic segment, or may be projected onto other visual material such as a still photograph or live video. Examples of this use of animation would be inserting visual cues to signal a transition between segments or topics, inserting moving arrows to highlight key points or objects within a picture, changing the color or the brightness of parts of an object, and moving or "exploding" a part of an object to isolate it from other objects in a picture.

Presenting Information

Animation can present information to viewers with the same techniques used with live video with potentially useful differences. Because the visual image is under the complete control of the illustrator, many real-world limitations imposed by time, distance, scale, access, or complexity can be ignored or reduced when illustrating a subject through animation. In addition, animation can present nonphysical concepts, processes, or objects as physical analogs, greatly expanding the kinds of content that can be presented. Examples of animation used to present information are presenting the steps of a process or procedure, such as the movements of parts of a machine (Laesecke, 1990); illustrating dynamic natural events, such as with biological systems (Tritz, 1987); and demonstrating the relationships between abstract or theoretical concepts with animated flow charts or diagrams (Riches, 1990).

Enhancing Practice

Animation can be used within interactive video and computer-based instruction to enhance student understanding and mastery of concepts through direct manipulation of graphic objects. Animation can also provide visual feedback by showing the effects of a student's actions. This permits the student to experiment and explore alternative actions within a simplified, risk-free, artificial environment (Meyer, Rocheleau, McMullen, & Ritter, 1991). Examples of this use of animation are found in interactive simulations, instructional video "games," and role-play "worlds." (Educational game effectiveness is reviewed in Randel, Morris, Wetzel, & Whitehill, 1992.)

Cosmetic Appeal

Rieber (1990a) noted that animation used for cosmetic appeal in instruction is intended to impress and stimulate, rather than teach the student, and is often evaluated for its artistic rather than its instructional merits. Animation can be used as a visual reward for good performance, or as a novelty sequence within drills and practice lessons. Animated characters are sometimes used to reduce the emotional level of a message by presenting potentially upsetting material (e.g., health and safety topics) in a nonthreatening way. Animated characters are used for humorous effects to sustain interest of a message, and the popularity of well-known cartoon characters is used to increase acceptance of ideas in instructional materials, particularly when aimed at younger learners. Finally, the ability to portray unusual and imaginary visual effects through animation has been used to stimulate viewers' interest in particular topics.

The Instructional Effectiveness of Animation

Although animation offers many potential advantages in instruction, its demonstrated effectiveness has been uneven. Researchers have had difficulty separating the effects of animation, the instructional methods the animation is intended to implement, and the characteristics of the learner. In particular, the age of the learner appears to be a major factor in the effectiveness of animation in instruction. In this brief review, we examine 28 studies in which animation was used to present information, enhance learner practice, cue the learner to the key aspects of a topic, or act as a motivating factor apart from the instruction itself. Sixteen of the studies involved adults of college age or older. The remaining 12 studies involved preadult learners, 9 with children and 3 with adolescents.

Adult Learners

The most common use of animation within the adult studies was as a format for presenting instructional content, usually within an interactive computer-based instruction environment. In 8 of the 16 adult studies, animation was used only to present instructional content. In 5 studies, the learner was also allowed to manipulate a computer-generated animated graphic to better understand the content. In 2 studies, animation was used as a cuing device, and in the remaining study, animation was used as a means of practicing a skill.

Only 3 of the 16 adult studies reported a positive effect associated with the use of animated graphics, 5 reported no significant effect, and 8 reported "mixed" results. The first study showing a positive effect for the use of animation (Lumsdaine, Sulzer, & Kopstein, 1961) used limited animation (superimposed arrows) to highlight the key information in a live motion picture presentation on the use of a micrometer. The second study used animated graphics to present facts, concepts, and rules regarding electricity and batteries (Rigney & Lutz, 1975). However, based on the research design used in the study, a static graphic possibly might have produced the same result as the animated graphic.

A more recent study, Park and Gittelman (1992), compared performance on electronic troubleshooting problems between subjects trained with an animated and a static graphic lesson on basic electronic circuit theory. The lesson consisted of an interactive tutorial presentation and a set of practice problems. The animated version of the lesson used animated graphic illustrations in the tutorial and for providing feedback to the learners about the effect of their attempts to repair a faulty circuit. The static version provided the same information in the form of a series of still graphic images. Subjects who received the animated version of the lesson made significantly fewer errors in completing the practice and follow-up test problems than subjects who received the static version of the lesson. There was no difference in the amount of time the two groups used to complete the practice or test problems. The authors concluded that the positive results were the result of using animation to teach content that was suited to its ability to represent "invisible" phenomena, the behavior of electronic circuits, and the effect of the student's actions.

The most common finding for the use of animation with adult subjects has been "no effect" (five studies) or "mixed" positive effects (eight studies). We discuss these studies according to how animation was used in the study. Eight of the 13 "no effect" or "mixed effect" studies used animation only to present information (A. Caraballo, 1985; J. Caraballo, 1985; King, 1975; Mayton, 1991; M. V. Moore, Nawrocki, & Simutis, 1979; H. J. Peters & Daiker, 1982; Reed, 1985; Zavotka, 1987). One study used animation as a means of practicing a skill (Gagnon, 1985), three studies combined information presentation and practice (Palmiter & Elkerton, 1991; Palmiter, Elkerton, & Baggett, 1991; Rieber, Boyce, & Assad, 1990), and one study used animation as a cuing device (Blake, 1977).

Mayton (1991) compared the effectiveness of static graphics and animation for teaching information about cardiac physiology. He found that subjects who viewed the animated version of the lesson performed better on test items that specifically addressed the dynamic functions of the heart, but on other topics they performed no better than subjects who viewed the static graphic lesson. However, the main effect was partially masked by the effect of a second experimental condition, the insertion of verbal hints directing the attention of the learner to parts of the visual image. When tested immediately after instruction, the animation group performed no better than the static group if the latter group had also been given these additional cues. However, during delayed testing, the animation group performed significantly better than the static group with the verbal cues.

Zavotka (1987) found that presenting animated, three-dimensional computer graphics to college-age students was an effective way to teach specific spatial skills. Merely viewing animated solid and wire-frame computer graphics improved the ability of students to interpret the three-dimensional shape of an object viewed from a variety of angles. However, the approach was not successful in teaching mental rotation skills. Viewing wire frame, as opposed to solid, three-dimensional objects, had a negative effect on the subjects' initial mental rotation scores.

Reed (1985) used animation to teach adults how to solve three types of algebra word problems and reported it superior to traditional lessons.

However, the difference in performance was small and could not be entirely attributed to the inclusion of the animated demonstration.

When animation was only used to present information, no effect was found in lessons teaching the relationship between geometric shapes (A. Caraballo, 1985), the physiology of the heart (J. Caraballo, 1985), the sine ratio in trigonometry (King, 1975), the psychophysiology of hearing (M. V. Moore et al., 1979), and organic chemistry (H. J. Peters & Daiker, 1982).

In the only adult study in which animation was used only as a skill practice device, Gagnon (1985) used animated graphic video games to teach spatial skills to male and female adult subjects. In general, there was no significant improvement in the subjects' spatial skill scores following extended practice playing the video games. However, among subject subgroups, female subjects and subjects with no previous experience with video games improved their spatial skill scores significantly more than male subjects and subjects with prior video game experience.

Three studies produced mixed results when using animation to present information and provide practice to the learner. Palmiter and Elkerton (1991), and Palmiter et al. (1991) conducted a series of studies examining the effectiveness of animated online tutorials to teach new users about the Hypercard authoring language on the Macintosh computer. In both studies, the group taught with the animated tutorial initially performed better than a group taught only with written materials and/or demonstrations. However, on subsequent recall and transfer tasks, the nonanimation groups displayed more improvement and performed better overall than the animation group. The authors suggested that the simplicity of using the animated demonstration may have encouraged the users to mimic the interface procedures and to disregard accompanying text when it was provided.

Rieber et al. (1990) used animation as an illustration format and as a practice device to teach the Newtonian laws of motion. They reported no independent learning effect attributable to the animation. Subjects who practiced the principles of action and reaction within an animated graphic microworld performed better on a written posttest than subjects who did not, but performed no better than subjects who "practiced" the same concepts by answering a series of embedded questions. However, students in the animation group responded more quickly to retest questions, suggesting that animation enabled a faster retrieval time in addition to equivalent learning.

Blake (1977) used animation as a cuing device for learning standard chess piece movements. Subjects were presented static learning materials, static materials enhanced with animated arrows, or a full-motion presentation. The animation was limited to a sequence of arrows, projected onto a static picture of a chessboard, that traced the permitted movement of different chess pieces. High spatial aptitude subjects performed equally well with the three conditions. However, those with low spatial aptitudes performed better with both animated and full-motion presentations than with the static materials. This study and the Lumsdaine et al. (1961) study using superimposed arrows were the only adult studies in which animation was used primarily to cue the learners' attention to the key parts of a visual image.

An additional adult study was considered as part of the previous section on procedural learning. The film used by Sheffield et al. (1961) might also be considered to have used a form of animation in that the parts of an exploded view of a device were shown to "pop into place," which benefited subsequent assembly performance.

In summary, the adult studies provide only limited support for the effectiveness of animation. Only three studies produced unambiguous positive results, and the "mixed" results were frequently limited in scope. In addition, Rieber (1990a) pointed out in his review of the literature that several of the studies suffered from methodological limitations. In several instances the use of animation was very restricted or may have been ineffective. For example, H. J. Peters and Daiker (1982) admitted that the graphics used in their study may have failed to focus on the same material emphasized in the text and that the animation did not draw adequate attention to the ideas it was intended to demonstrate.

Preadult Learners

Twelve studies investigated the effectiveness of animation for adolescent and grade-school-age learners. Ten of these produced positive results and two found no effect attributable to animation. Three of the studies used animation only to present information (Baek & Layne, 1988; Rieber, 1989a; S. V. Thompson & Riding, 1990), two studies used animation to facilitate practice (Acker & Klein, 1986; B. White, 1984), and five studies used animation for both presenting information and practice (Rieber, 1989b, 1990a, 1990b, 1991a, 1991b). One study used animation only for cuing the learner (A. Collins, Adams, & Pew, 1978), and one study used animation as a motivational device (Suber & Leeded, 1988).

High-School-Age Learners

Three studies used high school students as subjects, and all three reported positive results for the use of animation. Baek and Layne (1988) used a computer-assisted lesson to present information about how to compute average speed. One group of students received a text-only lesson, and two other groups received a lesson with text plus static graphics or with text plus animated graphics. The group presented with the animated material performed better on a follow-up performance test than the group shown only static materials, which in turn outperformed the group taught the text-only lesson.

B. White (1984) developed a series of educational computer games using animated computer graphics to teach high school students the basic principles of Newtonian laws of motion and force. The students attempted to maneuver an animated spaceship by controlling its direction and thrust in a frictionless two-dimensional microworld. Students who played these games for an hour were better able to answer a series of questions regarding the probable effect of different forces on the direction and velocity of an object.[1]

A third study, in which animation was used to cue learners, also produced positive results, but was based on a small sample size and used limited animation (A. Collins et al., 1978). It tested the effectiveness of animation in a geography lesson on South America and reported better recall of city names and locations from using a graphic map in which the key cities were highlighted with blinking symbols.

Grade-School-Age Learners

Of nine studies involving elementary school students, seven produced positive learning effects for the animated materials, and two found no effect attributable to animation.

Two studies used animation only to present or illustrate a lesson. S. V. Thompson and Riding (1990) found a positive effect for animation by using animated computer graphics to illustrate a geometric theorem. They reported improved performance among grade school students presented with an animated demonstration of the Pythagorean theorem compared to a group shown only a set of static diagrams. However, the improvement was described as "significant but small in educational terms."

A study in which animation was not effective with grade school children (Rieber, 1989a) was an early version of an interactive lesson on physical laws that was successful in three studies described later. The lesson used animation to illustrate the effect of force on the movement and momentum of objects. The lesson was described by the author as difficult in both content and the complexity of the animated material, resulting in students spending less time on the animated sequences than other frames within the lesson. There was no difference in the ability of subjects who viewed the animated sequences to answer factual questions or apply the principles taught to specific situations.

In a series of subsequent studies, Rieber and other colleagues revised the lesson described earlier by restructuring the content and by adding a

---

[1]DiSessa (1982) described a similar animated microworld game used to examine the stages of thinking children and adults use to master a problem in the laws of motion, force, and inertia. This study is not included in this discussion because the focus was on the learner's thought processes rather than on instruction and the findings were based on a small number of observational case studies. However, the study is a good description of the use of graphic animation as a way to practice and experiment with abstract concepts and principles.

practice component. Two studies produced positive results attributable to animation (Rieber, 1989b, 1990a). After reorganizing the lesson material into more concise segments, the group viewing and practicing with the animated materials performed better on a knowledge recall and application test than students who viewed a static version of the lesson (Rieber, 1990a). Subjects who received the animated version of the lesson were also more likely to return to the lesson voluntarily during a free study period (Rieber, 1989b). A subsequent revision of the lesson added a nonanimated "practice" condition in which subjects answered questions that directed their attention to the key points of the frame. Subjects who actively manipulated an animated graphic spaceship that illustrated the principles taught in the lesson performed better on subsequent tests than subjects who answered the embedded questions or received no practice (Rieber, 1990b). The study was further extended to test the effect of animation on learning incidental information. Rieber (1991a) found that subjects presented the animated version of the lesson were able to learn incidental principles of motion not explicitly taught in the lesson with no decline in learning of the information covered in the lesson. These findings were confirmed in a replication of the study reported in Rieber (1991b).

Other than the first Rieber study (1989a), only one other study failed to produce a positive effect for animation with preadult subjects. Suber and Leeded (1988) failed to find a significant motivational or learning effect for a graphics feedback condition in a computer-aided lesson to teach fourth-grade spelling. Moreover, students were no more likely to use the graphics mode lesson voluntarily when it was made available to them during a free study period. This study made only marginal use of animation, consisting only of cartoonlike graphic feedback ("Wow!," "Super!," and "Good Work!") for a correct answer.

In the only study in which animated material was tested across adult, adolescent, and grade school populations, Acker and Klein (1986) developed three spatial tasks in both a video and a computer graphics format, and tested both versions on third graders, middle school students, and university students. These tasks required the learner to estimate distances based on the movements of either a videotaped live actor or a computer-generated animated cartoon figure. The animated graphic presentation yielded significantly more accurate performance than did the more realistic video version for both middle school and university students. The third-grade students performed similarly with either version. The effectiveness of animated graphics as a teaching tool stood in contrast to the attitudinal preferences among the age groups because the two older groups preferred the video version and the third graders preferred the computer animation version. Thus, middle school and university students preferred the video version over the computer version, but performed significantly better on the computer graphic version of the tests. Although the third graders performed similarly with the two formats, they strongly preferred the animated over the video version, which the authors explained in motivational terms of the animation being more "engaging" and "interactive."

Discussion of Animation

Based on the distribution of study outcomes, the effectiveness of animation in instruction appears to be confined to younger learners. Only 3 of the 16 studies with adult subjects produced positive results, whereas 10 of 12 studies with preadult subjects reported a positive effect for animation. A secondary finding suggests that using animation to illustrate or present content, by itself, is relatively less effective than other uses. When animation was used in this fashion, only 2 of 11 studies reported positive results (8 adult and 3 preadult). By contrast, generally positive findings were reported when animation was used to allow the learner to practice an idea or skill. Of 13 such studies, all 7 preadult studies and one adult study were positive, and the remaining 5 adult studies reported "mixed" positive results. Although the number of studies is small, the distribution of outcomes also suggests that animation is effective when used to cue learners to the important aspects of a presentation. Not enough research has been reported to establish the value of animation as a motivational device. Finally, recent studies that have attempted to explicitly match the presumed advantages of animation to appropriate learning objectives have tended to produce more positive learning outcomes.

Rieber and Kini (1991) noted that the conditions under which animation should be more effective than static graphics are not well understood. However, they indicated that the principal advantage of animation over static graphics appears to lie in its superior ability to represent change or movement over time. They contend that dynamic visual content has at least three components: visual appearance, verbal or cognitive meaning, and motion or trajectory characteristics. Although such phenomena can be represented in static graphics through the use of arrows, or with a sequence of static images, such changes are more abstract and require more learner effort to interpret, connect, and integrate their meaning. Animation, according to Rieber and Kini, triggers the learner's ability to perceive apparent motion, thereby reducing the amount of effort the learner must exert, and freeing short-term memory for other tasks. They also suggest that animation provides a redundant representation of the cognitive concepts of motion and trajectory in addition to verbal and static visual representations.

Based on his analysis, Rieber (1990a) made three design recommendations for the use of animation in instruction:

1. Animation should be incorporated only when its attributes are congruent to the learning task. The attributes of animation are visualiza-

tion, motion, and trajectory. Animation should only be used if the instructional strategy requires one of these attributes. Many of the studies that report no difference in learning performance between animated graphics, nonanimated graphics, and unillustrated text failed to specify whether an animation attribute or any form of visual illustration was necessary to complete the learning task. When all three attributes are congruent to the learning task, animation effects are possible to the extent that they are not undermined by excessive task difficulty, inability to properly attend to information in an animated display, or poor instructional design.

2. When learners are novices in the content area, they may not know how to attend to relevant cues or details provided by animation. Rieber noted that learning from animation improved when he "chunked" material into discrete packages of text, static graphics, and animation (Rieber, 1990a, 1990b). He attributed this to the increased attention they were able to give to the animated sequence. However, other research suggests that learners not familiar with the content may not be able to perceive important details in an animation if they view the presentation without guidance or a chance to interact with the computer (Reed, 1985).

3. Animation's greatest contribution to computer-based instruction may lie in interactive graphic applications.

REALISM AND FIDELITY IN VISUAL INSTRUCTION

Realism and fidelity are commonly thought to be important characteristics of visually based instruction. The two most popularly cited attributes of realism are motion and image quality expressed as the accurate reproduction of detail. Similar issues are discussed in terms of fidelity when considered in the context of simulations. Other attributes may be thought to be instances of realism (e.g., color) or are attributes less commonly mentioned in connection with learning (e.g., subtle social, emotional, facial, and auditory features). Discussions of the attributes of realism appear to substantially exceed the number of studies directly bearing on the idea.

Continua of Realism

Several authors discuss a continuum of referential fidelity in which categories of visuals are ordered from the realistic to the abstract. Such rankings are essentially elaborations of the idea that pictorial materials are processed more directly as represented than are verbal materials requiring additional decoding.

Dale's *cone of experience* is an early expression of the idea that implied that the degree of pictorial fidelity is positively related to learning (see Magne & Parknas, 1963; M. V. Moore & Nawrocki, 1978). In this ranking, greater learning was implied to take place with direct experience represented by the wider base of the cone, followed by pictures, and then visual symbols and verbal symbols near the narrower peak of the cone. More generally, the cone of experience referred to ordering experience from concrete to abstract. Hunter, Crismore, and Pearson (1987) referred to the same idea as *referential representationality*. They distinguished a continuum of visual information that ranges from faithful photographic reproduction of reality, through artwork, diagrams, graphs and formulae, tables and charts, and then, at the far extreme, to iconic orthography where levels of abstraction are furthest removed from their apparent real-world referents. For purposes of his empirical investigation of visual illustrations, Dwyer (1972, 1978) also ranked visuals on a realism continuum. They were ranked from simple line drawings, to drawings that were detailed and shaded, to photographs of a model, and to realistic photographs; each of these were subcategorized so that black-and-white visuals were less realistic than color.

Friedman (1993) also discussed referential fidelity in terms of a realistic-to-abstract continuum ordered in terms of depictive–pictorial, schematic, iconic, structural–functional, symbolic, and then arbitrary. She argued that categorizations of visuals in terms of the amount of realism need to be recast in terms of the type of information afforded by the visuals (*informational affordances*). One potential scheme for the information afforded by visuals is in terms of appearances, static relations, and events or sequences. She further distinguished between these primary or directly represented characteristics and those not directly given by appearance that are secondary inferences or conclusions we may derive from them. Friedman's account typifies more recent views that extend and qualify the relation of realism and learning. Specifically, she emphasized that visual characteristics are associated with different transformations into mental representations.

Friedman's account is in many ways similar to Salomon's (1979) analysis of media symbol systems in which he described symbolic modes being recoded by the learner to extract meaning from them (see chap. 9). In contrast to popular notions of the importance of resemblance between symbols and their referents, he argued that what is important for communication is that "resemblance occurs between a symbol and a mental conception of the referent, not between a symbol and its referent" (p. 218). In other words, he distinguished (a) the similarity between the instructional presentation and what it depicts or describes, from (b) the congruence between the presentation and the mental representation.

Realism in Pictures, Simulations, and Motion

The following sections address several topic areas in which realism appears to apply to learning. The discussion is critical of realism as a principle in learning because it is focused on variations within the dimensions of comparable media. However, this perspective should be distinguished from an alternative level where media differences are more broadly conceived. A very general continuum of realism like Dale's might involve such a wide range of "experience" as to include substantially different media comparisons. Such a broad view of realism is not particularly challenged in circumstances where the capability to present some kinds of information is absent or is difficult to achieve with alternative media having fewer representational capabilities. Examples of this broader conception of realism can be seen in the previous sections discussing motion and visual–verbal media comparisons. Thus, it might be thought that a realism principle is supported by the findings that a hands-on learning experience can be more beneficial than visual or textual instruction, that some motion depictions are more beneficial than text, and that video modeling can be more effective than print in learning teaching skills. Likewise, realism might be supported by the finding that learners are aided by the addition of pictures to text when some of these visual depictions share more properties with corresponding real objects than do linguistic systems used to describe them. However, the following discussion suggests that, when realism is considered within comparable media, systematic changes in the amount of realism do not always appear to predict learning.

Details and Pictorial Fidelity

Compared to other experiences, visual realism may be more simply characterized as the extent to which a visual depicts the real thing or cannot be differentiated from it in the extreme (Dwyer, 1978). Authors examining the realism hypothesis generally conclude that it has not been supported with regard to pictorial detail (Peeck, 1987). Instead, detail has been characterized as facilitating learning to the extent that particular details are relevant to the task. The extension of this qualification is that instructional effectiveness may be limited if too much information is given as a consequence of realism with high degrees of detail. The well-known series of studies by Dwyer indicates that excessive detail in more realistic pictures or models of the heart may be less effective than appropriately detailed line drawings (Dwyer 1972, 1978; Parkhurst & Dwyer, 1983). Dwyer (1978) offered a general characterization of the relation between achievement and realism in visual illustrations as being curvilinear in that too much or too little realism could be detrimental. Thus, overly simplified illustrations limit the amount of information conveyed, and highly realistic illustrations can contain too much information for the essentials to be identified or can require additional time for understanding. Studies with other materials also show that irrelevant or excessive detail does not always facilitate learning (Borg & Schuller, 1979; Gorman 1973) and it may overwhelm students who are less able (W. H. Allen, 1975; Parkhurst & Dwyer, 1983; Winn, 1989).

Color is another instance of pictorial detail where a benefit may or may not be achieved, depending on how it is used. Although viewers commonly prefer color, it has not generally been noted to be an effective learning variable, such as when expressed merely as an instance of realism in pictures. However, color may be beneficial to the extent that it serves an attention-getting, organizational, or discrimination cuing function (e.g., highlighting) and is not overused (Chute, 1980; Dwyer, 1971, 1972, 1976; Friedman, 1993; Kanner, 1968; Lamberski & Dwyer, 1983; M. V. Moore & Nawrocki, 1978).

Simulations and Fidelity

A practical instance of concern with realism is in the literature on simulations, which are in some cases implicit studies of visual instruction. Alessi (1988) distinguished among a wide variety of simulations that follow different principles. He distinguished simulations concerned with *how to do something* (e.g., procedural simulations) from others dealing with phenomena the student is to *learn about* (e.g., process simulations on cause–effect relationships). Transfer-of-learning criteria are of concern in procedural simulations. Transfer is thought to increase as similarity increases between conditions during learning and those present in the intended real situation. With equipment simulations, similarity can be distinguished in terms of *physical fidelity* (extent of looking like the real equipment) and *functional fidelity* (extent of acting like the real equipment). Using such a distinction, J. A. Allen, Hays, and Buffardi (1986) experimentally varied both types of fidelity in an electromechanical troubleshooting task and found that solution times decreased as each type of fidelity was increased. Other measures showed more complex relationships that depended on the level of physical and functional fidelity (e.g., number of troubleshooting tests made).

Reviewers of training device fidelity issues note a more recent trend to question whether high physical fidelity is always required for all tasks (Blaiwes & Regan, 1986; Hays & Singer, 1989). They argue that those circumstances where high fidelity is needed must be discriminated through an analysis of the critical portions of the skill to be learned. Fidelity should then be adjusted accordingly to obtain the right mix of both psychological and physical fidelity. Alessi's (1988) review of simulation fidelity resulted in an explicit hypothesis that the relationship of learning and fidelity is nonlinear and depends on the instructional level of the learner. For the beginning student, an inverted U-shaped function is proposed in which moderate amounts of fidelity are more effective for learning than either low and high degrees of fidelity. Thus, low fidelity is not realistic enough to be effective, and excessive fidelity has a negative effect because an assumed limited attention/capacity mechanism is overwhelmed. As students become increasingly sophisticated, better learning is achieved with increasingly higher fidelity instruction that these students are better prepared to process. Alessi also proposed that each level of student expertise has a point at which increasing fidelity has less of an incremental effect, or even a negative effect if the instructional level of the student is low.

Motion

Although realism can serve as an initial cursory explanation for some benefits of depicting motion, it generally has not been researched in the context of such hypotheses. Rather, fairly well-detailed descriptions of the important components of motion have been developed that go beyond a simple realism explanation (W. H. Allen & Weintraub, 1968; Blake, 1977; Gropper, 1968; Hochberg & Brooks, 1978; Spangenberg, 1973; Swezey et al., 1991). These selective benefits of motion stand in contrast to a general absence of a blanket benefit to all types of instructional presentations, such as observed with the wide range of factual material in the studies by W. H. Allen (W. H. Allen, Cooney, & Weintraub, 1968; W. H. Allen & Weintraub, 1968; W. H. Allen et al., 1970). Even though based on only a few early studies, the conclusion from the review by Chu and Schramm (1967) still seems applicable. They concluded that there was not consistent evidence for motion over stills, but that learning would be improved by moving visual images if the continuity of an action is an essential part of the learning task. Similarly, W. H. Allen and Weintraub (1968) concluded "motion is certainly indicated where the particular content to be learned consists of the movement itself and its characteristics or is enhanced and differentiated by the cues provided in the action of the movement" (p. 68). In a slightly different way, Blake (1977) said "a dynamic presentation could be said to have an advantage over a static presentation to the extent that it can draw attention to the critical portions of the display and can enhance perception of the desired figure-ground relationships" (p. 975).

Taking the previously reviewed studies together, the attributes of motion found relevant to learning were being able to make discriminations, having attention directed to relevant features that change, clarifying sequential relations by providing continuity between events, being able to learn a concept that itself is defined by motion, learning the motion itself, and tasks that are unfamiliar or difficult to express verbally. These specific beneficial circumstances of motion do not easily map to a simplistic idea of realism. For example, realistic rapid presentations can yield negative effects, but unrealistically slowed presentations of large amounts of information may offer better discriminations because they accommodate information-processing load limitations. Conversely, the benefit of greater realism or fidelity may be reflected in a general way when learning a motion itself and when sequential relations are clarified by the continuity of motion. However, when more specific discriminations are identified in these presentations, these broader benefits of realism become further qualified. Thus, realism is left as a popular cursory description clearly subordinate to specific explanations based on a cluster of motion principles found relevant to selected learning tasks. The capability to depict motion is automatically included in contemporary educational presentations using video. With media choices less of an obstacle, the features of motion that were identified as critical to learning therefore provide a basis for focusing attention on appropriate exploitation of those circumstances.

Discussion

Critical Elements Instead of Realism

The idea that a degree of realism or fidelity is only required to the extent that it is relevant to intended objectives has emerged as the most common generalization of authors considering the issue (W. H. Allen & Weintraub, 1968; Blake, 1977; Chu & Schramm, 1967; Dwyer, 1972, 1978; Friedman, 1993; Hannafin & Phillips, 1987; Hays & Singer, 1989; M. V. Moore & Nawrocki, 1978; Peeck, 1987; Rieber, 1990a). In Friedman's (1993) words, "the amount of fidelity that is maintained by a representation is likely to be irrelevant unless considered within the context of the purpose for which the representation is likely to be used" (p. 274). It may be more than irrelevant in some instances when excessive realistic detail detracts attention from relevant learning cues or insufficient study time is allowed (Dwyer, 1972; Peeck, 1987).

Blake (1977) noted a consequence of the observation that visual detail could enhance or degrade learning depending on how "critical" it is to aiding the perception of desired materials. He suggested that makers of instructional media may include high levels of detail as a result of the difficulty of isolating critical elements from irrelevant cues. Similarly, Borg and Schuller (1979) also suggested that the cost of detailed illustrations may not always be warranted by their effects on learning. The level of detail that is optimal for learning may only be known empirically in many cases. This proactively focuses attention on the initial analysis of the stimuli and methods of the learning situation and their correspondence to the desired or to be understood behavior.

The attractiveness of a simple realism or fidelity principle in developing instruction has not been replaced by a correspondingly simple prescription. Instead, an analysis of elements critical to learning objectives is urged in adjusting the features of a presentation. This theme seems common to the separate research fields concerned with the role of pictures, motion, and human factors. It is also consistent with general views such as Clark's (1983) emphasizing the reexamination of media in terms of the instructionally relevant events taking place in a medium.

Interpreting Realism

In summary, realism as a claim for the benefits of visualized or video-based instruction can best be characterized as an occasional descriptive correlate rather than a guiding principle. The following layers of simplification offer an interpretation that may be used in addressing popular opinion.

First, broad popular interpretations of realism suggest that it can benefit learning when comparing very different methods of learning in which it is difficult for one of the media to present certain kinds of information. This might be the case when visual depictions are found to be more effective than their verbal descriptions or when hands-on experience is more beneficial than a surrogate visual depiction.

Second, within more specific and comparable media, greater realism does not always yield better learning. High levels of realism can be detrimental and intermediate levels appear to be more beneficial when they selectively emphasize those elements critical to learning. What is relevant for learners is not always predicted by the similarity of a presentation to what it depicts, describes, or how it acts or responds in real life. As Clark (1984) observed, "'skeletal' presentations offer less chance for the student to fix on irrelevant detail than more elaborate visual presentations" (p. 239).

Third, what is relevant for learners has empirically grown out of experience. This congruity between a presentation and the learner is qualified somewhat differently with regard to visual detail, motion, and learning to do something. The broadest generalizations characterizing these indicates (a) that the effect of pictorial detail and motion on learning depends on whether the relevant information to be learned can be easily discriminated and that the level of detail, speed, or load on memory does not become excessive; (b) that sequential or spatial relations shown in the continuity of motion are beneficial when central to the message to be learned, such as in learning or modeling a motion itself; and (c) that the learner's level of skill determines the extent of realism or fidelity that can be tolerated and that is optimal for learning.

5 Computer-Based Interactive Video

Interactivity as a feature of instruction is shared by many traditional media and instructional methods. Students interact with instructors and other students while learning. They also interact with a book as they study it, marking passages, jumping around to reread a section, correlating text with diagrams and pictures. The advent of interactive video-based technologies has moved instructional delivery in the direction of approximating such interactivity. Although videotapes to some extent permit interruptions and replays of linear sequences, the attraction of videodiscs is that they combine the representational qualities of video with the interactivity afforded by computer program control. Interactive video-based instruction reduces limitations associated with one-way linear video communication media by providing variable control over the pace and course of instruction and by being actively responsive to performance. Such capabilities were previously unavailable to designers of conventional film, videotapes, and one-way broadcasts.

The general term *interactive* video typically refers to a computer controlling a videodisc, although it can also include the control of a videotape player in some manner that segments the display of linear sequences. The advent of real-time, random-access videodisc media enables developers to easily branch among motion video segments, precise frame-by-frame stills, correlated audio presentations, and other computer-generated text and graphics. The coupling of video media with computer-based instruction allows instruction to be individualized for students who actively participate in advancement and allows active monitoring of their performance in order to respond with feedback, tailored branching, reviews, and advisement.

META-ANALYSES OF INTERACTIVE VIDEO

Prior to the use of meta-analysis techniques, previous traditional reviews of interactive video are exemplified by counts of studies showing benefits

(Bosco, 1986), discussions of study findings (Kearsley & Frost, 1985; E. E. Smith, 1987) and directions for future research (Hannafin, 1985). More recent meta-analysis techniques summarize the findings of many studies in terms of effect sizes. An effect size is given in standardized units in terms of the mean difference between control and treatment groups divided by the standard deviation of the combined groups or just that of the control group. A comparative summary of effect sizes for many different types of psychological and educational treatments is given in Lipsey and Wilson (1993).

Using meta-analysis techniques, Fletcher (1990) recently provided evidence suggesting that interactive videodisc-based instruction offers both a more efficient way to deliver instruction and a moderately better level of achievement compared to traditional methods. Fletcher's analysis included 28 studies of interactive videodisc instruction in military, industrial, and civilian settings. About half of the military studies involved electronics maintenance, whereas the higher education studies covered a range of topics including chemistry, medical trauma, and foreign language training. The traditional methods compared in these studies included non- or limited-interaction approaches of conventional instruction such as lecture, text, programmed text, on-the-job training, experience with actual equipment, video, or videotape and excluded interactive video or computer-based instruction.

Overall, 47 comparisons were derived from the 28 studies analyzed by Fletcher (1990). These comparisons showed an average achievement increase for interactive videodisc instruction of .50 standard deviations over conventional instruction (an increase for 50th percentile students to about the 69th percentile). Higher education studies constituted 14 of these comparisons, and showed an average achievement increase of .69 standard deviations (i.e., an increase to the 75th percentile). Military studies constituted 24 of the comparisons, showing an increase of .38 standard deviations (i.e., an increase to the 65th percentile), the lower achievement level being possibly attributed to the use of completion criteria.

Fletcher also examined four measures of instructional effectiveness: knowledge outcomes, performance outcomes, instructional time, and postinstruction retention. Interactive videodisc instruction was equally effective for knowledge outcomes (e.g., facts and concepts) and for performance outcomes (e.g., demonstrated capabilities on procedures or skills), averaging about .35 standard deviations, or an improvement from the 50th to 64th percentile. Directed, tutorial approaches were more effective than stand-alone simulations, with combinations of these techniques showing an intermediate level (.70 for tutorial approaches, .40 for combined tutorial and simulation approaches, and .15 for simulations alone). An assessment of studies involving different levels of interactivity indicated that higher levels of interactivity were associated with higher levels of achievement.

Eight studies reviewed by Fletcher provided data on the amount of time required to progress through the instruction. He found a 31% time savings to reach threshold levels of performance for interactive video over conventional instruction. This figure is comparable to a general figure of 30% previously reported for computer-based instruction (cf. Kulik & Kulik, 1987; Orlansky & String, 1977, 1981). Achievement data on retention were not found to be affected in comparing videodisc and conventional instruction. Other data from this study suggested that videodisc instruction could be less costly than conventional instruction. The general conclusions drawn from this investigation were that videodisc training can provide both more efficient training and moderate increases in achievement.

Another recent meta-analysis performed by McNeil and Nelson (1991) examined other variables in 63 interactive video studies that included both interactive videodisc and videotape techniques. They reported an effect size of .53, which is comparable to Fletcher's figure of .50, and again noted this is slightly higher than that found in computer-based instruction studies.

McNeil and Nelson (1991) also classified the reviewed studies in terms of several descriptive features. Studies employing interactive video as a supplement to instruction were found to average larger effects than when it was used in place of traditional forms of instruction. Studies allowing within media comparisons among different interactive video conditions where the range of instructional techniques was reduced yielded smaller effect sizes than comparisons from studies using a traditional instruction control group. Approximately one third of the studies examined used videotape, which yielded similar effect sizes to those in the videodisc studies. Their analysis also compared studies in terms of the extent to which the instructional sequence, review, and practice were predominantly under learner control or were guided or controlled by the program. As with Fletcher (1990), these comparisons again indicated that program-controlled interactive video appears to be more effective than learner-controlled interactive video.

Comparing separately reported meta-analyses offers a rough view of the pattern of effectiveness of computer-based instruction, interactive videodisc-based instruction, and noncomputerized visual-based instruction. Fletcher (1990) noted that the achievement effect sizes obtained in his study of videodisc instruction were higher than those previously reported for computer-based instruction. His effect sizes of .50 overall or .69 for higher education studies can be compared to representative computer-based instruction meta-analyses that found .31 over all educational levels (Kulik & Kulik, 1987), .26 in colleges (Kulik & Kulik, 1986), and .42 in adult education (Kulik, Kulik, & Shwalb, 1986). These effect sizes stand in contrast to the results discussed earlier for noninteractive visualized instruction, where Cohen, Ebeling, and Kulik (1981) obtained .15. The greater effectiveness of the computer-based and interactive videodisc instruction studies over these visualized instruction studies seems explicable in terms of the formers' greater interactivity, as suggested by Fletcher's report.

Beyond the obvious identification of interactivity, these results raise a research question for future meta-analyses concerning the effect of video. That is, it is not clear to what extent video contributes to any increment in effectiveness of interactive video over computer-based instruction that is not video based (e.g., studies such as Dalton, 1986). This question would certainly depend on the visual features of the subject matter and is related to the earlier question of whether production techniques that exceed simply recording conventional lectures would provide a benefit in linear video instruction.

INSTRUCTIONAL DESIGNS IN INTERACTIVE VIDEO

Whereas general media comparisons show interactive video to be more effective than traditional instruction, the details of the instructional designs that lead to the improvement are less well circumscribed (Bosco, 1986; Fletcher, 1990; Hannafin, 1985; Reeves, 1986; E. E. Smith, 1987). Fletcher (1990) commented that there was little in the studies he reviewed to indicate how different interactive videodisc instructional designs achieved success and that it was rarely addressed in the studies. Similarly, Bosco (1986) noted the wide variety of techniques being used in 29 interactive video studies reviewed, where 19 provided little or no information on the nature of the interactive video program, 5 provided moderate information, and 5 provided extensive details on the design of the instruction. Lack of reported details hampers the explanation of the obtained effects for interactive video because there are a large number of different ways in which questioning, feedback, lesson control, and advisement can be configured.

A pattern of findings from efforts directed toward explaining interactivity come from studies using within-medium designs that compare different interactive video techniques. Because the methods implemented in these vary considerably, there are fewer comparable studies available for meta-analyses that rely on frequently encountered comparisons like that with a conventional instruction group.

Interactivity between the learner and computer can be characterized in several ways. It can be characterized in terms of the kind of cognitive processing produced by the ways learners receive information, the elicitation of overt responses, the ways in which learner responses are analyzed, and the kind of actions that are taken in responding to and guiding the learner (Jonassen, 1988).

The most potent of these studied variables in interactive video has been the beneficial effect of "enroute" practice questions. Such questions are embedded within the instructional sequence, as opposed to being ones blocked together as a separate test. Although attempts have been made to make linear video seem more interactive with embedded questions (cf. Hannafin, 1985), the range of possible actions following a question is enhanced with computer control. A series of interactive video studies indicate that performance is increased to the extent that the instruction provides various enroute questions, feedback, and branching to reviews (Hannafin, Phillips, & Tripp, 1986; Phillips, Hannafin, & Tripp, 1988; Schaffer & Hannafin, 1986). Information questioned during the course of instruction shows a benefit of the practice on retest relative to other similar new test items and appears to benefit fact questions more than those for concepts or applications. However, both conceptual and factual knowledge are benefited by interactive learning strategies that employ a contextualized, concept-based approach, as opposed to one simply emphasizing facts (Dalton & Hannafin, 1987). In procedural learning, the form of practice given in interactive video practice may be more complicated. In one case, learning to build a device was not benefited when actual practice of the assembly procedure was interspersed with interacting with the computerized instruction, possibly because of a competition between the two (Baggett, 1988).

Various lesson-control designs are a second powerful component of interactivity. An ongoing research focus involves comparing techniques that vary in the extent to which lesson features are controlled by either the student or computer. Generalizations pitting learner versus program control of lessons should be viewed cautiously because individual portions of a lesson may benefit from one or the other form of control and may be useful in hybrid combinations (Jonassen, 1988; Jonassen & Hannum, 1987; Steinberg, 1989). The various techniques explored in these studies attempt to provide structure and guidance for students unfamiliar with the content and who may not know what is best for them instructionally, while also attempting to allow control when the student is able to make such judgments. Combinations of lesson organization, path sequencing, diagnosis of progress, and remediation branching generally appear to have more robust effects on learning than use of only a few of these techniques, such as only optional reviews and other unguided student decisions (Gay, 1986; Hannafin & Colamaio, 1987; Ho, Savenye, & Haas, 1986). For example, Gay (1986) compared learner- and program-controlled designs using a full set of these techniques and found program control to increase learning for students with low prior understanding, whereas learner control reduced task time for high prior understanding students.

Although achievement comparisons favor interactive video over linear video (e.g., Dalton, 1986; Dalton & Hannafin, 1987; Levenson, Morrow, & Signer, 1985–1986; Phillips et al., 1988), instances where the same video material is made interactive by adding extra features such as questions, feedback, and branching indicate that learning time may also be extended

(Schaffer & Hannafin, 1986). Using similar video material provides more comparable experimental conditions than comparisons with more traditional forms of instruction (e.g., classroom instruction) where time savings were reported for interactive video (see Fletcher, 1990). Thus, "repurposing" existing video to an interactive format may increase instruction time to the extent that the video is relatively unmodified. Similar findings arise from studies of linear pacing in interactive video. Learner control may extend lesson time more than program-paced control, potentially offering a longer opportunity for learning (Burwell, 1991; Dalton, 1990).

Although studied in the context of interactive video, other studied variables include ones better thought of as good instructional practices than ones inherently "interactive." For example, prefacing instruction with objectives or orienting activities directing attention to subsequent instructional topics have comparatively smaller effects than questioning and lesson control (Hannafin et al., 1986; Ho et al., 1986; Phillips et al., 1988).

Although these studies contribute toward an explanation of the effectiveness of interactive video, they constitute a still active research area involving a complex interaction of video program design, computer-based instruction, and traditional instructional design theory. Despite the characterization of interactive video as being a joining of two electronic media, many recent studies of interactive video more strongly resemble studies of computer-based instruction than they do studies of video-based instruction. Discussions of repurposing existing video into the interactive video format provide a contrast between the characteristics of linear video and the way it must be configured for interactive video (B. S. Allen, 1986; Hannafin & Hughes, 1986; E. E. Smith, 1987). Although principles for effective video instruction may seem to be simply included by subsumption, there appears to be a need for better delineating the video techniques that are unique to interactive video and when they should be used (cf. Braden, 1986). Such principles should be based on findings from research, such as have already begun to emerge from studies of computer-based instruction (Alessi & Trollip, 1991; Jonassen & Hannum, 1987).

6 Video Production Methods and Tradecraft

This is the first of two chapters on video production methods and techniques. This chapter concerns practitioner recommendations from video professionals on producing quality videos. The next chapter concerns the use of production techniques to enhance learning.

OVERVIEW OF TRADECRAFT AND INSTRUCTIONAL PRODUCTION METHODS

The use of video production methods and techniques in instruction and learning has two goals: (a) producing instructional video materials that meet general standards of technical quality, and (b) using the capabilities of video to enhance learning. In most instances, these two goals overlap because the characteristics of technical quality, such as a good picture image, high viewer involvement, and logical treatment of content, are also the characteristics of good instructional video. However, the overlap is not perfect. The characteristics of "good video" for the video professional may exceed the requirements of instructional video. An example of this would be the emphasis on *production values* (music, sets, talent, etc.) in commercial video products. In other instances, the characteristics of professionally developed video, such as fast pace, frequent scene changes, and an emphasis on visual effects, may be inappropriate for instructional topics.

The discussion to follow concerns the tradecraft rules associated with professional video production methods and techniques. The term *tradecraft* refers to the rules of video production that have evolved from the experience of video professionals. These tradecraft rules are intended to ensure that the viewer understands what is shown on the screen and to minimize the built-in limitations of the video medium—restricted field of vision, limited depth of focus, and the transitory nature of the video image. An important subobjective of these practices is to prevent the viewer from becoming aware of the techniques being used and to lead the viewer to accept what is shown on the screen as being natural, logical, and realistic.

With a few exceptions, little empirical data back up these tradecraft rules. The standard textbooks and references on television production and cinematography document the practices and techniques that implement the rules, but are not consistent in their content and terminology. Although some topics appear more often than others, the standard references do not codify a fixed set of rules, but a range of production choices and techniques. Some aspects of this literature understandably reflect an artistic or subjective quality. The video profession is highly technical in terms of hardware and production procedures, but the production decisions of practitioners appear to be guided more by personal experience than a body of professional standards. The tradecraft rules are followed because they appear to work or because negative viewer reactions are provoked when they are violated.

The second topic, treated in the next chapter, discusses the use of production techniques to enhance learning. These efforts are directed toward adapting video presentations to educational purposes by maximizing the presumed advantages of the medium. They include an ability to focus and hold the viewer's attention; to bring words, sound, and pictures to the viewer at the same time; to show movement and realistic visual images; and to bring a variety of visual material to the learner in a standardized, manageable format.

In contrast to professional tradecraft practices, the use of video production methods to enhance learning has been better researched. The literature extends back into the 1940s, or even earlier if the related study of the use of film is included. This research has continued as the use of television in instruction has become common both inside and outside the classroom. One assumption underlying some of this research is that video has unique attributes that can be exploited for instruction by manipulating certain video production methods and techniques. Many of these involve so-called "formal features" of the medium—specific techniques such as cutting and zooming—intended to influence or gain the viewer's attention. Another body of issues that has been examined concerns the relative effectiveness of various presentation formats, program pacing and length, and different instructional strategies aimed at gaining viewer participation.

Instructional video materials are designed by choosing from among the basic production variables, based on both pedagogic theories and practical tradecraft practices. Taking both fields together, the broadest conclusion is that production methods—by themselves—have a limited effect on learning. Many of the production techniques used to focus attention and avoid confusion are logical techniques that increase the opportunity for instructional content to be noticed and understood. The important context in which to utilize these techniques is one where they are viewed as fitting within an overall instructional strategy. Thus, they are appropriately used to support good instructional practice. Their use would support well-known practices designed to aid the learner, such as well-organized content, discriminating or emphasizing important content, repetition, appropriate rates of development, or eliciting responses that result in gaining correct knowledge.

PROFESSIONAL TRADECRAFT

Tradecraft rules are discussed under four broad topics: (a) camera technique, including the selection of shot length, camera movement, camera angle, and zoom or focus lens effects; (b) shot composition, including picture complexity, balance and proportion, movement, framing, and lighting; (c) editing, including cutting, shot order, and continuity; and (d) the use of special effects such as animation, music, text, and captioning. For purposes of this discussion, we have ignored the production techniques relating to picture and sound quality under the assumption that these factors are fundamental to any form of video production and have no uniquely instructional function.

The basic unit of analysis of any production technique is the *shot*. A shot is a single, uninterrupted sequence of film taken by a single camera. Scenes are typically constructed out of several separate shots. There is no fixed limit to the length or internal complexity of a single shot. A shot may last for only a few seconds or several minutes. A shot may remain focused on a single location or subject, or it may shift from one subject to another.

A shot can be considered from three perspectives: the content of the shot; how the content is presented, or treated; and how the content and its treatment will be influenced by earlier and later shots. The content of a shot is the most important element, and must be determined before any other decision can be made. However, once the content has been determined, the most important decision is how the content will be shown on the video screen. It is at this point that production technique becomes important. There are many ways to present the same content, and each way will emphasize different details and imply different relationships. After the shots that are to make up the presentation have been captured, the next step is to edit the shots with attention to the correct sequence, appropriate transitions, and the overall effect of the presentation.

Camera Technique

Camera techniques include the selection of the shot length, camera movement, camera angle, and zoom and focus effects.

Shot Length

Shot length refers to the relative distance of the camera from the subject of the shot, which affects the apparent size of the object, how much of the subject will be visible, the visibility of details, and the amount of the surrounding environment that will be shown on the screen. Shot lengths are typically described as *long shots, medium shots, close-ups,* and *extreme close-ups*. The actual distances associated with each of these shot lengths is not fixed, but is relative to the subject and the setting. A long shot taken in an office or living room setting is considerably closer to the subject than if the shot is taken in a stadium or an open field (Burrows, Wood, & Gross, 1989). Shots are also designated according to the number of subjects in the shot: a *one-shot* has only a single subject, a *two-shot* has two subjects, and so on (Compesi & Sherriffs, 1990).

Long shots, which are taken at a considerable distance from the subject of the shot, are usually used to establish location and atmosphere, establish general spatial relationships, and display broad, large-scale actions or movements (G. H. Anderson, 1984; Fuller, Kanaba, & Brisch-Kanaba, 1982; Millerson, 1985; Utz, 1980). Closer shots are used to emphasize details or significant features of the subject, to dramatize or reveal reactions, or to create a sense of intimacy with the subject (G. H. Anderson, 1984; Browne, 1989; Fuller et al., 1982; Millerson, 1985; Utz, 1980).

The rules suggest that a shot should be sustained only long enough to accomplish its purpose. A long shot that is sustained beyond the time needed for the viewer to interpret the image and identify the important elements of the picture is thought to frustrate the viewer's desire to examine specific details. Similarly, an oversustained close-up is likely to be equally frustrating because it prevents the viewer from looking around a scene or seeing the response of other subjects. A sustained close-up might also cause the viewer to become disoriented and to forget how the restricted view relates to the overall scene (Millerson, 1985).

Zettl (1990) suggested that the small size and the relatively square shape of the standard television screen limit the effectiveness of the long shot as a device for establishing a location or developing the relationship of objects within a larger spatial context. The larger and wider motion picture screen is thought to be better suited to presenting large-scale images, whereas the shape of the video screen is better suited to a close-up or extreme close-up shot. The small size of the video screen makes even the largest subjects or events appear small, reducing their visual impact on the viewer (Compesi & Sherriffs, 1990). Television, according to Zettl, is a more intimate medium and is better able to present small details, individual rather than group actions, and small-scale events with medium, close-up, and extreme close-up shots. He suggested that long shots in film cinematography can be used effectively to establish a location or context, followed by a gradual development of the details with successively closer shots. However, in video, he contended that it is better to build up the context of a scene from a series of medium and close-up shots. He suggested that this "deductive" approach to developing the content is better suited to the smaller, more intimate nature of video (Zettl, 1990).

Camera Movement

Camera movement is used to change the direction, angle, or distance of the video image during a shot. Tradecraft rules suggest that camera movement should always be motivated, controlled, and at an appropriate speed (Browne, 1989; Compesi & Sherriffs, 1990; Davis, 1966; Millerson, 1985; Utz, 1980, 1992). That is, according to the rules, the camera should only be moved to accomplish a particular objective. Random or accidental movement should be avoided. Any movement should be slow enough for the viewer to understand the changes on the screen. In addition, tradecraft rules hold that, under most conditions, the movement should not call attention to itself so that the viewer's attention shifts from the subject of the shot to the camera movement itself (Zettl, 1990). Camera movement is less intrusive when the subject of the shot is moving, but becomes more prominent to the viewer when the subject is static (Millerson, 1985). Tradecraft rules also discourage camera movement in close-up and extreme close-up shots, because of the limited viewpoint and the restricted depth of field (Millerson, 1985).

Camera movement includes the use of panning, tilting, dollying, crane or pedestal movement, and trucking. *Panning* involves turning the camera horizontally on its mount head to scan an extended horizontal area from a fixed location. *Tilting* involves changing the vertical direction of a shot by pointing the camera up or down on its mount head. *Dollying* involves changing the distance from the camera to the subject by moving the camera toward or away from the subject. This is sometimes referred to as *Z-axis* movement.[1] *Crane* or *pedestal movement* involves lifting or lowering the camera while maintaining a fixed shot angle. *Trucking* involves moving the camera horizontally, to follow the movement of a subject or to scan over an extended area. It differs from panning in that the entire camera moves with the subject rather than merely follows the subject from a fixed position. Combinations of these movements are sometimes employed, such as the *arc shot*, a combination of trucking and panning in which the camera moves in a semicircle around the subject of the shot, maintaining a continuous focus on the subject (Burrows et al., 1989; Compesi & Sherriffs, 1990).

Panning. Camera pan shots are used to establish a spatial relationship between two objects or areas. A slow pan is thought to create expectation and tension as the viewer watches for a significant detail or action. A fast, or *whip*, pan is used to suggest a dynamic relationship or transition, such as a dramatic change of direction, a rapid movement in time or space,

---

[1]An object's position relative to a camera can be defined in terms of three coordinates, labeled X, Y, and Z. An object's X-axis position is its location on the horizontal (left-to-right) dimension; its Y-axis position is its location on the vertical (up-and-down) dimension; and its Z-axis position is its distance from the viewer (camera).

a cause-and-effect relationship, or a contrast or comparison of two persons or objects. Professional producers are cautioned to avoid panning over irrelevant areas, because viewers may attach meaning and significance to anything shown on the screen. If two subjects to be shown are far apart and there is no reason to show the intervening space, a cut between the two subjects is preferred to a pan (Millerson, 1985).

Tilting. A camera head tilt upward is used to emphasize height, such as the use of the slow upward tilt when showing a tall building. A tilt downward is used to emphasize depth, such as the use of a downward tilt to show a deep canyon (Fuller et al., 1982; Millerson, 1985). A tilt upward is thought to create a feeling of rising interest, expectancy, and hope, whereas a tilt downward is thought to suggest feelings of lowered interest, disappointment, sadness, and criticism (Millerson, 1985).

Dollying, Craning, and Trucking. Physically moving the camera by dollying, crane or pedestal movement, or trucking, is thought to give the viewer a sense of subjective presence, whereas a static camera provides a sense of objectivity and detachment from the action (Millerson, 1985; Utz, 1980, 1992). Moving a camera, rather than zooming in on a subject, is thought to provide a greater sense of solidity, realness, and depth resulting from the apparent intermovement of planes (parallatic change; Millerson, 1985; Utz, 1980, 1992). Given the limited picture area on a television screen, vertical and horizontal camera movement (tilting, panning, or trucking) is thought to be more distracting than Z-axis movement or dollying. Confining the camera to backward and forward movement is thought to place more emphasis on the subject and make the camera's movement less intrusive (Zettl, 1990). Practitioners also caution against any physical movement of the camera during a shot using a long focal length lens, because any accidental or unsteady movement will be exaggerated in the picture (Burrows et al., 1989).

Camera Angle

Camera angle refers to the position of the camera relative to the subject of a shot. The term *camera angle* is sometimes used to describe the vertical position of the camera relative to the subject. In a high angle shot, the camera is shooting from above the subject. In a low angle shot, the camera is shooting from below the subject. The vertical camera angle of a human subject is usually determined relative to the viewer's normal eye level. Similarly, the vertical camera angle of an object is determined relative to the viewer's normal line of sight (Compesi & Sherriffs, 1990).

In some instances, the term *camera angle* also refers to the orientation of the subject in relation to the camera. In the case of a human subject, this orientation is determined by the direction the subject is facing in relation to the camera—full front, profile, and rear angles. The same criteria can be used to describe the orientation of objects that are normally thought to have front, profile, or rear aspects, such as vehicles, buildings, and animals.

In professional video productions, different camera angles are used for at least four functions: (a) to avoid the so-called jump cut, (b) to clarify the point of view of an off-screen observer, (c) to intensify the emotional or aesthetic impact of a scene, and (d) to create a stylistic effect (Zettl, 1990).

A *jump cut* occurs when an object seems to suddenly move from one screen position to another because of a small, unintended change in the position of the camera or the subject. This effect occurs when the editor cuts between two shots that were shot from approximately the same position without regard to the small difference in the subject's position. To avoid the jump cut, the camera angle of successive shots is changed enough so that difference in position is apparent and deliberate rather than accidental (Burrows et al., 1989; Compesi & Sherriffs, 1990; Zettl, 1990).

Camera angles are used to clarify the point of view of an off-screen actor by adopting the subjective position of the actor to show approximately what the actor would see. This temporary use of a "subjective" camera is sometimes inserted into a conversation, as when the camera uses a high angle shot to simulate the point of view of an adult speaking down to a child, or a low angle shot to simulate the child speaking up to the adult (Zettl, 1990).

Camera angles influence the visual impact of a shot by implying or illustrating certain traits of the subject. A low angle (shooting upward) is thought to make subjects appear strong, important, ominous, or strange. A high angle shot (shooting downward) is thought to make subjects appear weak and submissive and to give the audience a sense of superiority to the subject. A very high angle shot is thought to create a sense of detachment, and emphasizes patterns of movement, isolation, and congestion (G. H. Anderson, 1984; Fuller et al., 1982; Millerson, 1985; Utz, 1980, 1992). Camera angles are also used to emphasize a movement, as when a dancer's leap is shot from a low angle or a diver's plunge into the water is shot from above (Zettl, 1990).

Camera angles are sometimes used to create stylistic effects—unique formula statements that characterize the director's personal approach, such as the continuous use of low angle shots throughout a production. This use of angles is usually a trademark effect used to personalize the video product (Zettl, 1990). These stylistic techniques should be used sparingly. Extreme or unnatural camera angles tend to draw attention to the camera techniques and distract from the subject of the shot (Browne, 1989; Millerson, 1985; Utz, 1980, 1992).

Zoom and Focus Lens Effects

Zoom and focus techniques use the camera's ability to change the focal length of shots to magnify or distort the video image, or to isolate objects by narrowing the focus of the camera to portions of the visual field. A wide-angle lens has a short focal length and tends to increase the apparent size of nearby objects while shrinking objects that are farther away. A narrow-angle (long focal length, or telephoto) lens tends to increase the relative size of distant objects, making them appear to be closer than they actually are. Normal focal-length lenses show objects at approximately their actual size and distance. Zoom effects are created by changing the focal length of the lens from narrow to wide (zoom out) or wide to narrow (zoom in) (Burrows et al., 1989; Zettl, 1990).

Different lens effects, discussed in the following, include changing the appearance of overlapping planes, the apparent size and distance of objects from the viewer, the apparent convergence of parallel perspective lines, and the depth of field.

Overlapping Planes. Wide-angle lenses de-emphasize the importance of overlapping visual planes as depth cues because they increase the apparent distance between objects. Narrow-angle lenses tend to "squeeze" objects so that overlapping planes become the major depth cue separating objects in the foreground, middle-ground, and background.

Size and Distance. Wide-angle lenses tend to exaggerate differences in the relative size of objects at different distances from the lens. Because viewers interpret size as a cue to distance, the wide-angle lens is thought to make near objects appear closer and distant objects appear farther away than they actually are. Narrow-angle lenses tend to reduce differences in the size of objects at different distances from the camera and thus make distant objects appear larger and closer than they really are (Burrows et al., 1989; Zettl, 1990).

Linear Perspective. Wide-angle lenses have the effect of accelerating the convergence of parallel lines in an image, increasing the apparent depth and distance of the picture. A room shot with a wide-angle lens will appear to be much larger and deeper in the video image than it would to a person in the room. A narrow-angle lens suppresses the convergence of parallel lines and reduces the apparent depth and spaciousness of a picture. Thus, the same room shot with a narrow-angle lens would appear to be smaller and more crowded in the video picture than it actually is (Burrows et al., 1989; Zettl, 1990).

Depth of Field. The depth of field of a lens is the portion of the Z-axis (the line-of-sight of the camera) within which an object will appear to be in focus. The depth of field of a camera is affected by the focal length of the lens and the amount of lens opening. If the depth of field is *shallow*, objects in only a small portion of the Z-axis will be in focus. If the depth of field is great (*deep*), objects at various distances from the camera will be in focus.

Wide-angle lenses tend to a have greater depth of field than narrow-angle lenses. This allows a camera with a wide-angle lens to present objects at varying distances. Consequently, a deep-focus (wide-angle) lens is used to create an illusion of depth and spaciousness when shooting several objects at varying distances from the camera (Burrows et al., 1989; Zettl, 1990). A shallow-focus (narrow-angle) technique is used to isolate and emphasize a single object by placing everything else in the frame out of focus (Fuller et al., 1982; Millerson, 1985). It is thought to be difficult to use a wide-angle lens to focus on a particular object (Zettl, 1990), because of the increased potential for background objects to distract the viewer from the subject of the shot (Mathias & Patterson, 1985).

Use of Lens Effects in Production. Zoom and focus lens effects are used to accomplish a variety of production objectives. Zooming is frequently used as a substitute for physically moving the camera when such movement is impossible or impractical (Burrows et al., 1989). However, because zooming also distorts the scale, distance, and shape of objects in ways that are difficult for the viewer to detect, this use of zooming is used most often in studio or interior location shooting (Fuller et al., 1982; Millerson, 1985). Zooming is also a valuable technique for shooting flat surfaces, such as a map, because it avoids the need to continually adjust the focus (follow focus) that dollying requires (Millerson, 1985). Finally, zooming is used to isolate or focus attention on a particular subject within a shot, or to reveal the context within which the subject or event is taking place (Compesi & Sherriffs, 1990; Zettl, 1990).

Wide- and narrow-angle shots change the way viewers perceive the space within which subjects are presented. Wide-angle shots are thought to impart a sense of openness and spaciousness, whereas a narrow-angle shot makes the shot appear crowded, congested, and confined. Wide-angle shots also increase the apparent speed of movement toward or away from the camera, whereas narrow-angle shots tend to suppress apparent movement along the Z-axis. Finally, the ability to place objects in and out of focus is sometimes used to create or accentuate the three-dimensional depth of the image. This use of *selective focus* permits the producer to simulate the "aerial perspective" effect whereby objects become less distinct (less in focus) as they recede in distance from the viewer (Burrows et al., 1989; Zettl, 1990).

Composition

Composition refers to the way objects and people are located within the frame of the video screen. Many of these rules are drawn from the related disciplines of photography, painting, and theater. Millerson (1985) described compositional principles as a matter of communication rather than merely creating aesthetically pleasing pictures. "Composing shots is not a matter of 'pictorial packaging,' but a method of controlling continuity of thought" (p. 80). Because the shape of the television screen is relatively fixed at a 3:4 aspect ratio, the compositional rules assume a limited viewing area with inherent restrictions in showing details or views of tall or long objects (Compesi & Sherriffs, 1990).

Picture Complexity

A basic maxim of video tradecraft is the need to keep the composition of a shot as simple as possible. The producer is advised to not require the viewer to interpret a shot by providing elaborate details or other possible distractions. Within this rubric, "good video" is thought to involve constant change and movement that does not leave the viewer too much time to analyze each shot (Cartwright, 1986). Tradecraft rules require that each shot should have only one center of interest and that each shot should advance the purpose or objective of the overall production (Cartwright, 1986; Millerson, 1985; Utz, 1980, 1992). All background details that do not meet these two criteria should be eliminated from a shot (Cartwright, 1986; Millerson, 1985). Viewers are thought to be able to notice and retain information about no more than seven to nine elements in a television picture, even when given enough time to scan the entire image (Giannetti, 1987).

Balance and Proportion

Different areas of the screen are thought to have different visual "weight" or importance. Tradecraft rules suggest that viewers judge the importance of objects on the screen relative to the weight of the area where they are placed (Cartwright, 1986; Millerson, 1985; Zettl, 1990). The center of the screen is believed to have more weight than any other area. The right side of the screen has more weight than the left side and the upper portion of the screen has more weight than the bottom portion. A common geographic division of the screen referred to as the "rule of thirds" suggests that the center of attention should not be dead center, but just off the center of the screen (Compesi & Sherriffs, 1990; Giannetti, 1987; Utz, 1992). Thus, the center of attention should be one third of the way up from the bottom, or down from the top, or inward from the sides of the screen. The four corners resulting from dividing the screen into thirds with two horizontal and two vertical lines may also be used as preferred locations for achieving balance with major picture elements.

Objects within the frame also have intrinsic weight because of their color and shape. Large, dark, regularly shaped objects are thought to have greater weight than small, light, irregularly shaped objects (Fuller et al., 1982; Millerson, 1985; Zettl, 1990). Thus, screen position and the characteristics of objects in the picture must be considered to achieve the desired balance (Compesi & Sherriffs, 1990; Giannetti, 1987).

A symmetrically balanced screen is thought to be seen as static, whereas an unbalanced screen is thought to be more interesting and dynamic (Cartwright, 1986; Fuller et al., 1982; Millerson, 1985; Zettl, 1984). Formal balance, which is recommended in still photography, is highly stable, but is regarded as dull and monotonous if it is sustained over a long period (Millerson, 1985; Zettl, 1984). Similarly, overuse of the center of the screen as the focus of action presumably becomes monotonous (Millerson, 1985). To sustain interest, it is recommended that the composition of the screen be periodically unbalanced by moving objects from the center to the edge of the screen, or by removing an object from the shot without adjusting the angle or focus of the shot. For example, if a shot opens with two subjects in view and one of the subjects leaves the frame, the camera can reframe the picture by placing the remaining subject at the center of the screen, thus restoring the picture's balance. However, if the camera maintains the same position and does not reframe the composition, the absence of the subject who left the shot is emphasized (Browne, 1989; Millerson, 1985; Zettl, 1984).

Framing

Under the rules, the screen should be composed to frame the center of interest, and to draw the viewer's eye to the object of the shot. Framing is achieved by placing objects out of focus around or above the center of interest (Cartwright, 1986). The composition of the screen should draw the viewer into the picture by creating the illusion of depth. This is done by showing people and objects at an angle, by placing objects in the foreground slightly out of focus, and by using shadows to highlight the edges and contours of objects in the picture (Cartwright, 1986; Millerson, 1985; Zettl, 1984).

The edges of the screen are thought to exert an influence on objects or subjects placed away from the center of the screen. Viewers are thought to perceive objects near the edge of the screen to be attached to or drawn toward the edge, so that a subject near the top of the screen appears to be higher or more separated from objects in the middle or lower portion of the screen. In the same way, objects at the edge of the screen in a close-up shot are perceived as being spatially farther apart than the same two objects in a long shot (Zettl, 1990).

Considerable attention is devoted to the composition of human subjects in the video frame. The space around the subject's head and face is important to the way viewers interpret a shot. In general, it is thought that the human face or head should be framed with adequate vertical space (headroom), if facing toward the screen, and adequate horizontal space in the direction of gaze (noseroom), if facing to the side of the screen. "Adequate," in this context, is somewhat subjective, but appears to mean a distance that balances the relative weight of the head with the surrounding empty space.

If the subject's head is framed too near the top of the screen, the figure is thought to appear attached to the frame. If the figure is framed with too much headroom, the figure appears to be sinking out of the frame. Failure to provide enough space around a subject's head makes the picture appear unusual or misaligned and, thus, is a strong cue to the viewer to pay attention to the screen. This effect is exploited by video producers for dramatic purposes. By placing a figure at the extreme edge of the frame, the figure appears trapped. A subject shot in profile with a larger than normal amount of space behind the subject's head or back creates the expectation that something is about to appear or happen behind the figure (Compesi & Sherriffs, 1990). Filming a moving subject with little space ahead is thought to create a sense of anxiety because the viewer cannot see what lies in the subject's path.

Lines, Boundaries, and Vectors

Because the video image is shown on a flat, two-dimensional surface, the natural lines and contours of objects on the screen are believed to influence the way viewers segregate and partition areas of the picture. According to the professional literature, shots should be composed to avoid strong visual lines such as telephone wires, the horizon, edges of buildings, or vertical poles that divide the screen into equal parts, or that cause the viewer to separate actions taking place in different parts of the screen (Cartwright, 1986; Millerson, 1985; Zettl, 1984).

When filming human subjects, tradecraft rules suggest that the shot should be arranged to prevent natural cutoff lines (i.e., wrists, mouth, chin, waist, knees) from coinciding with the screen edge, because viewers are thought to confuse apparent visual boundaries with the physical edges of subjects and objects (Fuller et al., 1982; Zettl, 1984). In addition, shots should be composed so that the visual boundaries of objects and human subjects overlap rather than coincide. Failure to provide clear visual cues that one object is in front of another can result in pictures in which objects that are far apart appear to be side by side or one on top of the other (Compesi & Sherriffs, 1990; Giannetti, 1987; Zettl, 1984, 1990).

Lines on the screen are thought to vary in their "visual strength." Diagonal lines are regarded as being visually stronger than either horizontal or vertical lines, and vertical lines are thought to be visually stronger than horizontal lines. Similarly, right and left angles are believed to imply different directions of force or movement. A diagonal sloping downward to the right is generally interpreted as heading downhill, whereas a diagonal sloping upward from the left in interpreted as heading uphill (Millerson, 1985; Zettl, 1990).

From an aesthetic standpoint, horizontal lines are thought to be more restful and comfortable to the viewer whereas vertical lines are more dynamic, powerful, and exciting. A tilted horizontal line creates a sense of disorientation and discomfort, because humans are thought to be conditioned to see the world in terms of horizontal and vertical structures (Zettl, 1990).

Lines on the screen form visual *vectors* that are thought to direct the movement of the viewer's eyes from point to point on the screen. These vector lines can be created by physical lines or shapes on the screen such as the edges of buildings, the alignment of separate objects that the viewer tends to group through perceptual closure, the implied lines formed by an object or a person in the picture looking or pointing in a particular direction, or the apparent movement of persons or objects on the screen. Vectors can also be created by devices used to focus the viewers attention, such as lighting, lens effects, or camera angle.

Lighting

Use of Lighting

Lighting, in the context of television production, means the deliberate control of light and shadow effects, and the secondary effect of light on colors on the video screen. Although there are many similarities between lighting for film and lighting for television, there are some differences. First, television cameras have a more limited range of contrast, and require somewhat higher lighting levels than film cameras (Mathias & Patterson, 1985). Second, television producers must consider the possibility that viewers may watch their material on either a color or black-and-white television monitor, or on monitors of varying size and technical capabilities. Both of these factors make it difficult for television producers to make use of the subtle lighting effects available to the film producer (Zettl, 1990).

Lighting theory and effects are complex topics that cannot be fully discussed here. However, we present some of the major aspects that relate to our later discussion of the use of production techniques to enhance learning. In general, lighting techniques are distinguished by the areas of the image that are illuminated, the illumination level, the sharpness of lighting contrast, and the density of the shadows produced. Different combinations of illumination level, contrast, shadow density, and the location of lighting sources can create strikingly different visual effects (Giannetti, 1987; Zettl, 1990).

The two major lighting types are *chiaroscuro* lighting and *flat* lighting. Chiaroscuro lighting creates defined areas of light and shadow, uses a lower overall level of lighting, emphasizes the contrasts between light and shadow with a rapid "fall-off" of light, and creates darker and deeper shadows. Chiaroscuro lighting is used to simulate natural point sources of illumination such as the sun, a lamp, or a candle. Because portions of the image are illuminated and portions are in shadow, chiaroscuro lighting can be used to direct the attention of the viewer to certain parts of the screen. Specific techniques include the *follow spot*, a single spotlight on the subject; the *limbo light*, placing a fully lit figure against a neutral, softly lit background; *cameo lighting*, lighting only the subject against a dark background; and *silhouette lighting*, in which the subject is unlit but outlined in shadow against a brightly lit background (Burrows et al., 1989). The light and shadow pattern can also be used to emphasize volume, contour, foreground, and background in relatively static scenes. Finally, chiaroscuro lighting is inherently dramatic and emotionally charged, making it well suited for theatrical video presentations (Giannetti, 1987; Zettl, 1990).

Flat lighting removes or drastically eliminates shadows, and emphasizes visibility and clarity over drama and emotion. Flat lighting illuminates the entire image and uses a high level of illumination so that light is evenly distributed. Although flat lighting reveals picture details, it also removes the three-dimensional cues provided by shadows. Flat-lit shots are thought to look cold, sterile, and uninteresting. However, the technique is also used to suggest high energy, cleanliness, truth, and modernity (Giannetti, 1987; Zettl, 1990). Bright, *high-key* lighting is sometimes used in comedy and light entertainment programming to establish an energetic, positive atmosphere. Low light levels are used to create a sense of foreboding and drama (Burrows et al., 1989; Giannetti, 1987). The psychological effect of these techniques is a matter of opinion, although some techniques have acquired the status of cinematic conventions.

Use of Color

Color is used in television production to convey information, and to express a mood, emotion, or attitude. The information function of color is accomplished by making the video image more realistic and lifelike to the viewer. The information function can also be accomplished by creating symbolic meanings of colors. Thus, colors can be used to symbolize ideas, emotions, or events if the viewer is familiar with the appropriate conventional meaning of those colors (Giannetti, 1987).

The other major use of color is to create a visual mood, or to suggest an emotion or attitude. This use of color is closely related to the idea of symbolic meanings of color. Numerous associations are possible between particular colors and various moods, emotions, attitudes, ideas, and the like. However, Zettl (1990) suggested that there is a relationship between the degree of color saturation in a picture and the focus of the viewer. He suggested that as color saturation increases, the viewer concentrates more on the external appearance of the image and less on the meaning of the image. He further suggested that by reducing the definition and saturation of the color image, the viewer is invited to fill in the missing elements, thereby increasing involvement in the presentation (Zettl, 1990).

However, the ability of the video producer to use color to present information, or invoke a mood, is limited by the possibility that viewers may be obliged to watch the production on a black-and-white television monitor. Similarly, because the hue saturation, contrast, and brightness in a video image depend on the characteristics of the television monitor, the appearance of an object may vary on different color monitors. In short, the video producer must assume that only major differences in color will be noticed by viewers so that color hue becomes less important in television production than color brightness and contrast (Zettl, 1990).

Movement

Motion and visual change are major defining elements of video production. The rules regarding motion are intended to control the powerful effect that on-screen motion is thought to exert on the attention and interest of the viewer. In most instances, the rules are designed to maximize the presumed effects of motion while keeping the image believable and understandable.

A basic rule is that all movement on the screen should be controlled, because movement is thought to attract attention toward or away from the object of the shot by making a subject or object more interesting to watch (Cartwright, 1986; Millerson, 1985). Movement toward or away from the camera, whether caused by the movement of the subject or the camera itself, is seen as stronger and more interesting than lateral movement across the field of vision (Zettl, 1984). Movement toward the camera is seen as stronger and more interesting than a movement away from the camera (Millerson, 1985). Similarly, left-to-right movement is thought to be stronger, easier to follow, and more natural to the viewer than right-to-left movement (Cartwright, 1986; Millerson, 1985). Upward movement is thought to be more dynamic and perceived as faster than downward movement (Millerson, 1985). As with diagonal lines, diagonal movement is thought to be the most dynamic movement direction (Millerson, 1985).

It is believed that movement should be kept away from the edges of the screen. As a technical limitation, the edges may be cropped on smaller screens causing the loss of the movement. Motion is also thought to call attention to the edges of the screen, breaking the illusion of depth and involvement needed to hold the viewer's attention (Browne, 1989; Cartwright, 1986; Fuller et al., 1982; Millerson, 1985).

Editing Techniques

Editing refers to the way individual shots are assembled into scenes and then scenes into episodes and programs. The primary technique is the *cut*, which determines when one shot ends and the next shot begins. The basic purpose of editing is to ensure the clarity of the message through attention to continuity and logical development.

Professional tradecraft rules advise the video producer to change shots frequently in order to sustain the viewers' interest. It is thought by some that a shot should not be sustained for more than 6 to 8 seconds (Cartwright, 1986; Utz, 1980). However, moderation is also urged in that change should be made for a purpose rather than for idle variety (Utz, 1992). A cut between two shots is thought to be less intrusive if it is made during some on-screen action so that the change of angle occurs when the viewer's eye is drawn to the movement and the viewer connects the two shots as part of a single event (G. H. Anderson, 1984; Browne, 1989). Tradecraft rules suggest that scenes or shots should be changed at the moment when the viewer is assumed to expect or want a change (Browne, 1989; Burrows et al., 1989). For example, when a shot refers to or implies a location or direction, as when an actor appears to be looking at an object out of the frame of the screen, the rules suggest that the viewer be allowed to see that object, location, or direction in the next shot (J. M. Carroll, 1980; Utz, 1980, 1992; Zettl, 1973). Failure to give the viewer this information is thought to create frustration and tension (Burrows et al., 1989).

When a new shot is shown, it should differ from the previous shot along more than one dimension. That is, a cut between shots should be different enough that the viewer can immediately detect the change and not confuse the new shot with the previous shot. Thus, if an object is shown in a medium shot, a subsequent close-up shot should differ in camera angle or framing (G. H. Anderson, 1984; J. M. Carroll, 1980; Croynik, 1974; Giannetti, 1987; Hochberg & Brooks, 1978; Mascelli, 1965; Utz, 1980, 1992). However, within a scene, the shots should provide enough continuity for the viewer to recognize persons or objects already shown. The editor should maintain character identification across shots. When cutting on the same subject, there should be enough continuity to permit the viewer to identify that subject (Croynik, 1974; Zettl, 1973). Likewise, stationary features that guide eye movement should match up between successive shots (Fuller et al., 1982; Mascelli, 1965; Zettl, 1973). Sudden or unexplained changes in distance or angle should be avoided from shot to shot because viewers may not be able to recognize the same persons or objects between the shots (Davis, 1966; Utz, 1980; Zettl, 1984). However, too small a change in screen position or angle creates *position jumps* or *jump cuts* in which the subject appears to suddenly change position in the scene. These problems can be avoided so that the small change in position is not noticeable by the viewer by inserting shots with a different size or angle or by using cutaway images, such as a reaction shot of a listener (Burrows et al., 1989; Utz, 1992).

Editors should attempt to maintain directional continuity when there is movement on the screen. If an object is shown moving from right to left across the screen in one shot, it should not be shown moving from left to right in the next shot (G. H. Anderson, 1984; Browne, 1989; Croynik, 1974; Giannetti, 1987; Hochberg & Brooks, 1978; Mascelli, 1965). Movement by the subject or the camera should be sustained between shots until the movement is shown to stop (G. H. Anderson, 1984; Fuller et al., 1982; Zettl, 1973).

Reverse-angle shots, in which a subject or subjects appear to reverse screen position should be avoided. Production rules suggest that the producer establish a *line* or *axis of action / conversation*. This line limits the angle and position of the camera when shooting the subject by locating the point at which the subject will appear to switch direction on the screen. For example, in a shot of two persons talking to each other face to face, the axis of conversation would be drawn directly through the two persons. So long as the camera remains on the same side of this line, the subjects will appear to be in the same relative position, even when shot at extreme, over-the-shoulder positions. However, when the camera crosses the line, the subjects will appear to have reversed positions so that the subject on the right will now appear to have moved to the left, and vice versa. Because of the momentary confusion this shot can create for the viewer, virtually every production guide warns against the reverse-angle error (G. H. Anderson, 1984; Browne, 1989; Burrows et al., 1989; Croynik, 1974; Giannetti, 1987; Hochberg & Brooks, 1978; Mascelli, 1965; Utz, 1980, 1992; Zettl, 1984).

Editors are also cautioned to maintain temporal continuity. Action should be presented smoothly and gaps should be explained by appropriate intervening shots. For example, the editor wishing to convey the passage of time between two shots might employ several conventional devices (Croynik, 1974; Zettl, 1973). These might be changing the position of the hands of a clock, a distinctive change in the angle of natural sunlight, or a slow fading of one shot to black followed by a slow fade up to the next shot. Similarly, the editor should maintain causal continuity. As much as possible, the order of shots should follow the causal sequence of the action. Thus, if A causes B, then A should precede B in order of presentation (J. M. Carroll, 1980).

The perspective of the camera with respect to the material being shot dictates what the viewer is able to see and hear. There are two basic perspectives or viewpoints: subjective camera and objective camera. A subjective camera adopts the point of view of a person within the scene. Normally, the subjective camera is limited to the perspective of a single person so that it cannot quickly change shot position or angle without an explanatory transition. By contrast, an objective camera adopts the point of view of an unseen, omnipresent observer who can view the scene from any convenient angle or distance. It is thought that once a particular viewpoint has been selected, that view should be maintained throughout the scene to avoid confusing the viewer. Consequently, a subjective camera should never see itself (G. H. Anderson, 1984; J. M. Carroll, 1980; Mascelli,

1965; Zettl, 1973). Presentations demonstrating a skill or procedure are better shown from a subjective viewpoint (performer's perspective) than an objective viewpoint (observer's perspective) (G. H. Anderson, 1984; Utz, 1980, 1992).

An important attribute of video is the ability to compress time and distance by cutting out irrelevant sequences and replacing them with visual cues indicating that time has passed or movement has taken place. Through repetition, audiences are thought to have accepted the use of the slow fade to black at the end of a shot as a cue that a scene has ended and that the next shot is the beginning of a new scene at some period in the future. Similarly, seeing a person walk out of the frame of view at the end of a shot is thought to be accepted as a cue that the person is moving to a new, perhaps distant location. This technique can be extended so that movement over a large distance can be reduced to a series of brief shots in which the subject enters and leaves the frame of view. Audiences are thought to accept this sequence of shots as a realistic depiction of the entire movement, even though the time actually required to move the observed distance would be significantly longer (Burrows et al., 1989).

Audio

Although video is often referred to as a visual medium, the audio components of a television presentation are a major channel of information and a significant aspect of any video production effort (Burrows et al., 1989; Compesi & Sherriffs, 1990; Zettl, 1990). Audio dialogue, narrative, music, and sound effects are important additional sources of information for the viewer (Zettl, 1990). In some instances, the audio channel may provide more relevant information to the viewer than the visual channel. In other instances, audio information is necessary to clarify and explain the visual image. Indeed, even minor changes to the audio track accompanying a video presentation can drastically alter its mood, meaning, significance, and interpretation.

Sound

Sound serves several functions in a television production. Sound conveys information directly, through dialogue or narrative, and indirectly through environmental sound effects. Sound is also thought to add realism to visual effects, to create or enhance the level of energy and excitement, and to establish the tempo or rhythm of a shot. Finally, sound can be used to create continuity across shots (Zettl, 1990).

When a sound is assigned to a specific source, the quality of the sound should match the location of the source in relation to the listener (the camera). Thus, a speaker's voice should be louder in a close-up shot than in a long shot. Similarly, the volume of a sound should correspond to its distance from the viewer even if the source is not visible, but is only implied, as when the camera focuses on the face of a person listening to an off-camera speaker (Burrows et al., 1989).

Music

J. Zuckerman (1949) discussed the early literature on the use of music in motion pictures. It consisted almost entirely of the published theories and opinions of composers, directors, and critics of Hollywood films. According to Zuckerman, the function of music from the practitioner's perspective is to provide information through musical symbolism, to generate an emotional response from the viewer, and to create conceptual structures that organize, link, and integrate the ideas and themes of a film. The musical variables that can be manipulated to create different effects are tempo and rhythm; cuing and accentuation of action; tone coloring; thematic structure, length, and development; volume; intensity; style; association with periods, places, persons, or ideas; and integration with on-screen action or dialogue (Giannetti, 1987; J. Zuckerman, 1949).

Music can be used to convey information about the personality of a character, to underscore some action on the screen, to recall previous events associated with some piece of music, or to foreshadow future events through the tone and color of the music. Examples of these effects would be the use of discordant, atonal music to suggest anger; the use of music that imitates a natural sound, such as hoof-beats, bird-song, or machinery; the use of musical motifs that are repeated whenever a character appears; or the use of well-known themes like funeral music to foreshadow doom (Giannetti, 1987; J. Zuckerman, 1949).

Creating an appropriate emotional atmosphere is a major function of music in films. Viewers are thought to interpret the tone of a scene—comic, tragic, peaceful, mysterious, etc.—at least partly from the tone of the accompanying music. Music can also be used to shock the viewer with sudden, unexpected changes in tempo, sound level, and instrumentation. Finally, music is believed to increase the viewer's sense of anxiety about a character and to create a rising or diminishing sense of tension, happiness, conflict, or danger (Giannetti, 1987; J. Zuckerman, 1949). Changes in musical style or tempo can be used to retroactively control the viewer's perception of a scene, as when loud triumphal music at the climax of a scene suddenly changes to a sombre dirge, suggesting a less positive aftermath (Giannetti, 1987).

Music is thought to perform a conceptual function in film by unifying different parts of the production and creating a sense of continuity across scenes. Music can also be used to create associations between ideas, or establish the time and place of a film, such as the use of music associated with a historical period. Music is also used to connect dialogue and fill in gaps in action and montage sequences. The continuity of the musical line is thought to unify the individual shots into a single scene (Giannetti, 1987; J. Zuckerman, 1949). Music can also be used to make ironic or satirical comments about the on-screen action, by using music that contrasts or contradicts the visual content, as when sentimental or romantic music is used in a tragic context (Giannetti, 1987).

Words on the Screen

Numerous graphic design recommendations and rules exist for displaying text and accompanying graphics on the screen. Utz (1992) summarized these with the guidance that presentations of words and graphics are best when kept simple, bold, and arranged to accommodate the 3:4 aspect ratio of TV screens. Text, titles, and labels should neither be crowded or sprawled and should be clustered together to be read as a group in a simple and noncluttered fashion when used with graphics. The text should be placed in a central "safe area" with an adequate margin left around text to avoid its being cut off. As a consequence of the limited resolution of TV, short lines of text should be used so as to maximize their size. No more than about 10 vertical lines of text should be used, with about 25 characters per line, and half letter spacing between lines. Lettering should use simple fonts that avoid thin strokes that may fade out or strokes that are so broad as to close up the white space. Utz (1992) suggested that reduced clarity be anticipated, such as by applying a practical "squint test" for the boldness of lettering.

Presentations of text should be consistent and should be over a background that makes words easy to read. Words should not be placed over backgrounds that blend with the text or that are so busy as to distract from or compete with the text (G. H. Anderson, 1984; Fuller et al., 1982; Utz, 1980, 1992). The color, size, style, and location of words on the screen should be consistent from shot to shot and throughout a production as much as possible (Fuller et al., 1982; Utz, 1980, 1992). A combination of upper- and lowercase letters is thought to be better than all uppercase lettering for lengthy text. Extraneous or unnecessary printed text should be eliminated from the shot because viewers will usually try to read any legible text on the screen (Cartwright, 1986; Millerson, 1985). A caption on the screen should always agree with the accompanying narrative (Davis, 1966).

Animation

In addition to the display of live motion, video can also display animated graphics to illustrate imaginary, theoretical, or inaccessible visual phenomena. The professional practitioner literature in this area is centered on the technical or aesthetic issues of animation rather than its use as a communication device. An exception is an article by Blinn (1989), who offered numerous design guidelines from the perspective of the computer animation specialist, based on his experience designing animated sequences for the instructional series, *The Mechanical Universe*. This series on introductory physics is notable because of its extensive use of animated computer graphics to illustrate scientific theories and physical phenomena, and to demonstrate the relationship between physical events and mathematical functions.

Many of the guidelines are variations of the rules governing live video and reflect the limitations of presenting visual information in a small, two-dimensional space. As in live video, Blinn stressed the need to focus the viewer's attention by making the most important elements in the image the first thing the viewer sees. As in live video, he advised the animator to avoid gaudy, "interesting" backgrounds that distract from the focus of the image. The overall design concept should be one that avoids using effects purely to dazzle the viewer or that includes too much small, unnecessary detail.

Animated graphics are able to display visual representations of events that would be impossible to capture in the real world because of their scale, speed, or complexity. Dynamic events that happen on a very large or very small scale may be difficult to display with geometric precision on a video screen. In this case, Blinn recommended that the animated presentation begin at a conveniently large or small scale, with the scale then being adjusted to magnify the details, or show the larger environment. When dynamic events happen on a scale that is impossible to accurately display, Blinn suggested that the animator exaggerate and simplify the image to capture the essential point of the illustration. He also pointed out a factor that is unique to computer animation: Because a major objective of computer graphics practitioners has been to achieve increased visual realism, many viewers have come to expect computer graphics to be extremely accurate. Consequently, it is necessary to cue the viewer when size or time scales are being distorted in animation by using sketchy, irregular lines in the schematic.

The use of colors in animation is a matter of choice, because the animator is not limited to the actual colors of objects. For video presentations, Blinn recommended the use of colors that remain distinct when the image is shown in black and white. Colors can be used to emphasize the main elements of the image, but the animator should not rely exclusively on color to differentiate elements. The animator should not use color "codes" that require the viewer to remember the symbolic significance of a particular color. The animator should not use too many colors at the same time and should be consistent in the use of colors, particularly if there is a conventional meaning for some color (e.g., red denotes danger) or if the same illustration is used several times.

Blinn recommended that animators avoid using three-dimensional illustrations, particularly when demonstrating abstract ideas, because viewers have difficulty understanding visual/spatial relationships with more than two variables. Blinn also recommended that animators avoid using spinning or tumbling three-dimensional objects and that three-dimensional representations only be used when there is no alternative.

Human Factors Guidance

The literature on human factors addresses concerns that overlap with design practice in visual-based instruction. In addition to the professional film and video production literature, Friedman (1993) noted that education, psychology, and human factors study related phenomena, each with a different characteristic emphasis. Human factors provides principles derived from both practical experience and experimental studies directed at practitioners.

S. L. Smith and Mosier (1986) provided a compendium of principles for the design of computer interfaces. A subset of these principles are relevant to visual-based instruction because they are intended to minimize processing and memory load demands on users and intended to increase presentation clarity through consistency and heightened discriminability. It is important to maintain consistency when arranging displays, making transitions between displays, referencing prior information, and using abbreviations. Heightened discriminability includes graphic cuing of important information, using distinctive data fields and labels, highlighting changed data, highlighting with animation, maintaining the fidelity of pictorial symbols to the objects they depict, and revealing details by zooming to higher resolution displays while maintaining an overview of the context.

Jackson (1955) presented an early illustration of deriving principles for depicting training devices given on instructional television. The clarity with which 105 training devices were shown on television during a demonstration by an instructor were rated by 12 staff members of the U.S. Naval Special Devices Center. The rating scales included 14 items designed to assess clarity in terms of detail, realism, outline, contrast, movement, interest, and conveying desired principles. The best and worst devices were analyzed in detail to identify the characteristics that differentiated them. Jackson derived 31 principles, which were then used to revise the displays. The revised displays were rated significantly better, and predicted ratings based on the principles correlated very highly ($r = .90$) with actual ratings.

Examples of Jackson's derived principles are: avoid busy backgrounds; use slowly moving parts; use light figures on dark backgrounds; use two thirds of the screen area to show devices; adjust the shot length so that it is appropriate for the desired detail to be depicted; suspend three-dimensional objects in space; use rough surfaces for greater visibility; avoid glazed, reflecting, or transparent materials and possibly treat them to appear dulled; and ensure that the text is printed in large enough letters (e.g., by applying estimation formulas in which the height of the letters would be the height of the device divided by 15).

Discussion

Several general observations can be made about the nature of the tradecraft rules and guidelines and their possible application to instructional video.

Most of the production techniques discussed are intended to compensate for the significant limitations of television as a medium: relatively small viewing area, limited depth of view, limited color range, limited lighting contrast, and relatively low picture image resolution.

Many of the effects created by manipulating such factors as the camera angle, lighting levels, screen composition, and editing are used by practitioners for aesthetic or dramatic effects, but have limited practical application for some forms of instructional video.

Those techniques that are used to attract and direct the attention of the viewer, such as camera shot length, focus and lens effects, lighting effects, and the creation of picture vectors and centers of interest, have direct application in most forms of instructional video.

Audio tradecraft rules are as important as the visual rules regarding camera technique, but may be more important for the instructional developer insofar as the audio channel is a major source of information and content.

Cutting and editing are important for both entertainment and instructional uses insofar as both require a logical development and exposition of the content, but are less important for instructional development when used for dramatic or aesthetic effects.

7 Production Methods and Learning

USING PRODUCTION TECHNIQUES TO ENHANCE LEARNING

Professional tradecraft rules are intended to avoid confusing the viewer, given the limitations of video as a presentation medium. These rules have grown out of the practical experience of television production practitioners rather than educational or training experts. Those interested in using video as a teaching device are generally obliged to follow these rules as minimum standards of television quality. Beyond these minimum requirements, instructional practitioners and researchers have attempted to use known instructional methods and specific production techniques to enhance instruction. The latter are attempted under the tacit assumption that some techniques could be used to teach students more effectively. These techniques are intended to harness the ability of video to capture, hold, and focus the viewer's attention; to bring words, sound, and pictures to the viewer at the same time; to show movement; to present realistic visual images; and to create believable visual illusions. In addition, instructional developers have attempted to use video to implement specific instructional strategies that appear to be well suited to the flexible, multichannel characteristics of the medium.

Several writers have conducted surveys of the research literature regarding the effect of different production techniques for instruction. The more comprehensive reviews were conducted by W. H. Allen (1960, 1973), Berry and Unwin (1975), Carpenter and Greenhill (1956), Chu and Schramm (1967, 1975), Hoban and Van Ormer (1950), Lumsdaine (1963), Lumsdaine and May (1965), Morris (1988a), Reid and MacLennan, (1967), Saettler (1968), Travers (1967), and Unwin (1979). This research has generally examined the use of production variables from one of two perspectives: the choice of appropriate formats and instructional techniques for televised instruction, and the application of specific attributes of television productions, such as zooming, panning, cutting, and sound and visual effects, otherwise called the "formal features" of television. Much of the early research confirmed that television could be used to implement instructional techniques and formats already used in classrooms. More recent research has focused more narrowly on specific production techniques that appeared to have direct instructional applications.

The production techniques described in the discussion of practitioner tradecraft rules (chap. 6) have been used in a variety of ways to influence learning. In some instances, they have been used to implement specific instructional strategies such as inserting questions or other devices to encourage viewer participation and involvement in the presentation. In other instances, they have been used to enhance the viewer's general arousal level through visual and audio effects. Finally, production techniques have been used to cue viewers to pay attention to important parts of the video presentation. Student attention to a presentation is often inferred from measures of learning performance on posttests. Some studies have also examined the general approval or preference of students for specific production techniques.

Issues relevant to the effect of formal features of media were addressed earlier in discussing learning from broadcast news, and in explicating the relation between attention and comprehension (chap. 3). Learning from the news was noted to be made difficult by features such as rapid pacing and a large number of short visuals inconsistently related to the stories. Work originally prompted by a concern with television's effect on children has led to a qualification of the idea that viewers are reactively controlled by formal production features designed to capture attention. Instead, it was suggested that viewers actively monitor television presentations, using the formal features as cues to the content, and deploy attention and processing resources based on their interest and ability to comprehend the content (D. R. Anderson & Lorch, 1983; Huston & Wright, 1983). As Clark and Salomon (1986) observed, this work suggests that "instructional production techniques should be oriented to conveying comprehensible information rather than attracting attention" (p. 467).

RESEARCH FINDINGS

General Presentation Format

Instructional video may take a variety of formats. It may adopt the form of commercial television programs; for example, a documentary, a dramatization, a panel discussion, a news broadcast, a commercial advertisement, a game show, or the much-maligned talking-head lecture. It may also break from the familiar commercial forms and adopt a strictly instructional form such as drill and practice, simulation, demonstration, job aid, or tutorial. Instructional video presentations often use more than one format as a way to introduce variety and sustain the viewer's interest.

Thus, a lecture sequence may be followed by a dramatization or a documentary related to some point in the lecture.
Little research has been done on the effectiveness of different program formats. The research has compared different formats in terms of viewer/learner preference, immediate learning, and long-term retention. The findings suggest that maintaining consistency and predictability within the chosen format helps sustain the viewer's attention and increases learning (Palmer, 1978). Thus, the effectiveness of a particular format is more closely associated with how well it fits the learner's needs than with any particular feature of the presentation itself (Corbin & McIntyre, 1961).

Dramatization

In general, the research tends to suggest that simpler, more straightforward formats are preferable to complex or elaborate formats in terms of viewer attention and understanding. Researchers found that programs that develop a single topic are better attended and result in better immediate understanding than programs with short, "magazine-style" formats (Wright et al., 1984). Similarly, most studies have found that dramatization of content is less effective than a straight expository video presentation (Chu & Schramm, 1967; Hoban & Van Ormer, 1950; Kazem, 1960; May & Lumsdaine, 1958; Vandermeer, 1953).

However, the evidence is not uniformly against the use of dramatization. Poole and Wade (1985) found no significant differences in the number of discussion points recalled or the overall quality of a written paper produced by adolescent students who viewed either a television documentary or a television dramatization. Dramatization has been shown to produce better immediate learning compared to both a live lecture presentation (Morris, 1984, 1988b) and a televised presentation in which no visuals were used (Kazem, 1960). Harless et al. (1990) used video dramatization to create believable simulations of patient encounters for medical students and found that the technique was effective in motivating the students' commitment to the care and management of the simulated patient. Dramatization also appears to be more effective in presenting affective attitudes than direct expository presentations using on- or off-screen authority figures (McCullagh, 1986).

Nugent, Tipton, and Brooks (1980) compared four presentation formats for learning effectiveness and viewer appeal: off-screen narrator with accompanying visuals, on-screen host/narrator, on-screen authority/model, and dramatization. Separate videotapes were prepared on two topics in each of the four formats and shown to groups of college-level chemistry students. The topics addressed personal values and professional ethics. The authority/model format was the most effective for both learning the material and in viewer appeal, followed by dramatization, on-screen narration, and off-screen narration.

A major difficulty and potential pitfall in the use of a dramatic format is the consistent finding that the effectiveness of a dramatization is closely associated with how the audience views the actors' credibility, competence, or status and accepts the accuracy of the story, setting, and intended message. If the actors are perceived as being unrealistic, being naive, or violating the expectations of the viewer, they are less effective in communicating the intended information (Hoban, 1953). Studies also suggest that when actors portray a character of higher status or expertise, they are more readily believed than when they portray a character of lower status, even when the content of the message remains the same (McCullagh, 1986). If a dramatization fails to convince the viewer of its accuracy, it may create an adverse reaction from the viewer, causing the viewer to argue against the intended content. Dramatization also relies partially on creating an emotional response as a way to persuade the viewer to accept the intended message (Deighton, Romer, & McQueen, 1989). We discuss how specific production techniques such as camera angle and editing can influence how viewers perceive on-screen actors in later sections.

Expository Formats

Within the genre of expository formats, no major differences appear to exist in terms of immediate learning. Viewers were found to have learned about the same amount of information from a simple expository presentation as from a debate/adversarial format (Breen, 1968); from a lecture format, an interview format, and a panel discussion format (Brandon, 1956; Chu & Schramm, 1967); and from a variety of newscast formats using combinations of static and motion visuals (Jorgensen, 1955). However, learners were able to retain more information from the straight expository lecture than from the debate/contrasting viewpoint format (Breen, 1968).

Although the effectiveness of specific formats with respect to immediate and long-term learning differs little, there are differences in viewer preferences. As Clark (1982) pointed out, learner preferences for a particular instructional method may not be congruent with the instructional method that is effective for them. Learners have been found to prefer dramatization over simple expository presentations, and to prefer interview and panel discussion formats to a lecture format, even though these formats have no advantage in terms of learning (Brandon, 1956; Jorgensen, 1955).

Presentation Pace and Length Effects

Presentation Pacing

Commercial video uses a rapid pace to sustain viewer interest in the program. However, in instructional video it has become an axiom to condemn this use of the medium in favor of a more deliberate pace intended to give the viewer time to digest and integrate the information as it is presented. Hoban and Van Ormer (1950) were among the first to state the principle that the rate of development or pacing of a film or video should be slow enough to permit the learner to grasp the material as it is shown. Research findings have tended to confirm the relationship between learning and the pace at which information is presented (Jaspen in W. H. Allen, 1957; Kozma, 1986, 1991; Wright et al., 1984). This practice also extends to the pacing of verbal information, because the number of spoken words per minute correlates negatively with recall (Hoban & Van Ormer, 1950; J. R. Smith & McEwen, 1973–1974). Research has also demonstrated the value of breaking up presentations with rest pauses so that viewers do not have to process new information continuously (Chu & Schramm, 1967; Coldevin, 1975).

However, the proper pace at which information should be presented is also determined by the particular content and the viewer's needs and current skill level. Most of the studies that examined the effect of pacing involved verbal learning, which seems to be sensitive to this effect. Other forms of content, such as learning visual material or psychomotor skills, appear to have a slightly different profile. For the learning of psychomotor skills, a differentiation can be made between the learning of technique and the learning of timing. The former skill is more readily learned through a slow presentation of correct movement and positioning. Once those skills have been developed, presentation at normal speed is preferable for learning timing (J. G. Williams, 1987a, 1987b). Accelerated rates used in one study suggested that a simple psychomotor assembly task can be taught through filmed demonstrations moderately compressed by a third or more over normal speed (Masterson, 1976).

Calvert and Scott (1989) proposed a complex interaction between pace effects, content, and program format to account for the mixed results found for studies involving younger viewers. Studies where fast pace resulted in improved learning were those where material to be learned was organized so that the important material was repeated or where previous material was unrelated to later material (Welch & Watt, 1982; Zillmann, Williams, Bryant, Boynton, & Wolf, 1980). Studies where fast pace resulted in decreased learning involved more complex materials presented over several segments and required learners to understand and integrate much old and new information (Wright et al., 1984).

Program Length

The other major time effect relates to the effect of presentation length, and the relative rise and fall in viewer attention during a program. The matter of program length has not been widely researched. The available studies tend to favor shorter presentation periods, with an upper limit of about 25 to 30 minutes (Baggaley, 1973; Trenaman, 1967; Vernon, 1953). The research also suggests that younger viewers are less able to sustain interest in a longer presentation than older viewers (Wright et al., 1984).

Based on the well-known "serial-position effect," video producers might assume that the viewer's attention and learning would be greatest at the beginning of a program and would then gradually fall off through the middle portion. Retention of information at the end of the program would rise if tested immediately, but not after a delay. The research evidence tends to support this pattern, although different results have been reported. Overall comprehension appears to decline over a longer period of exposure to a program, suggesting that important points should be made earlier rather than later in a program (Berry et al., 1981; Trenaman, 1967; Vernon, 1953). However, two early studies produced contradictory patterns. Brandon (1956) found more learning from the middle portion of an instructional video program than from either the beginning or the end. Jorgensen (1955) found more retention from the end of a program than from the middle or beginning.

Instructional Video Strategies, Techniques, and Devices

Apart from the selection of a presentation format, other major production design decisions include the selection of specific instructional strategies, techniques, and devices. These decisions influence what information is presented, in what level of detail, how the information will be organized, and how it will be presented to the learner. Instructional television and film research confirms that the general rules for good instruction also apply to video presentations. Indeed, the most useful finding appears to be the proven value of introductions, reviews, and the repetition of important sequences and ideas as the best single way to improve learning (W. H. Allen, 1960, 1973; Chu & Schramm, 1967; Coldevin, 1975; Hoban & Van Ormer, 1950; Link, 1961). These and other conventional techniques that have worked well in video and film include providing advanced organizers such as topic titles in textual or spoken introductions (W. H. Allen, 1973; Hoban & Van Ormer, 1950), showing common errors when teaching procedural skills (Hoban & Van Ormer, 1950), focusing on critical elements when conducting a demonstration (Travers, 1967), directing attention to parts of a film before it is shown (May & Lumsdaine, 1958), and teacher-directed introductions and follow-up discussions after a class has been shown a film or video presentation (W. H. Allen, 1960; Chu & Schramm, 1975).

Encouraging Student Participation

A variety of presentation techniques have been explored in efforts to encourage viewer involvement and participation. Some of the experimental interventions used in early investigations were eventually better adapted to more interactive programmed learning or learner-managed techniques than to more conventional fixed-paced linear presentations of films and videos. Early reviews of instructional film research clearly identified learner participation as a valuable device to increase learning from film and video (W. H. Allen, 1957, 1960; Carpenter, 1972; Lumsdaine, 1963). General techniques having a positive effect include direct statements that material is to be learned, explicit directions to respond to some stimulus on the screen, indicating that a particular segment contains important information, and the introduction of "relevant" attention-getting devices (W. H. Allen, 1957; Chu & Schramm, 1967; Krendl & Watkins, 1983; Neu, 1951; Salomon & Leigh, 1984; Torres, 1984). In addition to encouraging greater attention and effort, particularly effective participation techniques involve requesting a response and providing knowledge of results. The effect of these methods on learning has been generally positive so long as attention is not excessively divided between participation and observing the presentation and the presentation is not too fast (W. H. Allen, 1957).

Inserting Questions

Merely inserting questions in linear, noninteractive video presentations to generally arouse viewer interest in material has little effect unless knowledge of correct answers is induced in some way (W. H. Allen et al., 1968; Campeau, 1967; Chu & Schramm, 1967; Kantor, 1960; Teather & Marchant, 1974). Such noninteractive questions should be seen as distinct from ones specifically directing attention to testable material, or those more effective procedures used in programmed or computer-based instruction where responses are required of learners and are often followed by knowledge of the correct response.

Many investigations of inserted questions in fixed-paced, fixed-sequence filmed or video presentations have used techniques in which the presentations are interrupted to obtain answers to inserted questions. One general finding has been that inserted questions facilitate learning of the material covered in the questions better than presentations without inserted questions. However, this effect is specific to the questioned material because no benefit is conferred on other material in the same presentation that was not the subject of questions (Dayton & Schwier, 1979; Heestand, 1980; May & Lumsdaine, 1958; Michael & Maccoby, 1953; Teather & Marchant, 1974).

As long as learners are requested to respond to inserted questions, generally similar benefits of questioning are obtained whether the responses are overt or covert or whether the material is preceded or followed by the questions (Michael & Maccoby, 1953; Teather & Marchant, 1974). Both of these studies also showed that learning is facilitated when knowledge of the correct response is gained following the questions compared to not receiving such knowledge. In the Teather and Marchant (1974) study, the presumed effect of participation was less important than knowledge of the correct answer because receiving the correct answer after responding was just as effective as receiving the question with the correct answer already provided.

When fixed-paced, fixed-sequence presentations merely insert questions as part of the ongoing dialogue of a presentation, the effect of the questions appear to be less pronounced (Chu & Schramm, 1975; Kantor, 1960; May & Lumsdaine, 1958). For example, Tamborini and Zillmann (1985) presented three televised programs to young children that used either declarative statements of the pertinent information, rhetorical questions preceding these statements, or these rhetorical questions additionally personalized by directing them to viewers with the pronoun *you* and by having the narrator look up into the camera when asking the question. The overall difference in learning among the three presentations was relatively small. The personalized rhetorical questions yielded significantly more learning than the statements, whereas the simple rhetorical questions resulted in learning in between these two that was not significantly different from either.

Attention-Getting Devices

Video production techniques used to gain viewer attention have had a weaker effect on learning than might be expected from the effort devoted to these techniques. Although attracting and holding a viewer's attention is a necessary prerequisite, it is more an opportunity than a guarantee that learning will occur (Huston & Wright, 1983). Consequently, the research shows an uneven effect on learning for production devices intended to generally capture the viewer's attention. In the following sections, we discuss specific attention-getting devices with respect to their success in increasing viewer attention and their effect on learning.

Devices to Increase General Viewer Arousal

The introduction of specific visual and sound effects purely to attract the viewer's attention to the program, but without any relation to instructional content per se, has had limited success in most studies and has been discouraged by most general commentators on the research literature since the 1950s (Chu & Schramm, 1967; Neu, 1951). However, some findings suggest that it will increase learning in otherwise unembellished video presentations (Ketcham & Heath, circa 1962, as described in Travers, 1967). As a general rule, any sudden, noticeable change in the audio or visual output of a program will have an immediate effect on the viewer's attention to a program (Huston & Wright, 1983). However, such immediate arousal does not appear to be strongly associated with learning, and may not result in sustained attention for an extended period. Ziegler (1969) used such devices as periodically blanking the screen, desynchronizing the audio and video tracks, and increasing the visual complexity of the picture background, none of which had an effect on the viewers' extended attention to the image. Similarly, special visual effects inserted between scenes, such as wipes, fades, or complex visual patterns, have no apparent effect on learning (Hoban & Van Ormer, 1950; Mercer, 1952; Travers, 1967). However, Morris (1984) produced some improved recall using summative freeze frames along with other technical enhancements of a standard chalk and lecture presentation.

Setting Verisimilitude

The appearance of truth or realism in a setting is referred to as its *verisimilitude*. The setting of a presentation affects both the viewers' ability to distinguish the relevant information in a presentation and the viewers' attitude toward the information. Simple settings or backgrounds tend to be less distracting to the viewer than elaborate sets or "on-location" presentations, resulting in better learning (Aylward, 1960; Barrington, 1970, 1972). In addition, a studio setting was found to invoke the same amount of viewer interest as an on-location presentation (Baggaley & Duck, 1974). However, in a persuasive presentation a speaker working against a relevant background—either real or simulated—is perceived by the viewer to be more honest, profound, reliable, credible, and fair than a speaker working against a simple studio setting (Baggaley & Duck, 1974, 1975a).

Cutting

Rapid cutting (transitions between shots) in a video or film presentation also acts to increase viewer attention (Aylward, 1960; Huston & Wright, 1983; Kraft, 1986). However, sustained rapid cutting tends to confuse viewers by preventing them from processing the information as it is presented (S. E. White, 1982). Eye-movement studies have shown that a rapid series of fast moving images on a screen causes the viewer to look toward the center of the screen without focusing on any particular object—a phenomenon called "surrender" (Guba et al., 1964).

Sound Effects

The use of sound effects in video has been inconsistent in its effect on learning, despite its ability to arouse and sustain interest in a presentation. Noticeable changes in audio levels such as the introduction of different voices, laughter, music, and background noise has been shown to increase viewer interest in a video presentation (Huston & Wright, 1983). Sound effects are associated with increased attention to a presentation in children (Alwitt, Anderson, Lorch, & Levin, 1980; Anderson & Levin, 1976; Bryant

& Zillmann, 1981; Calvert & Gersh, 1987; Calvert, Huston, Watkins, & Wright, 1982; Calvert & Scott, 1989). When used as audio markers, sound effects appear to be effective devices for highlighting key points in a presentation, thus increasing the opportunity for learning (Bryant, Zillmann, & Brown, 1983; Calvert & Scott, 1989; Watt & Welch, 1983). However, they have no effect on learning when used merely as a diversion (Travers, 1967), or as background noise to add realism to narrative (Barrington, 1970, 1972).

Music

Music has generally shown little positive effect on the instructional effectiveness of a video or film presentation (Freeman & Neidt, 1959; Gallez, 1976; T. Griffin, 1969; Hoban & Van Ormer, 1950; May & Lumsdaine, 1958; Morris, 1988b; Rink, 1975; Saettler, 1968; Schramm, 1972; Seidman, 1981; Travers, 1967; J. Zuckerman, 1949), although a few studies have shown a positive effect among young children (Mann, 1979; Wagley, 1978).

Some uses of music may decrease learning by distracting the viewer from the content of the presentation. Wakshlag, Reitz, and Zillmann (1982) found that, given a choice, students were more likely to select and watch a short educational program when it was accompanied by music with a fast tempo and an appealing melody, rather than when the program was accompanied by slow, unappealing music, or by no music. However, in a second experiment the researchers found that, over an extended period of exposure, viewers paid significantly less visual attention to an educational program accompanied by background music with a fast tempo than to a presentation with no music or music with a slow tempo. All subjects gradually decreased their interest in the program, as indicated by the amount of time their eyes were focused on the television screen. However, subjects exposed to the fast-tempo music appeared to lose interest in the program more quickly than those exposed to the slower paced music. In addition, subjects exposed to the fast-paced background music were significantly less likely to recall facts from the presentation than subjects exposed to the slow-tempo background music. There was no significant difference in the amount of time subjects watched the presentation or in their ability to recall facts between the subjects in the slow-tempo group and the no-music control group. The researchers concluded that fast-paced music impeded learning whereas slow-paced music had no effect on attention or learning.

Boltz, Schulkind, and Kantra (1991) found an effect for background music on the recall and recognition of elements of short dramatic video clips. By varying the "mood" of the music preceding or accompanying modified taped broadcast episodes, they were able to increase recall of the story plot, the ability to recall whether a piece of music had been heard before, and the ability to match an episode with a piece of music. When the mood of the background music accompanying the episode's outcome was consistent with the outcome (tragic, funny, surprising, etc.) the viewers' recall of the episode's plot was significantly better than when the music was inconsistent with the outcome or when there was no accompanying music. Background music used to foreshadow the episode outcome had the opposite effect. When the music and the outcome were inconsistent in mood, plot recall was significantly better than when the music and outcome were consistent or when no musical foreshadowing was provided. No effect for consistency of mood or the function of the music (accompanying or foreshadowing) was found for recognition of the music itself. However, music with a more positive mood was recognized more often than mood with a sad or negative tone.

Humor

In studies dating back to the 1930s, humor has generally not been found to be effective in the classroom or within a television production (Chapman & Crompton, 1978). The use of humor in instructional films or video was generally discouraged in the early research literature for its lack of effect on learning (Chu & Schramm, 1967; McIntyre, 1954; Travers, 1967) despite its effectiveness of increasing viewer attention. Arguments in favor of the use of humor propose that it breaks the monotony of an otherwise dull presentation (Zillmann, 1977), puts students at ease (Horn, 1972; Mechanic, 1962), builds rapport between teacher and student (Zillmann, 1977), creates positive affective associations to the instructional material, and thus increases the probability that it will be remembered and recalled (Kaplan & Pascoe, 1977; Monson, 1968). Arguments against the use of humor include suggestions that it promotes a "playful" state in which information cannot be processed efficiently (cf. McGhee, 1980), that it creates a distraction that prevents information from being received (cf. Schramm, 1973), and that the enjoyment created by humorous presentations may lessen the satisfaction with nonhumorous presentations (Chapman & Crompton, 1978; Singer & Singer, 1979; Wakshlag, Day, & Zillmann, 1981; Zillmann, 1977).

Most of these claims for the effectiveness of humor in instruction either have not been tested, or have been disproved. Bryant, Comisky, Crane, and Zillmann (1979) found contradictory evidence that humor significantly reduces student anxiety. Zillmann and Bryant (1983) found that college students react negatively to unrelated humorous digressions by instructors, resulting in less attention to instructional material. There also is evidence that the insertion of humor creates an expectation that handicaps instruction not including such material (Singer & Singer, 1979; Wakshlag et al., 1981; Zillmann, 1977) and that such incentives tend to replace the intrinsic incentive to learn with an incentive to be entertained (Lepper & Greene, 1978).

A principal mechanism whereby humor is thought to enhance learning is by increasing the viewer's attention to the presentation, which carries over from the humorous material to the instructional content (Zillmann, Williams, et al., 1980). The effectiveness of this generalized arousal of attention created by humor has been shown with very young children. The insertion of humorous stimuli at intervals in a children's educational television program was shown to increase both attention to and acquisition of information. Moreover, increased use of humor apparently increased the speed at which information was acquired, with no apparent decrease in attention to the serious portions of the presentation (Wakshlag et al., 1981; Zillmann, Williams, et al., 1980).

Research on the use of humor has also focused on the degree to which inserted humor should be related to the instructional content and on possible misunderstandings and misinterpretations on the part of the viewer created by certain kinds of humor. Inserting well-integrated humor that is closely related to the content, or uses relevant content in a humorous format, is thought to be a valid and useful instructional technique. This stands in contrast to inserting unrelated, unintegrated humor merely to increase attention (Chapman & Crompton, 1978; Lesser, 1972, 1974).

Research findings also suggest that even well-integrated humor may not improve learning if the form of the humor creates confusion or distorts understanding by the learner. Zillmann and Bryant (1988) noted that much humor is based on a distortion or exaggeration of reality, ridicule, and irony. Among young viewers, misperception of the properties of new ideas or objects can be created when ironic humor is inserted into a video presentation. These misperceptions may not always be corrected by subsequent explanations. Moreover, the susceptibility of viewers to these distortions does not diminish with age (Weaver, Zillmann, & Bryant, 1988; Zillmann et al., 1984; Zillmann, Williams, et al., 1980).

The general direction of the research regarding the use of humor in instructional television is that it is most effective for young learners, that it becomes increasingly ineffective as learners grow older, and that its effect is negligible for older adolescents and adults (Zillmann et al., 1984).

Color

The use of color in film and video presentations has been thoroughly researched since the technology became generally available. The most common finding has been that adding color has a small positive effect on viewer learning. However, any small improvement with color over black-and-white presentations may not be large enough to justify any additional expense or effort (Chu & Schramm, 1967; Hoban & Van Ormer, 1950; Kanner, 1968; Kanner & Rosenstein, 1960; Lamberski & Dwyer, 1983;

Link, 1961; May & Lumsdaine, 1958; Vandermeer, 1954). Such concerns may be a moot point today, because color is generally a routine feature of most contemporary video and film work.

The other most common finding is that viewers tend to prefer color to black-and-white presentations, regardless of any added instructional value (Chute, 1980; Katzman & Nyenhuis, 1972; Link, 1961; Travers, 1967; Vandermeer, 1954). Given a choice, learners may spend more time and devote more attention to a color than an identical black-and-white presentation (Katzman & Nyenhuis, 1972). This small increase in attention may result in greater learning of secondary or incidental visual information (Chute, 1980; Katzman & Nyenhuis, 1972; Vandermeer, 1954).

Chute (1980) suggested that any benefit of color may depend on the kind of task and the way that color is used, and may be obscured when the results of high and low spatial aptitude individuals are combined. He generally found small overall effects of color with a fixed paced film on discriminating shapes. However, he found children who viewed a colored version performed better if they had higher spatial aptitude, whereas those with lower aptitude performed better with a monochrome version of the film. He suggested that the detriment suffered by those of low aptitude may have been related to the rapid presentation of information with dimensions that were excessive for them, which implies that their performance would benefit from a sparing and highly relevant use of color.

The major advantage of color appears to be confined to cases where color plays a specific instructional role in aiding discriminations (Chute, 1980; Dwyer, 1971, 1976; Lamberski & Dwyer, 1983; Travers, 1967 Vandermeer, 1954). These include situations where color recognition is an intrinsic part of a task to be learned and color is used to emphasize differences among objects, delineate figure–ground relationships, and provide an organizational scheme. In general, when color is used to distinguish among objects on the screen, the benefit is primarily for those objects only. These specific uses of color stand in contrast to its general blanket use for all types of content. Although color is considered here as an attention-getting device, these discriminatory uses suggest it might be more appropriately considered part of the following discussion on cuing techniques.

Experiments in which objects presented to learners varied in terms of how consistently color denoted the objects' shape and/or location tend to confirm the value of consistent color coding of information (Tolliver, 1970). However, the effectiveness of a color coding scheme is limited by the number of colors used, the number of objects to be coded, and the overall visual density/complexity of the screen image. In a dense visual field, the value of color coding is inversely proportional to the number of different objects to be coded and the number of different colors used. In a sparse visual field, the value of color coding is directly proportional to the number of objects to be coded, up to a ceiling (Kanner, 1968).

Increasing Attention and Learning Through Cuing

This use of production techniques refers to specific attempts to increase the viewer's attention and learning by highlighting important elements of a video presentation, cuing and focusing the viewer's attention, and clarifying the content to ease comprehension. In general, these techniques have been more successful than efforts to raise the learner's general level of arousal or appeals to the viewers' emotions and preferences. Specific cuing techniques include camera effects; cutting, editing, and composition effects; uses of captions; and uses of accompanying commentary/narration. Camera effects include the impact of zooming, panning, changing shot lengths, camera angles, and depth of focus on the viewer's focus of attention and ability to understand the video image. Cutting and editing are created by successive changes in what is shown on the screen. For example, the length of time shots are sustained affects the ability of viewers to understand and internally organize what is presented to them. Cutting and editing effects also include the impact of deleting, rearranging, and imposing structure on a sequence of video images on the viewers' attention level, psychological comfort, and acceptance of the video image. Compositional effects include the impact that the placement of persons and objects on the screen in relation to each other, from the viewer's point of view, have on the viewer's focus of attention and the relative importance the viewer attaches to different parts of the image. In addition to these visual effects, cuing can also be achieved verbally, such as in captions or through the accompanying narrative.

Zooming

The camera technique of zooming (i.e., enlarging or shrinking a video image by changing the focal length of a lens) is a commonly used method for achieving changes in the length of shots without moving the camera or the subject. The use of a smooth, continuous zoom effect is also used to mimic the refocusing of visual attention from lesser to greater levels of detail, or to back away from a subject to place it in a larger visual context. Baggaley (1973) suggested that the "zoom-out" technique might be used to cue the learner that the presenter is temporarily disengaging, for example, to allow the viewer to take notes or to reflect on what was said.

Within instructional video presentations, zooming has been used to attract the viewer's attention, to focus the learner's attention on the important parts of the visual image, and to supplement or supplant the learner's skill in relating details to conceptual or perceptual wholes (Salomon, 1974, 1979; Salomon & Cohen, 1977).

Salomon's (1979) experiments with zooms were concerned with noticing details in complex visuals and learning detailed knowledge from a video story. In those conditions where zooming could be compared to another unaided condition using a straightforward presentation, zooms were not particularly any more effective in terms of overall performance. However, because the intent of using the zooms was to aid learners who were unable to isolate details themselves, analyses in which learner ability was considered did show an effect of the zooms. Most of the learner ability or aptitude pretests employed were visually related measures. In general, performance with the standard or straightforward presentations improved as learner ability increased. However, zooming presentations tended to weaken this relationship, or, in some cases, revealed a negative relationship with ability. That is, the performance of lower ability individuals improved somewhat more with the zooms than with the standard presentations, whereas the performance of higher ability individuals worsened somewhat more with zooming than with the standard presentations.

Torres-Rodriguez and Dwyer (1991) used zooms and animation in teaching a lesson on the human heart with only limited success. No major effect was found for either technique, used singly or in combination. However, additional analyses showed that low prior knowledge individuals apparently benefited from either of these techniques on a few of the test measures used.

Dollying

Zoom effects are often contrasted with the effects of the alternative technique for changing the focal area of a video image, moving the camera, or "dollying." This technique is sometimes used in instructional and commercial video productions to simulate physical movement of a character through space as seen from a subjective point of view. Research into the relative effect of dollying and zooming on the ability of a viewer to build an accurate mental model of a physical space, based on a video "tour" suggests that dollying provides additional perceptual cues not available from a zoomed image, because of parallax cues and more realistic changes in the relative location of objects as the subject moves through a scene. However, the strength of the cuing effect was not so strong that the use of zooming prevented subjects from constructing accurate mental maps of an area (Kipper, 1986).

Shot Length

Shot length, by itself, does not appear to have any major effect on learning, so long as the information is clearly visible to the viewer. S. E. White, Evans, and Murray (1986) did find a moderate effect in which products presented with longer shots were recalled better than products presented with medium-length shots, when a commercial was viewed at higher than normal speed. However, showing a narrator with a medium (upper body) shot was no more or less effective than showing the same narrator with a close-up (face only) shot in terms of learner recall (Aylward, 1960). Shot length also appears to have an effect on viewer attention.

Although there is no significant difference in the attention level of students to close-up and medium-length shots (R. Williams, 1965), a sustained use of long shots results in a loss of viewer attention over time (R. Williams, 1968).

For instructional video, students apparently prefer presentations that use simple, fixed, and consistent shot lengths to presentations that vary the location and length of shots (Corbin & McIntyre, 1961), contrary to the professional judgment that a variety of shots is necessary to sustain viewer interest and attention (Cartwright, 1986; Utz, 1980). Focal length can also affect perceptions of the velocity and distance of objects moving toward the camera (Acker, 1983). Wide-angle views lead to an increased perception of velocity, and adult viewers were more likely than children to notice that the effect was caused by the focal length of the lens used in the videos.

Panning

Panning effects are continuous horizontal or vertical movements of the camera to scan a physical region larger than the viewing area of the screen. Panning has only been examined for its effect on attention level, rather than learning. Rapid panning has been found to attract and hold the viewer's attention, but sustained, slow panning may result in a loss of viewer attention over time (Huston & Wright, 1983).

A related piece of research suggests that being able to orient persons and objects within a spatial context is an important element in learning. Rothkopf, Dixon, and Billington (1986) experimentally enhanced the spatial cues available to viewers of a videotaped panel discussion by presenting each member of the panel on a separate monitor, eliminating the requirement for the camera to pan or cut from one speaker to the next. This also removed the mental demand on the viewer to recognize and mentally locate the speaker each time a new panel member spoke. The effect was an increase in learning and retention compared to a group presented the same discussion with a conventional one-monitor display.

Camera Angle

Camera angle effects have been studied primarily for their effect on the viewer's perception of an actor or on-screen presenter. This research was apparently stimulated by the frequent assertions of video and film professionals that particular camera angles suggest certain positive or negative qualities about human subjects that, in turn, affect the subjects' credibility. From an instructional standpoint, these effects are important whenever an on-screen dramatic character or a presenter is used to convey information.

Research confirms the general belief of practitioners that presenting a human subject from a low angle (i.e., shooting the subject from below eye level) results in viewers perceiving a dramatic character as being taller, stronger, more unafraid, bolder, and more aggressive than presenting the same character shot from a high angle (above eye level) (Kraft, 1987). In general, a low-angle shot increases the positive perception of any on-screen character, whereas a high-angle shot results in more negative perception by viewers (Mandell, 1973; McCain, Chilberg, & Wakshlag, 1977; Tiemans, 1970).

Experimental data suggest that presenting a narrator, lecturer, or other on-screen "expert" from a half profile angle, so that the speaker is perceived as speaking to a listener just off-screen, increases the speaker's perceived reliability and expertise, compared to a direct, full-face presentation into the camera (Baggaley & Duck, 1975c; Duck & Baggaley, 1975). This finding conflicts with other research that eye contact correlates highly with positive evaluations of on-screen presenters in decision-making, instructional, and persuasive settings. Velthuijsen, Hooijkaas, and Koomen (1987) found that adult subjects communicating only through an interactive television network preferred a video image that increased the amount of eye contact they could obtain with their remote partner. Acker and Levitt (1987) also found that participants rated their satisfaction with a video teleconferencing system according to the degree of eye contact they obtained from other remote participants, but not to the quality of the decision reached during the conference. Eye contact is generally associated with increased effectiveness in both televised and live presentations (Arnold, 1990; Breed, 1971; Karasar, 1970; Lin & Cresswell, 1989; Rosenkoetter, 1984). In persuasive presentations, such as a commercial or political speech, eye contact is positively correlated with the presenter's perceived honesty, forthrightness, energy, and forcefulness (Huddleston, 1985; Kipper, 1988; Merritt, 1984).

S. E. White et al. (1986) examined the effect of camera angle on viewer recall and recognition of commercial products presented at higher than normal speed. The study was intended to inform the producers of television commercials on ways to counter the tendency of viewers to skip past commercials in videotaped programs—a practice called *zapping*. They found that commercials using either normal camera angles, or extremely high or low shots were recalled better than commercials using shots of either moderately high or low angles. The authors attributed the effect to the added interest in the commercial created by the extreme angle shots and to the superior clarity of the normal angle shots.

A more explicitly instructional issue concerns the most effective camera angle with which to present a demonstration of a procedure. The research evidence confirms the practitioner's dictum that, whenever possible, the demonstration should be presented from the perspective of the person performing the procedure to avoid forcing the viewer to mentally adjust the image (Chu & Schramm, 1967; Greenwald & Albert, 1968; Hoban & Van Ormer, 1950). For example, Roshal (1949, 1961) found a substantial superiority in learning to tie knots from films with a 0° subjective view

RESEARCH FINDINGS 151

from the perspective of the learner compared to a 180° view as would be seen if facing an instructor. Similarly, in using interactive television to perform collaborative tasks involving objects, common views shared between remote participants were found more valuable than face-to-face views (Gaver et al., 1993). Other compositional effects that have been confirmed by experiment suggest the value of placing the most important visual subject at or near the middle of the screen (O'Bryan, 1976), and the importance of avoiding unexplained reversal of the viewing angle (Kraft, 1987). Other contentions about asymmetrical placement of speakers and visuals appears to be unsubstantiated by research (Metallinos & Tiemans, 1977; Zettl, 1990, p. 111).

Cutting and Editing

As already discussed, cutting and editing techniques influence viewers' level of attention, comprehension, and retention through control of the pace of a presentation. Cutting and editing techniques can also be used to cue learners about how to segregate and organize different pieces of information, and the relationship between items of information within an overall context. Cutting and editing techniques are used to impose structure and order on disparate video sequences, and, by juxtaposing shots, to create different interpretations and meanings apart from the content of individual shots. Finally, cutting and editing techniques can be used to increase the credibility and acceptability of information presented by on-screen actors or presenters. On the negative side, poor editing or cutting can confuse viewers, decrease their interest in a presentation, or undermine the effectiveness of presenters.

Appropriate cutting rates depend on the complexity of the content. Viewers require more time to interpret a complex scene so that a slower rate of cutting is effective for sustaining viewer interest. Cutting a complex scene too rapidly frustrates the viewer and reduces the viewer's sense of momentum. If a cut comes too late, the viewer experiences an increased sense of impatience and boredom with the entire presentation (Kraft, 1986). Eye movement studies have shown that sustained focus on a narrator's face creates a tendency for the viewer's gaze to wander over the screen (Guba et al., 1964). If a cut comes too soon, viewers report irritation at not being able to fully assimilate the information in each shot (Kraft, 1986).

Kraft (1986, 1987) found that viewers tend to prefer video presentations that have been cut into a series of shots over ones that are uncut, continuous sequences. Baggaley and Duck (1975c) found that video presentations that appear to have been unedited and unscripted result in an increase in the viewer's reported sense of uneasiness and discomfort. However, viewers are generally unaware of when or how often cuts are made. Asking viewers to attend to the number of cuts in a video sequence reduces their ability to attend to and recall the content of a presentation (Kraft, 1987). Also, cuts apparently have only a partial effect on how viewers organize the information they view on the screen. Viewers tend to segment information at cuts that coincide with major structural breaks in a presentation, but many intervening cuts are not noticed and play no part in the way material is "chunked" for recall (Kraft, 1986). Although viewers prefer video material that has been cut, there is no difference in their recall of the content or the order of events in cut and uncut presentations (Kraft, 1986, 1987). Baggaley and Duck (1975c) showed that editing of an unscripted video sequence can significantly reduce reported viewer discomfort and increase its understandability.

Kraft, Cantor, and Gottdiener (1991) examined the effect of the establishing shot and directional continuity on viewer comprehension and recall of filmed events. The so-called *establishing shot* is usually the first shot of a new scene—a long or wide-angle shot that places subsequent medium and close-up shots within a larger context. *Directional continuity* refers to the frequently stated rule that a series of camera shots should always preserve the same relative orientation to subjects in the scene. This "axis of action" rule was previously discussed in chapter 6 in the section on editing techniques. Crossing the axis of action creates an apparent reversal of position of a subject or subjects, and is thought to result in viewer disorientation and confusion (Zettl, 1990). Kraft et al. (1991) found that the inclusion of an establishing shot improved the ability of subjects to recall prominent objects in the scenes so that they could draw them in their correct place, but had no effect on recognizing the angle at which they had viewed specific shots. Maintaining directional continuity (not crossing the axis of action) also significantly increased performance on both the drawing and recognition tasks. In addition, subjects who viewed a series of shots in which directional continuity was violated performed significantly better on the drawing test when an establishing shot was presented at the beginning of the sequence than when it was not. In a second experiment, maintaining directional continuity improved the ability of the subjects to place the scenes in the order in which they had been viewed and to recognize the angle at which they had been viewed. Unlike the first experiment, the addition of an establishing shot had no effect on either measure and did not compensate for the lack of directional continuity.

Editing effects include how a shot is interpreted by viewers because of the shots that precede and follow it. A classic study of this effect was conducted by Pudovkin (1958). By changing the shots adjacent to a shot of the face of an actor showing virtually no facial expression, the experimenter was able to vary viewers' interpretation of the actor's emotions from happiness to mild bemusement to despair. A second experiment by Pudovkin used the same three shots, but, by rearranging the order in which they were presented, he was able to change the perception of the main character from that of a fearful man to a brave man. Isenhour (1975), in his summary of this and other similar studies, claimed that the meaning of a shot is necessarily affected by its context and order. However, the degree to which a shot's meaning will shift depends on its intrinsic intensity and strength relative to the other surrounding shots. An emotionally charged shot or a shot displaying violent or dramatic action will be less affected by its context than a neutral or static shot. Also, the context and order of a series of shots will have less effect if the shots are sufficiently disassociated. In the latter case, complete disassociation between adjacent shots is practically impossible, because many viewers are familiar with the use of wildly different shots in dramatic presentations to imply ironic relationships.

Specific editing techniques can influence the way a viewer perceives the character and qualities of a presenter. For example, the insertion of audience reaction shots can influence a speaker's perceived popularity, interest value, judgment, and instructional ability (Baggaley & Duck, 1975a; Duck & Baggaley, 1974). Changing the context of a speaker's statement from a prepared speech to a response to a question by inserting an "interviewer" shot has the effect of increasing the speaker's perceived tension, sincerity, and understandability (Baggaley & Duck, 1975b). Finally, increasing the cutting rate of a presentation increases the perceived vigor, potency, and activity level of an on-screen actor or presenter (Penn, 1971).

Presenting Verbal Material

A final set of production techniques relates to the use of verbal material to supplement the visual image in a video presentation. Verbal material may be introduced either through on-screen text or audio narrative—both techniques being widely used in instructional film and video productions. This discussion centers on the empirical evidence regarding the effect of different production-level variables. (The effects of combining visual and verbal information on learning were discussed earlier in chap. 3.)

Text on the Screen

The use of text on a video screen has been examined since the earliest instructional television presentations were developed in the 1950s. Based on the early research, a consensus was reached that the use of redundant text and video results in improved learning (Chu & Schramm, 1967; Markham, 1989; May & Lumsdaine, 1958; McIntyre, 1954; Travers, 1967). Much of the current research has examined the best way to use text, with heavy emphasis on human factors variables applying to computer interfaces (e.g., Alessi & Trollip, 1991; S. L. Smith & Mosier, 1986). The production variables related to the use of text on the screen center on the location of the text; the number of words that should be displayed at one time; the style, color, size, and spacing of the text; the length of time the text should remain on the screen; and whether the words should be displayed before, after, or at the same time as the visual or audio material they are intended to explain or supplement.

In general, the rules for the design of on-screen text are the same as those governing the presentation of text in printed material. However, text on the screen is more difficult to read than text on a printed page, resulting in a 20% to 30% slower reading rate (S. L. Smith & Mosier, 1986). Many of the rules for the use of text on the screen are derived from this finding. The basic recommendations have been that lengthy text displays should be avoided. When extensive reading is required, the material should be presented in printed form rather than on the screen (Gould & Grischkowsky, 1984; Muter, Latremouille, Treurniet, & Beam, 1982). When the viewer must read extended bodies of text on the screen, it was found better to have a few long lines of text than several short lines (Duchnicky & Kolers, 1983).

Text is easier to read with conventional upper- and lowercase letters rather than all uppercase letters (P. Wright, 1977). It is also better to maintain consistent spacing between words and letters than to insert spaces to achieve aligned right margins (Campbell, Marchetti, & Mewhort, 1981; Gregory & Poulton, 1970; Trollip & Sales, 1986). The same principle applies to the use of hyphens; it is better to print the entire word on a single line than to hyphenate the word for the sake of a more even right margin (C. M. Brown et al., 1983; Engel & Granda, 1975).

The rules for good writing in print apply equally to text displayed on the video screen: Use clear, simple wording; develop ideas logically; use simple sentence construction and concise wording; maintain a positive, active voice; and avoid clichés, contractions, unfamiliar abbreviations, jargon, and acronyms (C. M. Brown et al., 1983; Engel & Granda, 1975; P. Wright, 1977; Wright & Reid, 1973).

On-screen instructions, such as text to direct the viewer to perform a step in a task, should be presented in their correct temporal order (P. Wright, 1977). A series of related items are easier to understand from a list rather than an extended text (P. Wright, 1977).

The use of text to supplement other material uses somewhat different rules than those governing the layout and characteristics of text-only computer display screens. In general, placing words on the screen over full-motion video imposes a noticeable increase in mental demand on the viewer. Because both text comprehension and picture interpretation require visual processing, the viewer must allocate attention between the visual image and the text. Consequently, excessive text on the screen, relative to the amount of other visual material, results in decreased comprehension (Hartman, 1961; Reese, 1983).

Professional producers reportedly rely on the "6-second rule" to determine how many words should be placed on a screen and how long they should be displayed. The rule states that no more than two lines of text should be displayed at one time and that each line should contain no more than 32 characters, including punctuation. The rule further states that no caption should be displayed for more than 6 seconds, which is the recommended display period for the longest caption allowed (64 characters on two lines). The display time for smaller captions should be proportionally shorter relative to the size of the caption. The rule translates to a ratio of about 1 second of display time for each 10 characters of text in the caption. Research shows that the 6-second rule appears to be appropriate for most adult learners who are acclimatized to the use of captions, although the rule does not take into account the fixed latency period needed by the viewer to shift attention from the visual image to the text and, thus, underestimates the time needed to focus and read a single-line caption (D'Ydewalle, Muylle, & Van Rensbergen, 1985; D'Ydewalle, Van Rensbergen, & Pollet, 1987).

Professional production rules suggest that text should be shown on the screen to coincide with the onset of the speech the text is intended to clarify (D'Ydewalle & Van Rensbergen, 1989). Some research suggests that verbal material is better learned when the text is placed on the screen slightly after the words are spoken than when the speech and the appearance of the text are simultaneous (Barrington, 1970, 1972). Research on the use of captioning has tended to confirm the practitioners' suggestion that literate viewers are likely to read and rely heavily on captions to interpret what is said and takes place on the screen (Gropper, 1966; Hartman, 1961; Markham, 1989). Among adults, the use of subtitles is preferred over the use of dubbing in foreign language films. Adults use captioning the same amount of time whether the soundtrack is available or not, and whether the language used by the speakers is understood by the listener or not. The variable that determines the amount of time a viewer spends reading an on-screen caption is the length of the caption itself in lines and words (D'Ydewalle & Van Rensbergen, 1989). The benefit of captioning may be slightly greater for more difficult materials and of benefit to those with both high and low language achievement levels (Markham, 1989). R. Griffin and Dumestre (1992–1993), in a review of the literature, cite several studies reporting that viewing captioned television presentations provides some benefits for the hearing-impaired, learning-disabled, and those learning English as a second language. In their own study of captioning among normal adults, R. Griffin and Dumestre (1992–1993) reported an improvement in vocabulary scores for subjects who viewed 11 or more 1-hour commercial broadcast programs with captioning substituted for the programs' audio presentation. The ability to read words and follow visual activity on a screen appears to require little additional mental effort by the viewer and is almost fully developed by the age of 11 (D'Ydewalle & Van Rensbergen, 1989).

Narration

The other technique for inserting verbal material into a video production is through audio dialogue. Production variations in the use of spoken information include the use of an on-screen or off-screen narrator, speed of speech, intermittence of speech, and the relative reading level and complexity of the verbal material. This discussion relates only to the use of narrative in a simple expository presentation. (See the discussion earlier in this chapter on dramatization for relevant variables on that form of presentation.)

Early film research confirmed the importance of narrative to the instructional effectiveness of a presentation. This was demonstrated by the superiority of narrated film to silent captioned film (Einbecker, 1933, and Zuckerman, 1949a, both as described in Travers, 1967). The importance of the narrative portion of a film presentation was also demonstrated by the significant proportion (80%) of relevant information students learned from merely listening to the soundtracks of instructional films (Nelson & Vandermeer, 1955, described in Travers, 1967).

In general, off-screen narration is superior to an on-screen narrator in terms of the speaker's perceived authority and credibility. However, if the narrator is a recognized and recognizable authority on the topic, his or her on-screen presence might add to the credibility of the message (Barrington, 1972; May & Lumsdaine, 1958). Baggaley and Duck (1975a) further suggested that a speaker is best presented as an independent source of information rather than a mere conduit of another person's message. Consequently, an obviously rehearsed, scripted, or edited presentation is likely to be perceived as being less reliable and credible than a less polished, but more natural presentation.

W. H. Allen et al. (1968) compared several styles of narration in an oceanography film given to sixth graders. The styles were conventional narration that supported the content shown, narration that was merely redundant with the visuals, directive narration that emphasized or pointed out relevant details, narration supplemented with question-posing dialogue, and nonlinear narration that used a subjective style, varying pace, and incomplete sentences. Little difference in effectiveness was found between these narration styles overall. However, several analyses of subtests in conjunction with student ability level suggested a slightly greater effectiveness with the conventional, redundant, and directive styles.

The speed of narration should depend on the complexity of the material and the other visual and auditory information being presented at the same time. Too rapid a presentation results in a loss of comprehension, and some loss may also be associated with too slow a rate of delivery (Travers, 1967). Also, continuous narration results in a gradual decline in attention, whereas an intermittent pace, with appropriate pauses, sustains the viewer's attention over a longer period (Hartman, 1961). Narration speed should be slowed slightly when used to accompany full-motion video images, but the speed of narration for an average audience presented with simple content should be about 160 words per minute (Travers, 1967). The relationship between reading level of the audience and the corresponding readability score of the verbal material presented is well established. As a general rule, simplification of verbal material results in improved comprehension (W. H. Allen, 1952; Travers, 1967).

Although visual and audio information should generally be synchronous, a study described earlier by Baggett (1984) suggested their relative ordering sequence to be important. She varied the order of visual and audio narration information in a video so that they were in synchrony or were displaced in either order by 7, 14, and 21 seconds. Presenting audio before visual information led to the poorest recall performance, whereas presentations that were synchronous or used visuals 7 seconds before audio led to the best performance.

8 Learning, Mental Effort, and the Perception of Media

The use of television for instruction has been greatly influenced by its parallel use for entertainment, recreation, and marketing. Although instructional/educational television has existed for as long as commercial television, it is commercial television that has set the basic standards and created popular expectations for the medium as a whole. Because most students are heavily exposed to commercial television, some educators suggest that they may bring habits, biases, and expectations about video to the classroom, and respond to televised educational material in the same way they respond to noneducational programming on broadcast television (Siepmann, 1973). Several constructs, mechanisms, and theories have been proposed to describe and explain how widespread and persistent experience with noninstructional television might influence the educational effectiveness of the medium. These theories and constructs relate to the effect of extensive exposure to television on basic learning habits and skills, and the effect of students' general expectations about the level of mental effort needed to learn from television.

COMMERCIAL TELEVISION'S EFFECT ON GENERAL LEARNING

A second set of concerns has focused on the intellectual skills, behaviors, and habits that long-term exposure to commercial television may create or encourage. Some concerns relate to the social impact of television, where learning is incidental to recreational viewing for entertainment (D. G. Singer, 1983; J. L. Singer, 1980; Singer & Singer, 1983; U.S. Department of Health and Human Services, 1982a, 1982b). These include the fear that commercial television promotes anti-intellectual and anti-education attitudes through its content (Postman, 1986), that it is responsible for declining academic achievement in reading and other subjects, that time spent watching television displaces more constructive activities, or that it encourages the modeling of violent, antisocial behavior (Morgan & Gross,

1982; Neuman, 1988). Other critics suggest that the form and content of commercial television—with its emphasis on action, movement, and rapid pace—discourages logical, systematic reasoning in favor of superficial, impulsive, intuitive, and impressionistic thinking (Postman, 1986; J. L. Singer, 1980; Winn, 1985). Taken together, these result in a concern with fostering critical viewing skills in young viewers (U.S. Department of Health and Human Services, 1982a, 1982b).

Research on the impact of television on viewers' intellectual skills have tended to reduce concerns with potential large-scale social effects or with major effects on large numbers of students. In general, the magnitude and the scope of television's probable effect has been reduced to specific at-risk groups. However, the direction of the effect, although small and limited, has been consistently negative with regard to intellectual skills.

The Effect on Reading

A number of studies of grade-school and high-school students have been prompted by the concern that reading and studying are negatively affected by television viewing (Hornik, 1981). However, it is not clear if extended viewing causes poor reading skill development or is just correlated with reading ability. Beentjes and Van Der Voort (1988) reviewed the research findings on the impact of television on children's reading skills. Three sets of hypotheses have been proposed to describe the possible effect: the facilitation hypothesis, the inhibition hypotheses, and the no effect hypothesis.

The *facilitation* hypothesis suggests that television viewing can have a positive effect on reading: first, by creating new interests that can lead viewers to read related printed material, and second, by providing reading practice of on-screen textual materials that the viewer must read to understand the program. Neither effect is supported by research evidence. Although commercially televised stories and series encourage reading of related printed material (Hamilton, 1975; Splaine, 1978), these TV–print "tie-ins" tend to redirect, rather than increase, viewers' reading behavior (Hornik, 1981). Beentjes and Van Der Voort (1988) stated that not enough research has been done on the effect of exposure to on-screen print on reading skills to support or reject this version of the facilitation hypothesis. These instances of hypothesized facilitation refer to general viewing, rather than to programs with objectives that are specifically educational. For example, a review by Murphy (1991) concluded that *Sesame Street* has had generally beneficial effects on school readiness and prereading skills.

The *inhibition* hypotheses propose that television watching has a negative effect on reading by delaying or preventing the development of reading skills. For example, J. L. Singer (1980) suggested that long-term exposure to commercial television may create an inability to concentrate for an extended period. Increased impulsivity is associated with short- and long-term exposure to commercial television (D. R. Anderson, Levin, & Lorch, 1977; Friederich & Stein, 1973; Furu, 1971; Gadberry, 1980; Kagan, 1965; Suedfeld, Little, Rank, Rank, & Ballard, 1986), but no connection has been shown between impulsivity and reading behavior, other learning skills, or general academic performance.

A second inhibition hypothesis suggests that, by emphasizing visual over verbal materials, television may hinder the development of verbal processing skills (Winn, 1985; D. M. Zuckerman, Singer, & Singer, 1980). Beentjes and Van Der Voort (1988) discounted this theory—sometimes described as a kind of "right-brain/left-brain" hypothesis—given an absence of experimental evidence and contrary hemispheric-specialization research findings.

A third possible inhibiting effect is attributed to the content of commercial television. With its emphasis on entertainment, its rapidly paced action, and its frequently negative portrayal of school, teachers, and learning, television may create negative attitudes toward the slower pace of classroom work, school in general, and reading (Singer & Singer, 1983). Some studies have found that heavy television viewers have less positive attitudes toward school (Morgan & Gross, 1982; Price, Richie, Roberts, & Lieberman, 1986). However, other studies have found a positive relationship between amount of television young children watch and their attitude toward school (D. M. Zuckerman, Singer, & Singer, 1980), or no relationship (Neuman & Prowda, 1982; Walberg & Tsai, 1985).

A fourth inhibition hypothesis suggests that television watching may inhibit the development of reading skills by displacing reading as a leisure activity. When television was first introduced into several communities, there was a significant, but temporary decline in the amount of time spent reading books by school-age children (J. R. Brown, Cramond, & Wilde, 1974; Himmelweit, Oppenheim, & Vince, 1958; Murray & Kippax, 1978; Schramm, Lyle, & Parker, 1961). In studies in which television watching was experimentally restricted, the amount of time subjects spent reading increased significantly (Gaddy, 1980; cf. De Meyer, Hendriks, & Fauconnier, 1987, cited in Beentjes & Van Der Voort, 1988). Television watching has been shown to replace other activities that could indirectly stimulate cognitive growth. Research conducted during the introductory stages of television found that children used time previously devoted to radio and cinema to watch television (Dorr, 1986; Finn, 1953). In addition, activities done while watching television, such as reading and homework, are performed less well because of reduced effort and attention (Beentjes & Van Der Voort, 1988; Dorr, 1986).

However, Neuman (1988), in a synthesis of eight statewide assessments and analysis of the National Assessment of Educational Progress, found only limited support for the displacement effect. Time spent in leisure reading and other activities was unrelated to time spent watching television. Among upper grade students, time spent on homework was negatively correlated with time spent watching television. Neuman pointed out that the small amount of homework assigned to students makes it difficult to place much confidence in the probable impact of television. The importance of any displacement effect is limited by the low level of reading that preceded the advent of television (Hornik, 1981). There is some evidence that displacement may occur with heavy viewing. The effect of television watching on reading may be nonlinear so that small amounts of watching may have no effect, or may actually be beneficial for some groups of viewers. However, above a certain level of exposure (3 or more hours per day), the effect on reading scores is increasingly negative and significant (Beentjes & Van Der Voort, 1988; Neuman, 1988). Morgan and Gross (1982) concluded that "A small amount of viewing seems better than none, and a lot is worst of all" (p. 81), but the benefit of small amounts of viewing disappears with high school students who show a more linear negative association of decreased reading with increased viewing.

The *no effect* hypothesis attempts to explain the weak statistical relationship between reading achievement and television watching. Three possible explanations have been offered: the absence of a true effect, inadequate research methods, or several countervailing effects that tend to mask each other. The first two explanations are not supported by the evidence, leaving the alternative that the effect is the result of several interacting trends or patterns that tend to mask each other.

The Effect on Educational Achievement and Aspirations

Although particular attention has been given to the impact of television on reading, other forms of educational achievement have also been examined, including general attitudes of students toward educational and vocational attainment. A 1982 analysis of 23 educational and psychological studies concluded that:

> The overall correlation of hours of televiewing and achievement is negative but small (−.05). Regardless of the sample size, year, and location of the research, the effect remains consistent. The overall effect, however, is not constant across the range of viewing times. The effects are slightly positive for up to 10 hours of viewing a week, but beyond 10 hours the effects are negative and increasingly deleterious until viewing time reaches 35 to 40 hours. Any viewing beyond 10 hours has little [further deleterious] effect. Females and high IQ children are more adversely affected than other groups. (P. A. Williams, Haertel, Haertel, & Walberg, 1982, p. 19)

The amount of television watched correlates negatively with educational attainment and a variety of general ability and achievement measures (Bailyn, 1959; Himmelweit et al., 1958; La Blonde, 1966; Lyle & Hoffman, 1972; Morgan, 1980; Morgan & Gross, 1980, 1982; Scott, 1956;

D. Smith, 1971; G. Thompson, 1964). Although both television watching and socioeconomic status (SES) are significantly related to achievement, the TV/achievement effect is independent of SES, level of exposure, and other related psychological and personality predispositions (Bailyn, 1959; Greenberg & Reeves, 1976). However, when studies have controlled for ability (IQ), the correlations among achievement, amount of television watched, and other predictors of achievement tend to become smaller. This suggests that television viewing and achievement are related because the amount of television watched correlates negatively with IQ (i.e., higher IQ is associated with lower viewing, and lower IQ with higher viewing).

Important effects have been related to other individual differences of age, social class, gender, and measured intelligence. The direction of the effect is not consistently negative. There is evidence to suggest that exposure to television has a positive compensatory effect on preadolescent learners, students from lower SES families, males, and persons with lower measured ability. Negative impact is found most often for older students, students from higher SES families, and persons of higher general ability. This negative effect is usually characterized by academic performance that is less than would be expected. The net effect is to pull persons toward the middle of the performance range, benefiting some and penalizing others. The viewer's choice of content appears to be an important variable. Heavy exposure to action-adventure and fantasy programming is more likely to have a negative effect than exposure to drama, documentary, and public affairs (Morgan & Gross, 1982).

Morgan and Gross (1982) examined the relationship between television viewing and the subsequent educational and career aspirations of adolescents. They found aspirations to be mediated by a complex set of demographic, family life, and personal factors as the adolescents were followed over several years. During the early middle school years, television watching was negatively associated with both occupational and educational aspirations. Male or female students described as heavy watchers tended to have more modest goals in terms of future jobs and years of education than more moderate watchers. This detrimental relation between television viewing and aspirations was independent of the positive relation of IQ and SES with aspirations. The detrimental relationship between viewing and aspirations disappeared as the students entered high school. Removing the contribution of IQ and SES, greater viewing was unrelated to aspirations for males and was positively associated with females.

COMMERCIAL TELEVISION'S EFFECT ON LEARNING FROM TELEVISED MEDIA

Whereas concerns have been voiced about commercial television's impact on students' overall ability or desire to learn, a concern has also been that the medium itself is limited as an instructional tool because students become habituated to respond to televised content without the conscious reflection or deeper processing needed for retention, transfer, and integration with other knowledge. Two specific effects have been suggested. First, the content of typical commercial television programming may influence how students view the medium as a whole. Some educational researchers suggest that students may regard television only as an entertainment and recreational medium and may discount the importance, seriousness, and value of any material presented in a televised format (Cennamo, 1989). Second, an effect is sometimes linked to the visual and lifelike nature of television. Because television is primarily a visual medium, and can be "understood" at a superficial level with little mental effort, students may assume that it is easier to learn from television than from written or spoken material, and may exert less effort to learn from a televised presentation than from the latter media (Furnham, Proctor, & Gunter, 1988). Salomon (1984) made a similar argument when he suggested that students may consider learning from television to be equivalent to learning from day-to-day observation of the real world—a natural process requiring no special effort by the student. Both of these preconceptions—that is, that television is a nonserious or an "easy" medium because of its visual and "realistic" (rather than a verbal and didactic) format—are likely to result in students making less conscious effort to learn from television than they would from a more "demanding" medium.

Popular Attitudes Toward Commercial Television

The research on attitudes toward television tends to confirm the validity of some of the concerns described in the previous paragraph. Nearly universal exposure to commercial television appears to have created widely held expectations about the medium and its content that are likely to affect how individuals respond to instructional uses of television. Moreover, the group of television watchers is virtually the entire population, there being virtually no significant group of nonviewers (Jackson-Beeck, 1977).

The research on television as a mass medium suggests that it is difficult to categorize the reasons why any one person watches television except in broad terms. Research conducted under the so-called needs and gratifications model assumes that the viewer is an active consumer of television, although there is an element of random exposure and casual sampling that also affects what the viewer watches (Bogart, 1965). The needs and gratifications model also assumes that television competes with other activities and mass media that could receive the viewer's time and attention (Katz, Blumler, & Gurevitch, 1974).

Studies in this field have pointed out that no single reason determines what a person watches, why, or how often. Reasons and motivations change from day to day according to the person's particular needs and wants, the programming content available, and other situational factors. People might watch a light comedy for mindless activity when bored or tired, but might choose to watch a news program or a documentary to learn about a topic that interests them. In addition, two different viewers may watch the same program for different reasons, focusing on particular characters, the plot, the setting, or the technical quality of the programming (Rosengren & Windahl, 1972).

Although the reasons why individuals watch television vary, the prevailing perception of commercial television is as a form of recreation, leisure, and relaxation. In a longitudinal study of British television viewers, Himmelweit and Swift (1976) found that the perceived value of commercial television as a source of information, new ideas, or new experiences tends to decline at about age 11; after that age typical commercial television programming is regarded as predictable and unexciting. Similar results were produced for American audiences, who also found that the proportion of time spent watching television to "pass the time" increased with age, relative to time spent for learning, companionship, escape, excitement, and relaxation (Rubin, 1977). Persons with alternative interests and opportunities tend to reduce the amount of television they watch from early adolescence on. However, persons with fewer recreational alternatives tend to continue watching a large amount of television (Himmelweit & Swift, 1976).

An exception to television serving as a source of entertainment is in the area of news and public affairs programming, which represent a major source of information for many persons (Roper, 1978). Categories of viewer "types" usually include persons for whom television is a source of culture, news, and information. Such persons tend to be from higher SES categories and to have active personal interests in public affairs (Donohew, Palmgreen, & Rayburn, 1987; Robinson, 1975).

However, most viewers watch television because it is readily available, and demands little energy or mental effort (Csikszentmihalyi & Kubey, 1982; Gould, Holosko, & Baggaley, 1981; Gutman, 1978; Robinson, 1975). Socially reinforced perceptions of television tend to influence how much a person will watch (or admit to watching). Middle-class individuals are more likely to report feeling guilty for the time "wasted" watching television, whereas working-class persons are more willing to admit that they watch (and actually learn) from commercial television (Steiner, 1963). Upper-middle-class viewers tend to express active dislike for television as a medium more often than other groups (Robinson, 1975). Even among working-class viewers, the amount of television watched is a source of concern. Survey responses show that most persons consider television watching to be wasted time and, more than any other form of recreation, persons tend to express a desire to reduce the amount of television they watch (Himmelweit & Swift, 1976). Viewer research has shown that only a minority of viewers consider television watching to be more than a form of leisure activity.

In summary, heavy use of commercial television is associated with lesser social skills and lower social status, and a lack of alternative forms of recreation. Television watching as an activity is associated with leisure, minimal involvement, and relaxation rather than learning, concentration, or effort.

Student Attitudes Toward Television and Learning

Student attitudes toward television as a source of learning tend to reflect popular, stereotypical attitudes toward the medium. Rubin (1977) found that, among students from age 9 to age 17, the perception of television as a way to learn is consistently low relative to other uses, such as a way to pass time, relaxation, arousal, or companionship. Each of these functions of television declined in perceived value from age 9 through age 17. Interest in educational television was also consistently low relative to entertainment programming. However, interest in news and public affairs increased from age 9 to age 17, albeit at a lower level compared to other program types. Greenberg (1974) and Gould et al. (1981) obtained similar results for students, verifying the perception of television as a vehicle for entertainment and relaxation.

These three studies (Gould et al., 1981; Greenberg, 1974; Rubin, 1977) examined attitudes toward television and learning in comparison to all alternative uses of television. In the only study in which attitudes toward television and learning were explicitly examined, Krendl (1986) surveyed students in grades 3 through 10 regarding their attitudes toward television and three other media. Students compared four activities—watching television, using a computer, reading, and writing—on three scales: which activity the student preferred to do, which activity the student considered more difficult, and the activity from which the student expected to learn more. The attitudes were not anchored with respect to specific goals or settings, such as enjoyment versus learning, or school versus home activities, but were left open-ended for the students to interpret.

Overall, students consistently preferred computer use and watching television over reading and writing. Computer use was regarded as the most difficult activity, followed by writing, reading, and television watching; virtually all students regarded television watching as the easiest of the four activities. Computer use was the activity from which students expected to learn the most, followed by reading, writing, and television watching. Television was regarded as the least effective learning medium by a wide margin.

Preference and Difficulty. Students tended to prefer activities that they regarded as less difficult; that is, students who preferred computer use to reading considered computer use to be easier than reading. However, this relationship between preference and perceived difficulty was strongest among students who preferred computer use or reading. Students who preferred television watching or writing also rated these activities as more difficult.

Preference and Learning. Students tended to prefer activities from which they thought they would learn. Those who thought they would learn more from computers or from reading tended to prefer computers or reading to the other activities. However, students who preferred writing or television were less likely to see their preferred activity as an effective learning tool.

Difficulty and Learning. The relationship between an activity's perceived difficulty and its value as a way to learn was weak. Students rated difficult activities as more valuable for learning. Students who considered television watching or computer use to be difficult rated those activities as educationally valuable; those who rated television watching or computer use as easy rated them educationally ineffective. No similar pattern was found for either reading or writing.

Gender Differences. Gender differences were evident in all attitude measures. Males preferred computers and television more often than females, but females preferred reading and writing more often than males. Males thought that computers were easier to use than females, whereas females thought it was easier to write than males. They tended to agree on the perceived difficulty of reading (hard) and watching television (easy). Males thought they learned more from television and computers than did females, and females thought they learned more from reading and writing than did males, mirroring their preference pattern.

Age Differences. Preference for television increased steadily with age, whereas preference for computer use declined steadily from grade 3 through grade 10. There were no grade differences in preferences for reading and writing. Younger students thought that computers were easier to use, and that reading and watching television were more difficult to use than did older students.

Grade differences for perceived learning effectiveness were found only for reading and writing. Both young and old students thought that writing was an effective way to learn more often than did students in the middle grades. However, the perceived value of reading steadily increased through the middle grades, where it tended to level off. Television was consistently viewed as being educationally ineffective and computers as being educationally effective from the lowest to the highest grades.

Discussion

Krendl's data indicate that student preconceptions differ depending on whether they are considering an activity based on preference, ease of use, or need to learn. With regard to television, most students do not tend to perceive it as a learning device. Television watching is a preferred activity, but is considered to be undemanding and unlikely to teach the student much of value. It is viewed as a good learning device only by younger students, who also tend to regard it as more difficult. Older students tend to view television as being easier to use but of little value as a source of learning.

Overall, Krendl's data suggest that more preferred activities are also perceived as less difficult, yet students are still more likely to think they will learn from them. Krendl's findings are consistent with an earlier review of studies indicating students may learn less from their preferred instructional method. Clark (1982) reviewed studies that were not limited to television, but measured preference, ability, and actual learning. In these studies, it was possible to contrast the structure or "load" of an instructional method, as well as the preference or enjoyment of the method. He found that those of higher ability preferred more structured or directive methods from which they learned less, but that they learned better from more permissive or open methods that placed a greater load on their greater abilities. Those of lower ability tended to prefer permissive methods, but learned better with more structured approaches. His suggested interpretation of the inaccurate judgments was that higher ability individuals believed higher structured methods would be an easier or surer path to learning, whereas those of lower ability believed more permissive approaches were more enjoyable. Taken together, students tended to report preferring or enjoying the instructional method from which they learned the least.

Student Attitudes Toward Television, Mental Effort, and Learning

The construct of mental effort provides a theoretical link between the instructional effectiveness of television and Krendl's and other research on how students perceive television (Cennamo, 1989). Mental effort is thought to determine how much and how well a person learns from a particular medium. It is defined as the learner's nonautomatic elaboration of material presented in instruction. By this definition, mental effort is purposeful and under the control of the learner. It involves the conscious elaboration of material, either through linking with existing information already learned or through the construction of new associations found within the learned material itself.

Salomon (1983, 1984) is the principal advocate of the connection between attitudes toward television, mental effort, and learning. Salomon's theory extends several aspects of other theoretical approaches (Cennamo, 1989). One of these is attribution theory (Weiner, 1979). The other is a collective set of ideas concerning expectations arising from prototypical knowledge schemata resulting from familiar, stereotyped, or routine experiences (e.g., D. R. Anderson & Lorch, 1983; Langer, Blank, & Chanowitz, 1978; Langer & Imber, 1979; Schank & Ableson, 1977).

Attribution Theory

Attribution theory attempts to explain the tendency of persons to construct alternative explanations for their personal success or failure at a task. According to Weiner (1979), persons tend to attribute performance on a task to one of four reasons: luck, effort, difficulty of the task, and ability. Two of the reasons, luck and task difficulty, are external to the performer. The other two reasons, effort and ability, are internal to the performer. Two of the reasons, luck and effort, are variable. The other two, task difficulty and ability, are more or less fixed and cannot be altered by the performer. Weiner suggested that persons are more likely to persist in a task if they believe the outcome is the result of variable factors rather than stable relationships. He also suggested that persons are more likely to continue a task if they think they are the source of success or failure. Of the two variable reasons most likely to result in task persistence, effort is more potent because it is within the control of the performer.

However, amount of effort is also influenced by the perceived difficulty of a task. Weiner suggested that persons attempt to perform a task to gain information about their personal ability. If persons consider a task to be too difficult—so that no amount of effort is likely to result in success—they will exert little or no effort, because they will not learn much about their ability from persisting at the task. If persons perceive a task as being easy—so that even persons with little ability are likely to succeed—the amount of effort they will exert is also likely to be low. Given this formula, persons are most likely to exert effort when the task is perceived as being difficult enough to test their ability and where effort can make a difference.

Schemata for Familiar Presentation Forms

Several views of learning employ related concepts concerning the development of schemata arising from routine experiences that have become familiar. One of these directly addresses television viewing within the context of a theoretical view on the relation of attention and comprehension that was reviewed in chapter 3. D. R. Anderson and Lorch (1983) suggested that viewers monitor programs for samples of information that fall within their range of comprehension or that are superficial audio and video formal features of the medium. These samples of information serve to predict content of interest, which might then receive greater comprehension processing resources. Information used to anticipate program content partially originates from familiar schemata growing out of prior experience with conventions used in television. *Schemata* are prototypical knowledge structures with sets of questions, or *slots*, which are answered, or *filled*, by the information presented in the television program. If a program appears to match the pattern of existing schemata—if the presentation fills the slots with familiar answers—the viewer loses the incentive to attend to the program, and relies on existing schemata to "understand" the program. Thus, reduced attention and learning are possible consequences of encountering information from a medium such as television, whose familiar schemata have been overlearned.

The Anderson and Lorch explanation is similar to the more general learning theory of Schank and Abelson (1977), in which a learner's comprehension is guided by a *script* for a stereotyped sequence of actions that define a well-known situation. It is also similar to the concept of *mindlessness* developed by Langer (Langer et al., 1978; Langer & Imber, 1979) to explain how individuals process information that presents itself in familiar, stylized, or stereotypical ways. According to this view, new encounters with very familiar information can lead one to revert to a mindless routine in which the material is ignored or receives a low level of attention. Applied to typical forms used in television, the viewer responds to the presentation with a previously learned routine that is followed with little conscious control or reflection. A person following a mindless routine is vulnerable to making an inappropriate response. Taking these concepts together, Cennamo (1989) suggested that viewers habituated to respond to television as a purely recreational medium—either through the development of well-established schemata, scripts, or mindless routines—might have difficulty responding appropriately to televised presentations that were educational.

Salomon's Theory

The most concentrated examination of the relationship between media perception, mental effort, and learning was conducted by Salomon (1983, 1984; Salomon & Leigh, 1984). Many of the theoretical concepts described previously, particularly Weiner's (1979) attribution theory, were examined by Salomon in his attempt to explain why students learn or fail to learn from television. In a series of six studies Salomon explored the relationships between mental effort, perception of self-efficacy, and perception of task difficulty in the context of learning from television and text. His theory suggests that lack of in-depth processing of televised materials may partially be the result of viewers' perceptions and attitudes toward the medium, which in turn result in the viewer exerting more or less effort to process the information in a presentation.

Salomon proposed three constructs to account for the response of students to televised and print material: (a) Amount of Invested Mental Effort (AIME) that the viewer exerts to learn from a particular medium; (b) Perceived Demand Characteristic (PDC), which is the learner's judgment about the relative difficulty of a particular task or medium; and (c) Perceived Self-Efficacy (PSE), which is the learner's sense of how well he or she can learn from a medium. The greater the amount of AIME that the learner exerts while attending to a presentation, the greater the amount of learning that will take place. However, AIME is thought to be mediated by PDC and PSE. Learners are thought to increase AIME when the PDC of the medium or the task/information is more demanding. Similarly, learners increase or decrease AIME in inverse relation to their PSE toward the medium—greater PSE will result in less AIME. The relationship with AIME on both these scales is thought to be curvilinear, because both extremely easy and extremely hard media/tasks are likely to produce reduced effort. Television is thought to have a low PDC because it is familiar and lifelike. Most learners are also thought to have a high level of PSE toward television because its forms and usual content have been overlearned by frequent exposure. Thus, the AIME for television is expected to be low for most learners.

Salomon tested and refined his theory for the media of print and television in three articles reporting a series of six studies: Salomon (1983), four studies; Salomon and Leigh (1984), two studies; Salomon (1984), one study—a later detailed account of the first study briefly discussed in Salomon (1983). All but one of the studies used American or Israeli sixth-grade students (ages 10–11) as subjects. The exception was a survey of Israeli university freshmen used primarily to confirm the existence of the basic concepts behind the theory (Salomon, 1983, third study).

The studies used a similar methodology, with the exception of the survey conducted with the university students. Subjects provided general information about their attitudes toward printed and televised media prior to their being presented with a brief story in equivalent videotape or print form. After the presentation, the subjects reported the amount of mental effort they exerted while viewing or reading the story and completed a test of their learning from the material. The studies varied in the way AIME, PDC, and PSE were operationalized and in whether additional demand manipulations were introduced by giving the material for "fun" or for "learning" (Salomon, 1983, fourth study; Salomon & Leigh, 1984). An attempt was made to create equivalent versions of the printed and televised materials. These materials were based on a dramatic film (Salomon & Leigh, 1984), a humorous silent film (Salomon, 1984), an educational film (Salomon, 1983, second study), or a televised story (Salomon, 1983, fourth study).

Learning performance was measured in two ways. Subjects completed a set of factual multiple-choice questions about events shown in the film or described in the text. They also answered multiple-choice or open-ended short-answer questions that asked them to make inferences about the characters' behavior and thoughts, or events shown or implied in the materials. Assuming equivalent print and television versions of the presentations, the print group should theoretically perform better than the television group because print requires greater mental effort than television. However, the results were not consistently in this direction. The common pattern in these findings was that print produced better performance more often than television, and that the inferences test appeared to be more sensitive to media effects than the fact test. Salomon suggested that testing inferences better reflects the elaborative processes of greater mental effort than does simple recognition of facts.

Amount of Invested Mental Effort (AIME)

Salomon examined two forms of AIME. *Pre-exposure* or media-related AIME measures were those obtained before (or in the absence of) presenting actual print or televised materials to subjects. This form of AIME reflected the subjects' general preconceptions about the media, and was operationalized by the subjects' estimate of the amount of effort they usually exert when watching television or reading, in general, or when attending to specific types of content, such as adventure stories, family-related topics, detective stories, sports, news, science, and the like. *Postexposure* AIME measures were collected after a presentation. This form of AIME attempted to assess the amount of mental effort subjects actually exerted as a result of their experience in viewing or reading a specific television or print presentation.

Five of Salomon's studies found the expected relationship between media and AIME with measures of both pre- and postexposure AIME (Salomon, 1983, third and fourth studies; 1984; Salomon & Leigh, 1984, only the first study reported means). The subjects in these studies reported that they exerted more mental effort when reading than when watching television.

The most detailed examination of pre-exposure AIME for print and television was reported in the third study in Salomon (1983)—the survey of Israeli university freshmen. In this study, Salomon found that subjects reported greater AIME toward print than television, in general, and with respect to most specific areas of content. However, the subjects reported that they typically exerted more effort to understand television news than news in a print form. Salomon also found that subjects' preconceptions about television are more stereotypically fixed than for print media. The correlation among the AIME scores for a variety of content areas was significantly higher for television than for print, suggesting that subjects see less variation in the effort they should exert for television, regardless of content.

Perceived Demand Characteristics (PDC)

Salomon distinguished between preconceived perceived demands of media and those demands that result from specific learning tasks. Media-related PDC was defined as the perceived "realism" of printed and televised materials (Salomon, 1984), the subjects' attribution of cause for success or failure to understand print or television material (Salomon, 1984), and the demand ("depth") attributed to print and television presentations of material in general, and for specific content areas (e.g., sports, news, adventure, etc.; Salomon, 1983, third study). The effect of manipulating the perceived demands of a specific learning task will be discussed later in this section (e.g., instructions about the purpose of a presentation).

The findings for the perceived demands of media were in accordance with Salomon's theory. Subjects regarded television as more realistic than print, which suggests that print was a more difficult medium (Salomon, 1984). Attribution of reasons for success or failure to learn, following Weiner's typology, also suggested that print had a higher demand (PDC) than television. Subjects tended to attribute success with print to the learner's effort or ability, whereas failure to learn was attributed to the difficulty of the medium. For television, success was attributed to the ease of the medium whereas failure was attributed to a lack of ability or effort on the learner's part (Salomon, 1984). Answers to questions about the demand or depth of television and print materials also showed that printed material had a higher perceived demand. However, among the several specific content areas, subjects said that the demand (PDC or depth) of television news was greater than that of printed news, a finding parallel to that found for AIME (Salomon, 1983, third study).

Perceived Self-Efficacy (PSE)

Four studies probed the subjects' level of perceived self-efficacy for print and television through questions about how easy it would be to learn a given topic from print or television and questions asking subjects to assign reasons for success and failure to learn from television and print. In response to the questions about how hard it would be to learn various topics, the subjects tended to regard themselves as being more efficacious with television than with print (Salomon, 1983, fourth study; 1984). Subjects tended to discount the difficulty of learning from television when attributing reasons for success or failure (Salomon, 1984). Similarly, the university students reported feeling more efficacious about learning from television than from print, except for the topic of television news (Salomon, 1983, third study). Salomon and Leigh (1984, first study) found that children expected to be better able to make inferences, concentrate, and think with print than with television.

The Relationships Between PDC, PSE, and AIME

Combining the PDC and PSE findings here, it was found that print was associated with higher demand and lower self-efficacy, whereas television was associated with lower demand and higher self-efficacy. The predicted relationship between PDC, PSE, and AIME within Salomon's theory was complex, but complimentary. Greater perceived demand (PDC) was expected to result in greater mental effort (AIME), and greater perceived self-efficacy (PSE) with a medium was expected to result in less mental effort. For printed media, demand was expected to be high and self-efficacy was expected to be lower, resulting in higher mental effort. For television, demand was expected to be low and self-efficacy was expected to be high, resulting in lower mental effort. The trend of the results generally supported these predictions.

The relationship between the perceived demand of media (PDC) and postexposure AIME was reported in two studies. In one study, the hypothesized relationship was confirmed—the greater the perceived realism of a medium, the less the reported AIME for print and televised presentations (Salomon, 1984). However, in the other study, no relationship between PDC and AIME was found (Salomon, 1983, second study).

The predicted relationship between self-efficacy (PSE) and postexposure AIME was found in three studies (Salomon, 1983, second study; 1984; Salomon & Leigh, 1984, first study). For subjects in the print group, PSE correlated positively with reported AIME; those who considered themselves to be good readers also said they exerted more effort when learning from the printed version of the story. For the television group, PSE correlated negatively with AIME. Those who said they felt they could learn effectively from television tended to report exerting less effort when watching a televised story. The relationship between PDC and PSE was expected to be negative (Salomon, 1984). However, the relationship between PDC—defined as the degree of perceived realism of the medium—and PSE was negative for television and positive for print. Thus, subjects who considered television to be realistic tended to feel greater efficacy about learning from television, but perceived realism in print material was associated with reduced efficacy toward print.

Effects on Learning Performance

The key relationship posited by Salomon was that media preconceptions would influence the amount of mental effort the learner exerts and this effort would in turn affect the amount learned. The relationship between AIME and media appeared to be strong and consistent when only the average AIME ratings were examined: Subjects tended to report exerting more effort when reading than when watching television. However, the prediction of learning performance from preconceptions and reported mental effort was somewhat more uneven and difficult to demonstrate. That is, whereas the average mental effort for print was higher than for television, it would also be expected that learning performance would systematically correlate with preconceptions and increase with mental effort.

There was some scattered support for the relationship between AIME and learning under conditions where no explicit expectations were given to learn the material. Salomon (1984) found a substantial positive correlation between postexposure AIME and inference test performance for both the print and television groups, but none on the fact test. Although Salomon and Leigh (1984, first study) found positive correlations between both pre- and post-AIME measures and both fact and inference tests, only two of the correlations were significant. Pre-exposure AIME was significantly related to inferencing for the TV group and postexposure AIME was significantly related to inferencing for the print group. These correlations were not fully reported in their second study, but a significant relationship was again found between pre-AIME and inference scores for those viewing television for enjoyment. Thus, in this study, those reporting greater mental effort also did better on the inferencing test—in two cases with television and pre-exposure AIME, and in one case with print and postexposure AIME. Salomon (1983, second study) found no correlation between postexposure AIME and a fact test for either the television or print groups, possibly because of a ceiling effect. Taking these studies together, the relationship between AIME and performance for television or printed media was somewhat inconsistent, though it tended toward a positive relationship.

In Salomon's (1984) theory, perceived demand and self-efficacy (PDC and PSE) were assumed to affect AIME, which in turn mediated the effect on learning performance. However, given the sometimes inconsistent effect of AIME on learning, the relationship of PDC and PSE to learning is of interest. For perceived self-efficacy, a trend was suggested even though somewhat different measures were used in the studies (Salomon, 1983, fourth study; 1984; Salomon & Leigh, 1984). Better self-efficacy with print appeared to predict better learning, whereas greater self-efficacy toward television tended to predict poorer learning or bore little relationship. For media-related perceived demand (PDC), Salomon (1984) failed to find a significant correlation between learning performance and perceived realism of print or television. However, experimentally creating task demands did appear to affect performance, as discussed next.

Salomon attempted to manipulate the perceived demand (PDC) of a learning task by giving subjects different instructions before they viewed or read the television or printed material in two studies (Salomon, 1983, fourth study; Salomon & Leigh, 1984, second study). Subjects were either told to view or read the material "for fun" ("PDC-Fun") or told to learn as much as possible ("PDC-Learn"). Salomon assumed that the these instructions would change the task-related PDC, and indirectly change the subjects' level of AIME and later learning. Performance was expected to be better under the PDC-Learn condition than the PDC-Fun condition. However, given the presumed tendency of persons to expend less effort when watching television than when reading, the improvement was expected to be greater for television subjects than print subjects. An additional subset of subjects also saw a television presentation with the scenes scrambled in one of these studies (Salomon, 1983, fourth study). This merely demonstrated that those with the scrambling in fact reported greater mental effort, but understandably not greater learning because the scrambling reduced the comprehensibility of the presentation.

Taking the two studies together, it was found that more postexposure AIME was reported for the PDC-Learn than PDC-Fun conditions and more was reported for print than television. The trend shown in these studies suggested that increased demand had a more positive benefit for television viewers and that print was less responsive to demand because AIME was already at higher levels. Thus, the trend obtained was for the PDC-Learn group to increase both AIME and inferencing performance over the PDC-Fun group relatively more within the television conditions than was found within the print conditions. These findings were interpreted to indicate that increasing the perceived demand for television viewers led them to invest more AIME and to abandon their typical way of viewing, in which media preconceptions would lead to less AIME. Although these interpretations tended to be supported by the average performance with inferencing, incomplete reporting of correlations between AIME and performance leaves the evaluation of the predictive relationship between the two ambiguous. That predispositions of the television viewers were replaced by the induced demand to learn was supported by the finding that the correlation between inferencing and pre-exposure AIME was reduced in the PDC-Learn condition relative to the PDC-Fun condition. This interpretation was also complemented by the finding that inferencing and intelligence were uncorrelated in the television PDC-Fun condition, but were positively correlated under the television PDC-Learn condition at a level similar to either print group. Thus, typical television viewing appeared not to engage mental effort unless the viewing task was perceived as more demanding, which appeared to more fully employ or "mobilize" ability, and yield better learning.

Salomon and Leigh (1984, first study) also reported relationships with intelligence when no task demand instructions were used. Persons with greater ability tended to report expending less effort when watching television than subjects with lower ability. Ability correlated positively with learning on both fact and inferencing tests for those given print, but not for those given television. When subjects were divided into low- and high-ability groups, high-ability subjects within the print group outperformed low-ability subjects on both tests. However, within the television group, low-ability subjects performed as well or better on both tests as high-ability subjects. Salomon suggested that high-ability subjects failed to invest enough effort learning from television and thus forfeited the performance advantage their ability should have provided. By contrast, within the print group, Salomon suggested the high-ability subjects' natural advantage was better used, resulting in better performance.

Discussion of Salomon's Studies

Viewing the series of studies as a whole, Salomon advanced the discussion regarding media, mental effort, and learning. He demonstrated that perceptions differ among media and differ as a consequence of learning from those media. However, he found difficulty verifying the complex relations proposed in his theory, less consistently demonstrating the predictive link between perceptions and learning performance.

Salomon consistently found subjects to report that they exerted more mental (AIME) effort when reading than when watching television. They regarded television as more realistic than print, which was assumed to reflect that print was a more difficult medium. They also tended to regard themselves as being more efficacious with television than with print. Greater mental effort seemed to result from greater perceived demand (PDC), and less mental effort seemed to result from greater perceived self-efficacy (PSE) with the medium. However, although the direction of the relation between AIME and learning performance appeared to be positive, it was not significantly so in a number of instances.

Overall, the weakness with the proposed theory appeared in the predictive links between the various preconceptions and self-reports and their actual effect on learning performance. Additionally, the obtained effects were not robust over both types of tests, being found more often with the inference than the fact test. Part of the predictive difficulty may lie in the different ways in which the AIME, PDC, and PSE constructs were operationalized over the different studies, and the large individual differences observed with them. Salomon acknowledged the problems associated with a heavy reliance on self-report by subjects. Particularly for the key variable of AIME, Salomon discounted the difficulty because it should be a conscious form of behavior under the direct control of the subject. Consequently, Salomon argued that subjects should be capable of reporting their AIME with a high degree of accuracy.

Although the effect of naturally occurring media perceptions are of greater interest, experimentally inducing learning demands tended to support the theory. Increased demand appeared to increase learning and mental effort in television viewers in a manner more typical of learning from print, and appeared to mobilize the use of their abilities in a similar fashion.

Related Research

Several researchers have examined questions similar to those explored by Salomon. An early study by Ksobiech (1976) identified the importance of student perceptions of the demands of a task on the way they responded to media. He found that task demands affected the proportion of time they responded to see video when only given the audio or responded to hear the audio given only the video. Students were more likely to want to hear audio than see video when given a presentation for the purpose of an "examination" compared to when they were merely "evaluating" it or receiving it for "enjoyment." This greater demand for audio was particularly evident with verbally oriented lecture material, although the level of interest in seeing video was raised somewhat by visually oriented material. Over several conditions, the general pattern of behavior suggested that students sought the video or audio information source that maximized the purpose for which they received the material.

Krendl and Watkins (1983) also manipulated the perceived task of students by informing them that a video presentation was to be educational or was for entertainment. Like Salomon, students viewing for either entertainment or learning did not differ on simple recall, but those viewing for learning were able to provide more insightful observations about the story. Thus, the benefit of perceiving the task as educational was found with higher level, abstract, or reconstructive measures that were interpreted to reflect deeper processing or greater mental effort.

Cennamo, Savenye, and Smith (1991) extended Salomon's methodology to a learning situation that contrasted interactive video with two forms of instructional television. With interactive video, college students were required to overtly respond to questions prior to receiving feedback. In an embedded-questions instructional television condition, they also received questions followed by feedback, but their opportunity to respond to questions was only covert. In a standard instructional television condition, they merely watched the presentation without questions, feedback, or responding. Student preconceptions of difficulty prior to receiving the instruction indicated they viewed standard instructional television to be the most difficult, followed by the embedded-questions instructional television, and then interactive video as the easiest of the three media.

There were no significant differences among the three media groups in the level of mental effort reported after having received the instruction. In addition, the mental effort reported for the lesson was not significantly predicted by the initial preconceptions of difficulty. Consistent with the Salomon hypothesis, reported mental effort correlated with recall and inference posttest performance. Thus, those performing better on the posttests also reported having exerted more mental effort. The interactive video lesson was the most effective learning method on the recall test, but no significant differences among the groups were found with the inference test. Recall scores were significantly higher for interactive video than for standard instructional television, and the embedded-questions instructional television group fell between these two groups and was not significantly different from either.

Cennamo et al. observed that finding greater perceptions of difficulty associated with less learning was apparently contrary to Salomon's findings of greater perceived difficulty being associated with better performance (i.e., for print but not television). They explained this difference by suggesting that the lesson and all media forms used in the experiment were obviously of an instructional nature, and these effectively framed the context in which students responded to the questions and the presentations. Thus, when initially asked about the relative difficulty of the three media forms, students apparently evaluated their relative effectiveness as teaching media, and rated those they considered less effective as more difficult. On the other hand, the postexposure mental effort ratings did not reflect much difference from experiencing the three similar media, but they did support the idea that an individual's performance and estimates of invested mental effort are related.

Beentjes (1989) replicated Salomon's study (Salomon, 1984) with respect to the measurement of pre-exposure AIME and the subjects' media-related PDC and PSE. Using a translated version of Salomon's instruments with Dutch sixth-grade students, Beentjes reproduced Salomon's results with respect to the internal consistency of the AIME and PSE measures, but failed to find acceptable internal consistency for the PDC measures. Ignoring the methodological problems, Beentjes' findings on AIME for print and television agreed with Salomon's in general and for a variety of content areas—subjects reported greater AIME for print than for television. However, the subjects did not express the same uniform pattern of PSE toward print and television. The PSE tended to vary by content area so that some topics were said to be more easily learned from books, and some from television.

Although Beentjes was unable to treat Salomon's PDC measure as a single measure, the components of the measure tended to produce the same set of results. Subjects regarded television as more realistic than print and thought it was more important to know who the author of a book was than the producer of a television program. However, responses to questions regarding the reasons for success or failure to learn from television and print, described earlier in this discussion, suggested that television had a higher PDC and printed material a lower PDC than reported by Salomon's American subjects. Finally, Beentjes failed to reproduce the significant correlation between PSE and AIME reported by Salomon. Whereas Salomon found that AIME decreased as PSE increased, explaining why students failed to learn as well from television, Beentjes found no correlation between the two measures. He suggested that the Dutch subjects differentiated PSE toward media according to content area, whereas

DISCUSSION 179

American subjects had a more stereotypical view of their ability to learn from the media, regardless of content. He concluded that global perceptions of media may play a role in how much effort learners expend when attending to those media, but interact with perceptions of the demands of the content and the learning situation. Some topics may be well suited to some media but not to others. However, he also conceded that cultural perceptions and experience with a media also color individuals' general approach to television, as shown by the generally greater level of confidence American subjects expressed about learning from television.

Bordeaux and Lange (1991) examined the relationship between age, program orientation (child vs. adult), parental involvement, and AIME for second-, fourth-, and sixth-grade school children in the context of normal in-home viewing. They hypothesized that children would exert less mental effort for child-oriented programs as they grew older and the programs became more predictable. They hypothesized that very young children would exert little mental effort while viewing adult programs, but that older children's greater comprehension and experience would result in increased efforts to understand such programming. Finally, they predicted that AIME would be lowest for very familiar or very unfamiliar programs, but would be highest for programs with which the children were somewhat familiar. The expected age-related decline in reported AIME was found for child-oriented programs, but no difference was found for adult-oriented programs. Although a positive linear relationship between program familiarity and AIME for adult-oriented programs was found, no such relationship was found for child-oriented programs. Parental participation in their children's television watching declined from grades two to six. Parental participation correlated positively with increased AIME, but multiple correlation analysis suggested that a distracting, but not a facilitating, style of parental participation was predictive of higher AIME. Although confirming the presence of prevailing attitudes that may affect the amount of mental effort children exert while watching television, methodological limitations of this study restrict the validity of the relationships found (i.e., reliance on retrospective self-report data).

DISCUSSION

In general, the negative effects of exposure to commercial television appear to be less pronounced than is popularly believed. The research on the impact of long-term exposure to commercial television on viewer attitudes, expectations, general achievement, and ability to learn from televised material can be summarized as follows:

The impact of commercial television on achievement is small but negative. The impact is greatest for those who watch large amounts of television and is minimal and even beneficial for low to moderate viewers. In the specific area of reading skills, there is some evidence that television displaces other activities that are likely to promote cognitive growth, but the effect is small and weighted toward heavy viewers.

The impact of commercial television on the ability to learn from televised material is relatively small. More preferred activities tend to be perceived as less difficult, yet they may also be perceived as ones from which learning may be better. Television is generally considered to be undemanding compared to other learning media. A tentative hypothesis is that television viewing is associated with the investment of less mental effort and possibly a little less learning. However, demands associated with learning tasks lessen the effect of preconceptions about television. The use of video for other than entertainment purposes may need to overcome some preconceptions developed from exposure to commercial television. However, the magnitude of the effect created by commercial television is not large, is highly variable with respect to individual learners, and can be countered with appropriate instructional strategies. These would include clearly communicating the purpose of the video presentation and providing viewers with appropriate expectations regarding the content and the level of effort they will be required to exert.

9 Symbol Systems and Media

This chapter provides a brief summary of the concept of media symbol systems. The concept of symbol systems is often used to refer to the idea that media differ in the ways that they represent information and that these affect how knowledge is extracted. Many authors employ the term in a general way to conveniently reference this concept. However, explaining the concept in more detail involves a discussion that is somewhat more complex. Because the concept is so frequently employed by media researchers, the following discussion attempts to briefly capture some of the rationale for the idea of symbol systems.

Information presented in a message may be symbolically coded in various ways that require some transformation for a learner to acquire knowledge. Salomon (1979) suggested that different media employ different symbol systems to convey meaning and that some kinds of information are better carried through some kinds of symbols than others. The overall concept of *media symbol systems* has become a common term adopted as a convenient generalization for such terms as modes of representation, modes of appearance, representational systems, or presentation modes. Salomon (1979; and, more recently, Clark & Salomon, 1986, and Bates, 1980) reviewed symbol systems with reference to educational media, drawing on and extending previous work by others (i.e., Goodman, Gardner, Kjorup, and Olson & Bruner as discussed in Salomon, 1979).

DIMENSIONS OF SYMBOL SYSTEMS

Symbols conveying information can be objects, marks, events, or movements that stand for or suggest something else when they allow knowledge pertaining to these other entities to be extracted from them. *Schemes* of several symbols related by rules for arranging and combining them become a *symbol system* when they are used consistently with respect to a particular *field of reference*. For example, the field of reference for alphabetic notation is sound events or pronunciations; for musical notation, it is musical performance; and for photographs, it would be the objects shown.

Thus, symbol systems have a syntactic component consisting of the symbols themselves and the rules for using and combining them, and they have a semantic component correlating the symbols with corresponding elements within a particular field of reference. Symbol systems differ along several dimensions, which Salomon (1979) believed are primarily those of *notationality, repleteness* or *density*, and *resemblance*.

Notationality refers to the extent to which symbol systems are unambiguously mapped onto a field of reference. A notational symbol system is one in which there is a strong, clear, and consistent correlation between a discrete set of symbols and a corresponding set of objects or concepts in the field of reference. Examples of notational systems with direct correspondences are written languages, musical notation, and mathematical symbols and formulas. Of these, languages would be slightly less notational because they can entail more ambiguities.

Nonnotational systems do not permit an unambiguous mapping between their elements and what they may refer to. Thus, particular symbols may not always refer to a particular corresponding element in the field of reference, some may not be represented by a particular symbol, and multiple meaning may result when several symbols may refer to the same element. Nonnotational systems are exemplified by pictures. Their correspondence to a field of reference is more inconsistent, ambiguous, and context dependent "inasmuch as their visual surfaces are not composed of readily identifiable inscriptions assignable to characters in a notational scheme" (Salomon, 1979, p. 33). Verbal systems are more notational than pictorial systems and those visual aspects of television that are notationally weak. Because learners are less restricted in the information they may extract from images, meaning in a visual image tends to be inherently more ambiguous than that of an "equivalent" verbal message. In the absence of auxiliary direction, learners may ignore important elements of the intended message, or may attach spurious significance to the extraneous parts of the image.

Salomon (1979) also distinguished among symbol systems in terms of their *repleteness* or *density* in referring to the relative richness or number of dimensions that convey information. For example, a sketch would be less replete than a detailed painting because it has fewer dimensions. A picture or diagram contains a great deal of information, contained in virtually every line, shadow, and shape, whereas a passage of text is relatively more restricted to underlying information contained in the words, phrases, and sentences. Comparing these two systems, the number of potentially significant features in the text is much smaller than in the visual representation, even considering additional information contained in the choice of typeface, letter size, and the like. In addition, the meaning of many visual representations would be more subject to the way different elements are emphasized and the context in which they are viewed. Taking notationality and repleteness together, pictorial systems would tend to be less notational and replete, whereas musical scores or written language systems would tend to be notational and less replete. Baggett (1989b) drew a similar distinction in characterizing visuals as being "bushy" with diffuse connections and verbal information as being relatively more "skimpy" with strong connections.

Finally, Salomon (1979) distinguished among symbol systems with respect to the degree they *resemble* the object or concept being represented. Symbol systems vary in terms of their depictive and descriptive reference, from one-to-one replication of the corresponding object, to a totally abstract representation through verbal, analog, or numeric symbols. Depiction is the extent to which a symbol directly resembles, copies, or imitates its referent in a concrete way, whereas a description is conventionally designed to stand for an abstraction of the referent, which it may not resemble. Depictions are associated with more nonnotational and replete systems, whereas descriptions are associated with more notational systems. Salomon argued that such characterizations of resemblance must also include a distinction between psychological and real resemblance. He held that the similarity between one's mental conception and symbols is more important than the actual similarity between symbols and what they refer to. Realism is therefore a relative and essentially subjective characteristic of a symbol system. Thus, depicting an object with a high degree of realism may not be required and may even be perceived as being unrealistic by a viewer if it does not match the person's internal conception of the object. Conversely, a convincingly dense, but essentially symbolic depiction will be perceived as being realistic if it fits the learner's internal map of the object. For example, a (notational) wiring diagram can be mistakenly accepted as a realistic depiction of the internal configuration of an electronic device.

SYMBOL SYSTEMS USED IN FILM AND TELEVISION

Salomon (1979) held that film and television are generally not symbol systems themselves. Rather they are media where many symbol systems are used—a "meeting place" for multiple codes or symbol systems. Because they embody no single symbol system, they adopt the symbol system of the content they depict. Thus, they are media that can use the syntax and semantics of photography, cinematography, print, speech, dance, music, theatre, science, engineering, and the like. In being media using other symbol systems, film and television still generally approximate the dimensions of notationality, repleteness, and resemblance of their original systems. In educational uses, verbal explanation can serve to constrain the ambiguities of a primarily nonnotational system. In general usage, film and video tend to embody symbol systems that are inherently nonnotational, dense, and concrete as opposed to abstract. Salomon (1979) argued that these media are perceived as being realistic because they utilize many familiar symbol systems derived from other media and because their dominant symbol system "is the nonnotational, relatively dense, replete system of photography" (p. 55).

The wide range of symbol systems employed in film and television may also underlie some popular notions about their capabilities and effectiveness. These notions may reflect a fallacy in attributing a potential for using many symbol systems with what is actually realized in many instances. For example, the talking-head lecture realizes little potential in simply being a transmission vehicle, and perceived benefits of motion may only be realized when discriminations are provided for relevant content. Beliefs in the effectiveness of video for learning may reflect a conglomeration of many potential capabilities from different instances, a subset of which may or may not be fully realized in typical instances. Salomon (1979) also indicated that the "difference between what *can be* affected and what is *typically* affected is particularly great for media that allow shallow processing" (p. 237). As discussed in the previous chapter on mental effort and media attitudes, perceptions of nonnotational systems as depicting lifelike messages can also foster shallower processing than with notational ones demanding more elaboration. Thus, television and video are associated with complementary beliefs in their effectiveness, in one case because of capabilities to convey a wide range of experience and, in the other, because they may avoid more effortful information processing.

Although they adopt other symbol systems, Salomon indicated that the dynamic visual media do have a limited native symbol system apart from the system of the content being presented. When used simply as a technology for transmission, these unique symbolic renderings provided by film and television are unrealized. However, they are realized to some extent with shots and sequences employing conventions in which composition and transformation are articulated. Transformations of events, objects, and relations over space and time are illustrated by fades, overlaps, split screens, cuts, and altered speed. Many forms of composition can be used, such as the location and juxtapositioning of objects within the screen, the angle at which objects are presented to the viewer, and the degree to which objects are highlighted in the picture relative to the foreground and background. Professional video and cinematographers also have a variety of conventions regarding camera position, lighting, and editing that are used to convey different moods, focus attention on specific persons or objects, or, more commonly, to avoid confusing or distracting the viewer. These rules of the trade are so commonly used in the profession that they are likely to be transparent to the nonprofessional, except when they are inadvertently or deliberately violated. Skillful manipulation of this limited vocabulary can focus the viewers' attention, create illusions about the spatial relationship among objects, and, to a limited extent, imply psychological relationships among objects and people such as superiority, subordination, intimacy, alienation, order, chaos, and the like (Kraft, 1987). For example, McArthur and Post (1977) found that a viewer tends to perceive a more brightly lit object or actor as being more important.

DECODING AND ELABORATION OF INFORMATION FROM SYMBOL SYSTEMS

Salomon (1979) linked his analysis of the content aspects of symbol systems to several contemporary human information concepts in interpreting how the symbol systems of media affect knowledge acquisition. His general description of the congruity or correspondence between symbols and their mental conception is explained in terms of the ease of decoding and how much processing symbol systems demand or allow in the service of extracting information. Differences in the information carried by symbol systems require different amounts of mental recoding prior to their subsequent elaboration. Decoding or recoding is the translation of information from its surface communicational code into an internal one. Subsequent elaboration of information in memory refers to its being rehearsed, related, and compared to other previously learned information and transformed or manipulated by symbolic means. Different symbolic modes might generally affect the amount of recoding in terms of the number of recoding steps one has to carry out to extract their meaning. Recoding may not simply be the distance along the chain of steps involved, because it is also a function of how well mastered the requisite recoding skills are. This automaticity of better learned skills involves shortcuts that help to recode and elaborate the message rapidly with less effort.

In relating these information processing concepts to symbol systems, Salomon interpreted them in terms of *allowing* shallower mental processing or as being ones *demanding* deeper mental elaboration. He also implied that notational systems tend to be related to verbal skills and nonnotational ones to spatial and perceptual skills. Notational systems describing their referents would demand more decoding and elaboration to accrue meaning, whereas nonnotational systems would allow shallower processing when they are perceived as depicting more lifelike messages. When learners are given specific tasks to be accomplished rather than left to voluntarily choose their amount of elaboration, the amount of elaboration may be less affected by the symbol system of the incoming information. Notational systems would require greater decoding depending on the learners' level of automaticity and be less affected by such task demands. Thus, young children who are still developing automaticity in verbal skills might be thought to learn from television's nonnotational content relatively better than from its more notational descriptions demanding verbal decoding and elaboration. Poorly skilled learners may also be drawn to use media with nonnotational systems to the extent that they require less mental recoding than notational ones.

AIDING AND CULTIVATING THE USE OF MENTAL SKILLS

Salomon (1979) discussed several ways in which the coding elements of symbol systems can aid learners and potentially affect the cultivation of cognitive skills. He distinguished among these effects by contrasting what he termed *activation, short-circuiting,* and *overt supplantation.* As described earlier, a learner's skills are improved by prior practice making them more automatic, and these existing skills are activated in extracting information from symbol systems in new circumstances. Short-circuiting refers to circumventing existing skills by overtly providing the end result of transformations that a learner might have employed. Supplantation offers the opportunity to better internalize such transformations by simulating or modeling a needed operation the learner has yet to master.

These skill-aiding and cultivation ideas were illustrated in several studies and may be exemplified by one on attending to cues in a detailed visual (Salomon, 1974, 1979). Modeling or supplantation was promoted with zooms used to show the gradual singling out of details. Short-circuiting involved showing only the initial and final states. Activation involved showing only the initial state, leaving learners to apply their own devices. The supplantation and activation operations were inferred to have been internalized because performance on a subsequent cue-attending test exceeded that resulting from the short-circuiting treatment that circumvented skill cultivation. The supplantation and activation treatments led to opposite effects for those with high and low prior aptitude. Cue attendance for those of lower aptitude was facilitated by the supplanting zooms, whereas it produced relatively poorer performance for those with higher aptitudes. When left to activate their own skill devices, those with high aptitudes outperformed those of lower aptitude. Thus, supplanting zooms used to isolate parts of wholes facilitated or cultivated the cue-attendance skill of those who could not easily execute this process on their own. The zooms interfered with the learning of the more able, who did better when left to activate their own better developed cue-attending devices.

Several other of Salomon's experiments illustrate similar general patterns, although the benefits of techniques to aid learners appear somewhat dependent on the tasks used (Salomon, 1974, 1979; Salomon & Cohen, 1977). Additionally, aiding the learner appears to be more robust than the more restricted case of cultivation where skills transfer to new situations. However, the general theoretical thrust derived from this work is that learner skills interact with the task and the coding forms of the content.

More specifically, learners of lower ability may be aided by techniques that compensate for their skills, and those of higher ability may or may not benefit from them to the extent that they can call on relevant skills.

10 Perspectives on Video Media

In this chapter, we discuss several historical, critical, interpretive, and theoretical topics on video and film research. First, a brief description of the evolution of film and video media research provides a context in which to understand subsequent critics. Next, we examine critical evaluations of media comparison approaches that stress the importance of differentiating media from the instructional methods used within media. Although these discussions include video, television, and film, they have a broad scope that also includes other media like text and computer-based instruction. Finally, we review an interpretive or theoretical perspective on learning from media that attempts to answer the arguments of media critics. Other theoretical accounts given in previous chapters are subsumed in this broad discussion of media.

HISTORICAL TRENDS AND CRITICAL PERSPECTIVES

Several historical trends and shifts in research emphasis form the basis for contemporary views and criticisms of media research. W. H. Allen (1971) and Saettler (1968) traced these trends in two of the better known historical accounts. W. H. Allen's (1971) account includes a critical observation on the acceptance of new media and the pattern of media research. He observed the attitude of the educational establishment to have been one that demanded proof that new techniques were at least equivalent to existing teaching practices. This standard fostered a pattern of comparisons between media that were conceived at this very general level.

Prior to 1950, research often involved evaluative comparisons between two media. These comparisons involved presentations with conditions that were relatively unspecified, such as between a film and an instructor. This pattern continued in much of the subsequent research. A substantial amount of research with film was undertaken by the military during World War II and in research programs that ensued for the following decade. Research on film was then followed by another decade of intense research on educational television begun in the mid-1950s. W. H. Allen (1971) observed that "with this change the cycle of 'evaluative' research was repeated; television researchers almost totally disregarded the findings from previous film research in their enthusiasm for the new medium" (p. 9). As we reviewed in chapter 2, the typical comparison of instructional television with face-to-face instruction found them to be equally effective. Allen again observed that the same evaluative cycle was repeated when programmed instruction emerged in the early 1960s. It can be observed from our perspective today that, even prior to the era of programmed instruction, there was a strong interest in "student participation" techniques in early film research. This long-standing interest has now been enabled by computer-based instruction technology that can implement feedback and individual adaptation techniques more easily than the earlier attempts using films, workbooks, or teaching machines.

The historical progression with new types of media was also accompanied by four other general trends (Clark & Salomon, 1986; Clark & Sugrue, 1988). Primary among these was the shift from a behavioral to a cognitive emphasis, a reflection of contemporary views drawn from psychology and education. Behavioral approaches focused on environmental causes of behavior change, emphasizing the role of external stimulus presentations designed to control behavior. These approaches were without reference to mental processes mediating such changes. They came to be replaced by evolving cognitive theories where learning was viewed as a constructive process in which learners actively engage in the process of integrating new knowledge with old. A second trend concerned the desire to understand how individual differences of learners affect learning outcomes. This research might be characterized more as a long-standing interest than a trend because the complexity of individual differences continues to require better understanding. Individual differences in ability, prior knowledge, attitudes, beliefs, and motivation often interact in complex ways with the type of learning task, content, and instructional method. A third trend elaborated on later in this chapter reflected a growing dissatisfaction with gross media comparison studies. As a consequence, researchers have attempted to better identify the instructional techniques or media attributes used within media that are of benefit to learning.

Finally, media research has generally not been theory based (Clark & Salomon, 1986). The recurrent hope for some sort of theoretical base has only been partially satisfied. Several examples of such contributions to this base were discussed in earlier chapters. These include Salomon's (1984) theory on mental effort and media, the active theory of attentional monitoring (D. R. Anderson & Lorch, 1983; Huston & Wright, 1983), and the concept of media symbol systems (Salomon, 1979). Theoretical issues were also present in the suggested accounts of motion, realism, and complementary visual–verbal relationships. A recent attempt at a general theoretical account of learning from media that brings together many of these issues is given toward the end of this chapter (cf. Kozma, 1991).

MEDIA AS VEHICLES

Clark (1983) criticized media research in a widely cited paper that has since become a nearly obligatory citation by media researchers. Perhaps the best known quote summarizing his argument is that: "The best current evidence is that media are mere vehicles that deliver instruction but do not influence student achievement any more than the truck that delivers our groceries causes changes in our nutrition" (p. 445). The strong wording of his conclusion, "that media do not influence learning under any conditions," sparked controversy (Petkovich & Tennyson 1984, 1985). His recommendation still draws comment (e.g., Kozma, 1991) because it urged researchers to "refrain from producing additional studies exploring the relationship between media and learning unless a novel theory is suggested" (p. 457).

The repetitive cycle of media comparison studies observed by W. H. Allen (1971) also led Clark (1983) to complain that "each new medium seems to attract its own set of advocates who make claims for improved learning and stimulate research questions which are similar to those asked about the previously popular medium" (p. 447). Salomon and Clark (1977) characterized this pattern where media are the major focus of investigation as being research *on* media and distinguish it from research *with* media where they are employed as modes of stimulus presentation. Although Clark sharply focused concern with this pattern, many others had previously raised similar concerns. Thus, Lumsdaine and May (1965) optimistically looked forward to a "diminution in over-all 'gross methods' comparisons, particularly in futile attempts to assess the overall value of media by comparisons with 'conventional' instruction, and a corresponding increase in the proportion of studies which attempt to manipulate specifiable variables" (p. 513). There had also been previous indications that most learning objectives could be accomplished through "instruction presented by any of a variety of different media" (Levie & Dickie, 1973, p. 859). Likewise, Chu and Schramm (1975) concluded that many of the techniques examined with instructional television were by no means unique to television, but rather, as Schramm (1977) noted, "learning seems to be affected more by what is delivered than by the delivery system" (p. 273).

Clark (1983) argued that when learning gains with various media are found, most of the evidence results from uncontrolled effects of novelty and differing methods of instruction. That is, evidence from comparisons between media really reflect embedded differences in the content and instructional methods employed or reflect a novelty effect of newer media that tends to disappear over time. He concluded that it is the instructional method that holds the powerful influence on psychological processes and not differences between media per se (Clark & Sugrue, 1988).

Clark (1983) supported his argument with a combination of observations derived from computer-based instruction and the preceding base of instructional television research. A primary source of confounding in media research is that newer media programs appear to be more effective because they often reflect the investment of greater effort and more instructional design. The term *confounding* refers to several uncontrolled factors causing an outcome. Research designs also affect outcomes, such as the finding that larger differences are found between treatment groups using different teachers than when the same teacher is used in both conditions. One speculative interpretation of this finding is that better teachers may have been used in the experimental conditions for two teacher studies (Clark, 1985; Cohen et al., 1981; Kulik & Kulik, 1987). Alternatively, although studies with the same teacher in both conditions might be considered better controlled in one sense, there could be a diffusion of an innovative approach to the control condition resulting from a general effect on the quality of the instructor's teaching. Evidence for novelty effects in media research is derived from empirical observations that studies of brief duration tend to show greater effectiveness whereas those of longer duration show a diminishing magnitude of effect. These findings may reflect increased effort and persistence by students, which subside as they become more familiar with the medium. Finally, reporting biases lead to more differences between media being reported because smaller effects are found with unpublished than published studies. A number of common methodological defects in media comparison studies have also been noted by several other reviewers (Briggs, Campeau, Gagné, & May, 1967; Campeau, 1974; Clark, 1985; Clark & Salomon, 1986; Dwyer, 1978; Simonson et al., 1979).[1]

The positive benefit of Clark's critique was that it sharply focused on the problem of what differences can be legitimately attributed to media. For one, attention was drawn away from comparisons of the relative achievement advantages of one medium over another—a consequence of

---

[1]Campeau (1974) succinctly categorized these methodological defects in terms of *samples*, *treatments*, and *measures of effectiveness*. In terms of the *samples* used, there were failures to use random assignment methods, to report biases from attrition of subjects, and to control for pretreatment differences. *Treatment* comparison problems were: very brief exposures to treatments, failure to control exposure time between treatments, using off-the-shelf presentations not tailored to the instructional objectives, brief insufficient descriptions of the tasks used, allowing unequal coverage of content between the media compared or not demonstrating it to have been equal, failure to specify the amount of teacher contribution used in combination with media, and failure to specify or control for teacher differences between conditions. Problems with the *measures* used to judge effectiveness were: use of tests with no evidence of reliability or validity, use of criterion measures that may not have been sensitive enough to detect differences such as regular course exams designed for other purposes, use of poorly constructed materials that might not fairly test a teaching method, and reliance on subjective and affective measures of media effectiveness.

media differences either being absent or potentially resulting from an instructional method being confounded with media. Instead, attention was refocused on the importance of those instructionally relevant events that are carried by or take place within the "vehicle" provided by media. In discussing the controversy generated by Clark's paper, Winn (1987a) pointed out that his criticism was aimed at the delivery role of media on learning and was not aimed at other roles like the efficiency of media. Thus, the benefits to learning are separate from efficiency and practical considerations such as costs, distribution, and their adequacy to carry different types of information. The desire to choose appropriate media for use in particular instructional situations has historically given rise to numerous media taxonomies and selection models (cf., Reiser & Gagné, 1982). The ambiguity with regard to differential effectiveness resulting from general media comparisons has limited their hoped-for role in media selection models (Campeau, 1974; Schramm, 1977). This leaves media selection models to analyses of tasks and content that might apply to many media and to practical considerations like costs and availability (Campeau, 1974; Schramm, 1977). The characteristics of the learner, setting, and task become considerations because most instructional tasks can probably be performed with a number of different media. Schramm (1977) noted that in actual practice one would just select a few of the relevant media rather than employ a whole range of media where each had been selected for some optimal efficiency or practical reason. That is, it would be unlikely for teachers to jump back and forth between ideal media. In practice, one or two preferably simple media will be chosen, which may really be second- or third-best media able to present stimuli for a large number of the required learning events.

MEDIA ATTRIBUTES

A more refined approach to understanding how media affect learning has been to focus on selected "attributes" of media. By examining relevant variables within media, this approach goes beyond molar generalizations about media and potentially offers a better specified set of conditions relevant to learning. Media attributes are specific capabilities or characteristics of media. Examples are the ability to display events in motion in a speeded or slowed fashion, using zooms to focus on details, or dynamically transforming objects. Our earlier discussion on the effects of motion reviewed several critical attributes of motion that were beneficial for certain kinds of learning. For example, Blake (1977) facilitated learning chess moves by showing them in motion or with animated arrows, and Salomon (1974) found attending to details to be benefited by zooms isolating details of complex visuals. The implementation of sophisticated dynamic decision rules might be thought of as a distinguishing media attribute in the case of instruction delivered by computers. Petkovich and Tennyson (1984) illustrated such an example with flight simulators using low-fidelity "skeletal" scenes embodying only the necessary visual cues. Dynamic feedback cues on the correct flight path aided student performance and they argued this to be an instance where learning benefits would be difficult to achieve in other ways without these media attributes.

These examples of media attributes might be seen as addressing an often expressed desire to "exploit" or "utilize the unique capabilities" of media (Jamison et al., 1974, p. 56; Kozma, 1991, p. 206). In view of the prior dissatisfaction with gross media comparisons, the benefit of identifying such media attributes lies in the better specification of conditions affecting learning. In this sense, a similar pattern exists in both the study of media attributes and in attempts to better identify the relevant differences among teaching methods in media comparison studies. Some find the distinction between attributes and instructional methods blurred in that "research on media attributes is essentially indistinguishable from research on instructional methods...leading one to question whether the concept of media attributes serves to clarify or confuse our understanding of media effects" (Levie, 1987, p. 21).

The usefulness of the media attributes approach is still being evaluated and may be seen as an evolutionary point in building a more theoretical framework relating media and learning (e.g., Clark & Salomon, 1986; Clark & Sugrue, 1988; Kozma, 1991). Clark (1983, 1984) questioned the media attributes approach on the grounds that they are sufficient but not necessary conditions for learning. To support the claim that learning is not affected by media under any conditions, he argued that efficiency and learning benefits are confused with one another and that the benefits of media attributes on learning are not unique to particular media. Although there is little disagreement that similar instruction can in many cases be delivered by a variety of media, Petkovich and Tennyson (1984, 1985) argued that it would be difficult or inefficient to do so without some media. For example, teachers could attempt sophisticated computer-based instruction branching rules only with great difficulty and the cues provided by the flight simulator in their example would be difficult to provide otherwise. Clark (1984) in turn argued that such attributes are only more efficient with these media, that they can be achieved by other media, and that they are therefore sufficient but not necessary conditions for learning. Thus, if a list of those features essential to learning were constructed, it would be found that several media could present them. As evidence, he noted that the benefit of zooms on cue attending found by Salomon (1974) could alternatively be achieved with other techniques such as darkening a border around a cue or by static close-ups. Similarly, Blake's (1977) demonstration of chess moves with either animated arrows or motion illustrates them to be alternative methods because they yielded similar benefits. This version of Clark's argument is more fine grained in the sense that it has moved from criticism of ill-specified gross media comparisons to rebuking the uniqueness of better specified attributes even when presented within very similar classes of media (i.e., the attributes are said to be correlated with several media instead of unique to them).

Many believe Clark's comments on media attributes to be extreme (Kozma, 1986, 1991; Petkovich & Tennyson 1984, 1985; Pintrich, Cross, Kozma, & McKeachie, 1986). A primary objection to Clark's argument concerns the interchangeability of media in instruction. They believe that the argument ignores the fact that many instructional methods would be inefficient, difficult, or impossible to implement in alternative media. Although still agreeing that there is a premium on discovering necessary conditions for learning, they believe that research on sufficient conditions is still worthwhile. As Kozma (1986) argued, "That other media may also have one or more of these attributes does not negate their importance in this process; it makes an 'attribute' distinctive from a particular medium" (p. 17). This point of view therefore seeks the identification of a relevant configuration of attributes that can be made to correspond to the learning process. That is, instead of requiring attributes to be solely unique to a medium, it is argued that a "characteristic cluster" of attributes is an appropriate level to look for uniqueness in media even if they are correlated with several media. Thus, at the level of an identified "characteristic cluster" of attributes, a medium becomes unique in having the potential to do things that other media cannot do. This more complex view will be illustrated next.

COGNITIVELY RELEVANT CLUSTERS OF MEDIA CAPABILITIES

In a recent synthesis of contemporary media research, Kozma (1991) attempted to develop a framework in which to understand learning from media. His account stresses an image of learners actively collaborating with media to construct knowledge that contrasts with a view that learning results from instruction being "delivered" by media. This framework attempts to answer whether media influence learning by suggesting that the "capabilities of a particular medium, in conjunction with methods that take advantage of these capabilities, interact with and influence the ways learners represent and process information and may result in more or different learning when one medium is compared to another for certain learners and tasks" (p. 179). Kozma's account covers many of the same features discussed in earlier chapters and covered in other integrative reviews attempting to build a more theoretical perspective (e.g., Clark & Salomon, 1986; Salomon, 1979). However, his purpose is to support the general argument that media be distinguished by those features or attributes of media that are both cognitively relevant capabilities and which form a cluster when taken together.

Kozma (1991) proposed that media be defined in terms of three characteristics—their technologies, symbol systems, and processing capabilities. Technology is characterized by mechanical and electronic aspects that have minimal or indirect cognitive effects. Technology's primary effect is to enable and constrain the other two capabilities of media. That is, cognition is affected by the symbol systems employed by media and by the processes that can be performed by learners rather than by the technology, per se. The concept of symbol systems as described earlier from Salomon (1979) distinguishes media in terms of the way information is represented. These forms of representation affect how learners decode or extract information, with television's capability of employing multiple pictorial and audiolinguistic representational sources offering a wide range of such information. As with Salomon, Kozma noted that information is not only represented in memory, it is processed or operated on by learners. Learners strategically manage their "available cognitive resources to create new knowledge by extracting information from the environment and integrating it with information already stored in memory" (p. 179). The capabilities of a medium can be made to complement the processing capabilities of the learner by facilitating operations the "learner is capable of performing or perform those that the learner cannot" (p. 181). In distinguishing media by a characteristic cluster or profile of symbol systems and processing capabilities, Kozma cautioned that these are potential capabilities. These capabilities may not always be used, such as when a talking-head lecture in effect turns television into radio or when a linear playing of a videodisc provides a passive experience differing little from that with televised broadcasts.

Kozma (1991) illustrated his framework of relevant attribute clusters with examples of learning from books, television, and computers. For Kozma, the cluster of "cognitively relevant capabilities of media" that interact with instructional methods are: (a) for books, the stability of print and its processing being under learner control; (b) for conventional television, the capability to convey a wide range of symbol systems including motion, the simultaneous combination of verbal and visual information, a transient presentation viewers cannot adjust to their own cognitive pace, and the characteristically different way in which attention and perceptions affect the allocation of processing resources; (c) for computers, their dynamic control features to process, transform, and proceduralize information and actions to dynamically aid learners. Kozma's contrast between the cluster of attributes that distinguish books and televised video media will be briefly illustrated.

Kozma characterized learning from books as a stable medium because it allows learners to recover from comprehension failures. They do this by slowing their pace, by rereading text, and by strategically skipping back and forth among sections of text. Text and visuals are characteristically processed in a more serial, alternating fashion with books than with videos. When pictures are available, readers use them to supplement the text for an alternative representation and use them organizationally to evoke a schema or mental model of the situation. Learners having less prior knowledge may benefit more from these visuals and use them as a continuing aid, in contrast to more able learners who use them more for an initial organizational aid.

The stability of books contrasts with television's transient presentation of a wide range of other symbol systems that include audio, visual, and motion information. Kozma characterized the cluster of distinguishing attributes of television in terms of: (a) the "window of cognitive engagement," (b) the simultaneous processing of information from symbol systems, and (c) the transient nature of the information being processed.

First, the window of cognitive engagement refers to the collective set of findings concerning the relationship of attention and comprehension and that concerning viewer purposes and media perceptions (i.e., the work reviewed earlier by D. R. Anderson & Lorch, 1983; Huston & Wright, 1983; Krendl, 1986; Krendl & Watkins, 1983; Salomon, 1974). Particularly for general viewing, processing of the stream of information from television involves a monitoring process in which attention is periodic and discontinuous. Information falling within each learner's window of comprehensibility and interest influences attention to and processing of the message. This information is monitored strategically by attentional shifts and by deploying greater processing resources that are cued by either formal features of the medium or by comprehensible information of interest. The effort devoted to processing the information in a message is also affected by educational, personal interest, and entertainment purposes for viewing. The effort devoted to learning increases as task demands create expectations to learn and may be influenced by preconceptions about the effort that a medium typically requires for learning.

Second, television is characterized by the simultaneous processing of auditory and visual representational symbol systems. Audio and visual information typically complement one another rather than compete for processing resources. Auditory information carrying sounds and language often helps in interpreting the visual information. Although learning from either modality is possible, each modality contributes something in the kind of details retained by learners. The information provided in television's multiple symbol systems may aid those that are less knowledgeable, paralleling the pattern observed with text and pictures. They differ in that learning from text is driven more by the construction of a linguistic representation of information, whereas learning from television is primarily driven by visual information containing more representational dimensions (e.g., Salomon, 1979).

Third, the transient nature of television may benefit comprehension when conveying relevant dynamic information, but may be a potential problem when the continuity and pace of the presentation are inappropriate to the learner. The amount of information to be processed per unit of time is particularly critical with television because learners may not adjust the "chunk" size of information to their own information processing limits. When the pace of information on television is not appropriate to a learner's own "cognitive pace," recovery from comprehension failures may not be possible as with print media. Whereas readers adjust their pace to achieve comprehension, viewers are constrained by a pace that progresses whether or not comprehension is achieved.

Kozma generally hypothesized that learner characteristics can make a difference in learning from media. The learner's prior knowledge and ability interact with complementary combinations of visual and linguistic information, such as when text is supplemented by pictures and when video combines audio and visual information. Books and television are similar with regard to offering visual information for organizational purposes or to evoke prior schemata applicable to understanding new material. They differ in that processing of text is more driven by the construction of a representation of linguistic information, whereas comprehension of video is more driven by the processing of visual information and does not allow regressing over material as with books. Those low in prior knowledge may benefit more from information in multiple symbol systems, whereas those with higher prior knowledge may need it less after using such information to evoke their prior knowledge of a domain. Kozma suggested that those higher in ability or prior knowledge may find text beneficial because they can process its information faster and more strategically than with fixed-paced video. Those low in prior knowledge or ability may find the stability or reviewability of text beneficial in avoiding comprehension failures when a video's pace is too quick.

In summary, Kozma (1991) argued that an "unnecessary schism between medium and method" (p. 205) has been created by Clark's (1983) argument that media do not influence learning. A more integral relationship exists between the two because media enable and constrain methods, and the methods draw on and instantiate the capabilities of media. Instructional methods influence learning in part because these methods can take advantage of cognitively relevant capabilities of media that aid or complement the learner. For example, books and computers are media that enable individualized methods under the control of the learner, whereas television enables methods using multiple simultaneous symbols systems with motion. Conversely, media constrain methods when television's pace is not controlled by learners or when a medium cannot convey dynamic simultaneous auditory and visual symbol systems.

Kozma's account is more a proposed framework in a field not particularly characterized by theory than it is a point-by-point refutation of

Clark's argument for each form of media. His illustrative contrast between books and television is more fully developed than the many other contrasts that could be elaborated; for example, for other forms such as lectures, discussions, tutoring, videodiscs, computer-based instruction, and so forth. There is an inherent limitation to Kozma's proposal to distinguish media in terms of a characteristic cluster or profile of symbol systems and processing capabilities. The limitation is that these characteristics are potential capabilities that may or may not be used in different instances of instruction. Considering clusters of attributes offers the potential for distinguishing between media more than when these attributes are considered individually. However, when a particular individual attribute is desired for instruction, those other associated or correlated attributes must also be weighed for their relative strengths and weaknesses. At the very least, Kozma's proposed clusters of cognitive media attributes focuses attention on distinguishing between media in meaningful ways and draws attention away from technology definitions of media. However, the components of such clusters must still be explicated and controlled to avoid those ill-specified and uncontrolled differences in instructional method that were criticized in prior media comparison studies. Thus, the enabling and constraining relationships between media capabilities and instructional methods offered by Kozma further the purpose of understanding cognitively relevant media differences. But the conception does not lessen the need to identify the causes of learning or diminish the import of practical and efficiency differences among media.

DISCUSSION

Differing perspectives on understanding the relationship between media capabilities and learning have led to a series of complex discussions. Media convey instructional methods, many of these methods could be delivered by alternative media, these methods are the important determinant of learning, and care must be exercised in distinguishing the effects of these methods from those of the media themselves (cf. Clark, 1983). A passage from Levie (1987) identifies the practical question of when media capabilities might be selected to supplement an instructional method and provides some guidance with the following bit of simple logic:

> When might the choice of medium make a difference in instructional effectiveness? If a medium has the potential to present information of a particular kind (e.g., the potential to show objects in motion), and if this potential is used when the information is relevant to an instructional objective, then using that medium might be more effective than using a medium that lacks this potential. (p. 21)

DISCUSSION 199

It has been proposed that this idea can be extended to include a cluster of media capabilities that, when taken together, may offer some characteristic distinctions among media that pertain to learning (Kozma, 1991). By this view, some media enable methods of instruction that can potentially take advantage of cognitively relevant capabilities of media to aid the learner, whereas the capabilities of some media constrain the methods of instruction that can be used.

11 Discussion and Conclusions

This discussion brings together those useful generalizations resulting from our review of a wide range of research and practical experience pertinent to the educational use of television, video, and film. A number of common themes emerged from the review and several of these are reflected throughout the following discussion: (a) Video offers the capability to convey a wide range of content, (b) video offers the opportunity to convey many teaching techniques available in other media, (c) research findings strongly temper the assumption that visuals enhance learning with the qualification that they must be used in meaningful ways, (d) some characteristic attributes of video may be adapted in some specific ways to be critical to learning, (e) an important cluster of factors related to pacing and control over the medium are a consequence of the transient nature of typical linear video presentations, and (f) many of the benefits of video are practical ones concerned with convenience, access, standardization, and efficiency.

EDUCATIONAL TELEVISION AND VIDEO

The concern that educational television should not be worse than conventional face-to-face lectures gave rise to hundreds of studies. Reviews of these studies agree that there is little difference in student achievement between televised and conventional classroom instruction. That comparisons with conventional face-to-face instruction result in little difference is explicable when television merely conveys the same information in similar ways. A similar pattern is seen in several specific extensions of televised instruction in which distance education students are separated from teachers. Achievement is also similar to conventional education with interactive television or video teletraining, and with correspondence telecourses. That students may generally learn as well from many media still leaves other concerns about the acceptance of these educational forms, the potential of some video techniques for specific tasks, and a range of practical and efficiency issues that affect the context of education broadly.

Most students have neutral or favorable attitudes toward educational television after having experience with it. However, both teachers and students initially share negative attitudes that tend to lessen with time as they gain experience with this form of instruction. The primary concerns with instructional television revolve around not having personal contact with teachers, class size, and with the presentation proceeding without the ability to ask questions, get help, or participate in discussions when desired. Favorable student responses include perceptions that the presentations or teachers are better prepared, and these correspond to reports that television teachers do invest more effort in preparation.

Distance education in the form of video teletraining attempts to approximate the live and interactive nature of face-to-face instruction by using two-way communications between teachers and distant classrooms. Its practical value results from avoiding travel when students are widely dispersed geographically. There is generally no difference or only a very small decrement in student achievement at remote sites compared to that of students at the live transmitting site. Effectiveness and satisfaction generally increase along with the degree of fidelity or interactivity between video teletraining sites. The conditions most critical to success involve providing students with video of the instructor and two-way audio communication between them, with video allowing instructors to see students possibly being more of a monitoring convenience. Student preferences for traditional live classroom training can be reduced to the extent that higher fidelity conditions are created at the remote site. Poor audio quality and image clarity are particular implementation details that can lead to negative comments about fidelity. It appears that video teletraining can be cost beneficial when capital outlays and operation costs are offset by intense usage by a number of sites and students. When student costs are borne by an employing organization, cost benefits also result from averting travel and per diem costs.

Distance education in the form of telecourses consists of preproduced televised instructional broadcasts or tapes that are accompanied by supplementary printed materials. Convenience is a primary attraction for telecourse students in remote locations or for those needing personal scheduling flexibility. Although student achievement in telecourses is generally not worse than in conventional on-campus courses, higher dropout rates have been noted and these appear to be related to being able to pursue learning independently. Integrated visual and printed course materials are valuable in telecourses to document the objectives of programs prior to a broadcast, to identify points to look for during a broadcast, and to provide postbroadcast notes summarizing the main points covered for further study. Broadcasts are regarded as being somewhat inconvenient because they are transient and must be viewed at fixed times. Student access and control over viewing are increased when programs are made available on videotapes. Students tend to view tapes more than once and employ them interactively by interrupting the tapes to review and clarify points for note taking. This control offered by tapes has been extended to classrooms in a hybrid form of distance education in which taped class sessions are mailed to remote classrooms. The remote class members can manage the lecture themselves by interrupting the tape when more discussion is desired, thereby making the instruction respond to their individual needs.

Our review of studies on the costs of television-centered education resulted more in a template for decisions among media than it did in concrete prospective guidance. Guidance from prior cost studies is hampered by the wide variability among the cost elements included and by the fact that they often reflect highly specific features of a given implementation. The costs of hardware and transmission systems reflected in this literature are also time bound and subject to change, although they do illustrate some useful application themes in terms of the relative benefits and liabilities of the different technologies reviewed. However, the generalizations on the economic structure of technologically-based mass education appear to be the valuable lesson that emerges from these studies with respect to understanding how to apply such media from a cost perspective.

On the whole, economic studies of distance education indicate that per student costs can be comparable to or less than those of conventional campus-based colleges. When students are off campus, institutional support costs are relatively less, salaries of personnel involved in direct delivery of instruction are less, and an increase is seen in new development, materials, and delivery system costs. Relative to conventional education costs, the investment in technological delivery systems reduces costs through lower direct contact with students brought about by the mass distribution of instruction from a smaller centralized teaching staff. The marginal costs of adding additional students declines more with distance education, where large numbers of students are required to achieve a benefit relative to the costs for capital, production, and transmission or distribution.

Instructional videotapes are an attractive medium for classroom teachers because they are a manageable medium. They can be presented with relative ease on commonly available tape players, are available in an increasing range of topics, and can be used to shift the viewing of programs to times convenient or appropriate to the lesson. Videotapes have come to replace films because tapes are more easily reproduced, less costly, more easily distributed, and often retained locally instead of being requested from central libraries. Tapes are an accessible technology under the direct control of the classroom teacher because they can introduce the instruction at any time that it is optimal to do so, stop it at will for discussion, and rerun it for review at any time. This control allows the opportunity to use several techniques that have been found to benefit student learning: teacher introductions, postviewing teacher-directed reviews and discussions, rest pauses during long presentations, and the repetition of viewings.

Instructional television, tapes, or films offer several benefits related to the general quality of education that are rarely quantified. The opportunities offered by this form of educational experience may be the only feasible alternatives in substituting for many live experiences that would be difficult to achieve otherwise. These media can take viewers to places in the world that they could not otherwise experience, bring distinguished experts into the classroom, and allow demonstrations not generally possible or too dangerous to perform within a classroom. They offer specialized material in which instructors may not be expert, and the potential to minimize quality differences among instructors by sharing "a good teacher with a very large number of classes, rather than one" (Chu & Schramm, 1975, p. 100).

Taken together, experiences with the different forms of television-centered education lead to several generalizations concerning convenience, control, and access. Chu and Schramm (1967, 1975) observed that where instructional television has been used effectively, it was rarely used to carry the "whole weight" of instruction, but rather was interwoven into an integrated teaching–learning system in the context of other learning activities. This may be exemplified by teachers who integrate video and film materials with their own instruction in the classroom and by telecourse students who find that integrated video and printed course materials are accessible forms of instruction valuable for review. Access to broadcast instruction is comparatively inflexible from the learner's point of view because it must be viewed at fixed broadcast times that may be inconvenient. Convenience is also a factor for distance-education students whose schedules or travel limitations might not otherwise allow them this educational opportunity. The transient one-time learning experience of television not only creates a preference for viewing programs when desired, it also leads to a preference for tapes allowing control over the pace of a program. Tapes are a manageable technology for individuals and classrooms and can be used to control the transient, fixed-paced nature of the medium when they are presented at will, stopped for discussion, or relevant sections are reviewed. Transient presentations do not allow learners to recover from comprehension failures as they might with more stable media such as books where they can adjust their pace and reread to achieve comprehension at their own "cognitive pace" (Kozma, 1991). These control and individualization issues are also addressed in a number of other effective learner participation techniques discussed in the next section.

LEARNER INVOLVEMENT AND PARTICIPATION

The educational value of techniques encouraging learner involvement and participation has clearly been shown in a long history of film and television research. Effective techniques for increasing learning include combinations of encouraging greater attention and effort, direct statements that particular material is important or may be testable, the introduction of relevant attention-getting devices, requesting an overt or covert response, and providing knowledge of results. Generally positive benefits for learning result from such methods, so long as the presentation is not too fast and attention is not excessively divided between participation and viewing. Questioning is particularly beneficial when correct knowledge is gained following a question. However, the benefit is generally specific to questioned rather than other unquestioned material and merely inserting questions as part of the ongoing dialog of a presentation has only a marginal benefit. So long as learners are requested to respond to inserted questions, generally similar benefits of questioning are obtained whether the responses are overt or covert or whether the material is preceded or followed by the questions.

These learner participation techniques were previously implemented with films, programmed workbooks, or teaching machines. The positive effects of these techniques are now more easily realized in contemporary interactive videodisc and computer-based instruction. Interactive videodiscs combine the representational capabilities of video with the interactivity afforded by computer program control. Recent meta-analyses have found interactive videodisc instruction to be moderately effective, on the order of a half a standard deviation, and this magnitude of effect is only slightly greater than what has been reported for computer-based instruction in general. The effectiveness of interactive video would appear to be related more to its being a form of computer-based instruction than to its being a form of video or visualized instruction, which contributes an unknown increment in effectiveness.

The effectiveness of computerized instruction is generally explicable in terms of the greater interactivity and individualization afforded by the variable control of the pace and course of instruction, an active participation in advancement, and monitoring performance to respond with feedback, tailored branching, reviews, and advisement. One of the more beneficial techniques has been enroute practice questions embedded within the instructional sequence, which allow an opportunity to initiate such interactivity. Various lesson control designs are a second component of interactivity. Directive approaches appear to be more effective than techniques offering less guidance to learners, such as with some simulations, optional reviews, or other unguided student decisions. Combining techniques that use lesson organization, path sequencing, diagnosis of progress, and remedial branching generally appear to have more robust effects on learning than use of only a few of these techniques.

Video-based instruction has also been found effective for providing demonstrations of skills to be modeled and as a form of individualized feedback in teacher education and in learning motor skills. A model provides a cognitive representation that can be used to guide the enactment of behavior, and providing learners with a view of their own performance allows knowledge of a discrepancy with a standard to be used in making corrections during skill acquisition. Video feedback in learning motor skills is more likely to be effective when attention is drawn to relevant aspects of the task and when prospective guidance is offered along with the video replay. Video can also be a useful tool in teacher education for demonstrating behaviors to be modeled, for viewing a replay of one's performance as feedback, and for providing the basis for critical evaluations by others. Similar techniques might be applied in a variety of other training environments, for example, by using camcorders to provide modeling and feedback during team training or individual skill acquisition.

CAPABILITY OF CONVEYING A WIDE RANGE OF INFORMATION

A prominent characteristic of video is its capability to convey a wide range of different types of information. These many representational forms are conveyed in realistic ways that simultaneously combine motion and a variety of visual, audio, and textual information. Contemporary features of video automatically include capabilities for motion, sound, and color without any special effort or concern for costs. A number of qualifications about the way these capabilities are used pertain to motion, task fidelity, pictorial detail, color, and the combination of verbal and visual information. A common theme with regard to the effectiveness of these capabilities is that they are employed in selective ways that are critical to learning the intended objectives and are appropriate to the learner's current level of skill or knowledge. For example, overly realistic features of visuals, motion, or complex tasks may provide irrelevant detail in excess of those skeletal elements that are critical to an instructional objective. Likewise, the use of color is preferred by viewers but is not effective when used simply for unrelated realism or as an attention-getting device. Rather, its educational value lies in aiding discrimination among objects, cuing or highlighting relevant information, and when its recognition is part of a task to be learned. Similar qualifications are given in the following for applications involving motion and the combination of visual and verbal material.

Although the transient nature of video may be detrimental when there is little control over the pace of information, this attribute also provides depictions of motion that may be beneficial. A cluster of factors emerged from our review that circumscribe the benefit of motion to a number of uses that are critical to learning. These are when motion allows discriminations to be made, when attention is directed to relevant features that change, when sequential relations are clarified by providing continuity between events, when learning a concept that itself is defined by motion, when learning the motion itself, and when the task is unfamiliar or difficult to express verbally. Many of these circumstances are present in procedural learning where motion is often more beneficial than static presentations, but may not be as beneficial as actual hands-on practice. Although motion may be used to depict features that are critical to learning tasks like these, it has not been found to provide a blanket benefit for a wider variety of more general kinds of content.

Instructional uses of computer animation reveal guidance that overlaps with that on motion in videos and that on effective graphics. Computer animation can be beneficial when used to focus viewer attention on changes among important elements and to cue or highlight features. However, its use is circumscribed by cautions to avoid unnecessarily detailed backgrounds or distracting techniques designed to dazzle the viewer. Typical applications of animation techniques may be to simulate concepts and events with representations difficult to capture in the real world because of their scale, speed, or complexity. These phenomena can be illustrated in exaggerated or simplified forms to capture essential relations.

Video presentations dynamically combine several forms of symbolic information simultaneously. The combination of visual and verbal information generally leads to equal or enhanced comprehension compared to their use alone. These sources of information are typically complementary in educational presentations, where visual, print, and oral information should be coordinated to avoid conflict. Visual and audio information should generally be meaningfully related and in close correspondence. Some research suggests that the optimal synchrony between them occurs when the visuals slightly precede the audio and that presenting audio before visuals may be detrimental. Research with illustrations in static materials also indicates that related visual and verbal information benefit learning by providing complementary alternative sources of information, and that visuals provide concrete representations of information that may not be easily conveyed otherwise. In many circumstances, supplementing verbal information with visuals may also offer the greatest benefit to those of lower ability. However, visuals should contain only the level of detail necessary for distinguishing relevant information, and greater time should be allowed when the amount or complexity of the visual content is increased.

Several related themes appear in guidance on the use of text and narration. The speed of narration should depend on the complexity of the material and other visual and auditory information being presented at the same time. Rapid narration can reduce comprehension and should be slowed slightly when used with motion or to introduce new ideas or concepts. Continuous narration can lead to gradual declines in attention compared to an intermittent pace with appropriate pauses. Redundant text and video may aid learning, subject to some related guidance on the way they are used. Text and narration should be consistent with one another and should generally coincide in time. A slight asynchrony between the two may avoid simultaneous demands on the viewer. The limited amount of text allowed by the resolution of TV screens and its transient presentation place a premium on using writing rules directed at rapid comprehension. These limitations lead to the use of simple, concise wording. They also lead to avoiding excessive text, text broken on too many lines with hyphens, inconsistent spacing, use of all capital letters, and text shown over motion or confusing backgrounds.

TEACHING METHODS, PRODUCTION PRACTICES, AND EFFECTS OF VIDEO MEDIA

A number of commentators have observed that differences between media may be less important than the teaching methods used within a medium. Instructional television and film research confirms that the general rules for good instruction also apply to video presentations. The proven value of some of these techniques appears to be a mix of ones that are more particular to video media and others that are merely conveyed by video in ways achievable by several media.

The most general theme among the educationally effective techniques relates to either creating conditions fostering learning or a complementary avoidance of conditions competing with learning. Thus, effective instruction should avoid distractions, excessive visual detail, a pace and rate of development too fast to allow information to be processed, and lengthy presentations without pauses that fatigue learners or force them to continuously process new information. The complementary set of effective methods to be employed include introductory or preparatory techniques that establish a disposition to learn or direct attention to points in the presentation to follow, organizational outlining and internal structuring of the content, devices to emphasize or direct attention to relevant information, repetition of important sequences of information, focusing on critical elements when conducting a demonstration, postviewing reviews or discussions, and techniques that aid or replace mental processing operations. Where possible, these techniques include those designed to lessen passive viewing, increase active learner participation or elicit responses, and provide confirming or corrective feedback.

Many of these instructional methods can be characterized as performing a compensatory function of greater benefit to learners in the low and middle ranges of ability or prior knowledge. Individuals in the higher range are more tentatively characterized as benefiting from procedures that provide greater freedom or less constraint and that avoid obstructing their more rapid or efficient learning strategies. These generalizations grow out of a variety of studies of learner differences, and the instructional strategies implemented in video appear to convey them in ways that are not particularly different from other media. Fewer studies than might be expected were found in which individual differences seemed specific to learning from video. Some of these confirmed the expectation that individual differences in spatial or visual abilities were related to performance when the information being learned was also of a highly visual nature.

Some research has examined a number of the guidelines for developing videos that have grown out of the experience of video professionals and educational practitioners. Professional video tradecraft and educational perspectives share good communication as a purpose, and the experience of these practitioners has resulted in the evolution of generalizations concerning a certain artful application of techniques judged to be effective because they appear to work. Professional video tradecraft guidance sets minimum technical standards of quality that attempt to minimize the limitations of video, avoid negative viewer reactions, and lead viewers to accept what is shown as being natural and realistic. Tradecraft rules typically apply to camera techniques, the composition of shots within the screen, and the way shots are edited to form a presentation. A common theme in guidance for using these techniques is that they should be purposeful and controlled and should maintain clarity and continuity. At this level of generality, they may be beneficial to the extent that they advance an overall objective, employ one center of interest, avoid distracting settings, employ editing and cutting to avoid confusing viewers with sudden or unexplained changes, and use a comprehensible rate of development.

Research examining techniques such as these from an educational perspective suggests that some appear to be selectively beneficial, others more benign or preferential, and yet others irrelevant or even detrimental to learning. Benign or preferential production techniques might be illustrated by uses of music, humor, and program formats other than simple expository ones. Selective uses of camera and editing techniques are illustrated in partially successful attempts to influence learning by directing attention through cuing. An instance of a camera angle technique being effective is when a procedure is demonstrated from the perspective of the person performing the procedure. The camera technique of zooming is used to draw attention to details within a larger visual context, but has been only partially successful when used to teach students the skill of focusing on details within a picture. Other techniques like panning, dollying, or shot length have little effect on learning so long as information is visible to viewers, and attention is not lost or distracted by effects that are too rapid or too slow.

Video production techniques that are irrelevant or detrimental might be exemplified by attention-getting devices using effects designed to dazzle and by related quick-paced techniques not suited to learning. The educational research literature generally discourages visual and sound effect devices introduced purely to attract viewer attention to the program without any relation to instructional content. Learning appears to be little affected by devices that temporarily draw attention—such as rapid cutting between shots, sudden noticeable changes, special visual or sound effects—or when these are included merely for general realism. The common commercial television technique of changing shots frequently does not leave viewers time to analyze and comprehend shots. Viewers tend to prefer edited presentations so long as they result in understandable presentations that are cut at a rate appropriate to the complexity of the scenes and are not sustained to the point of boredom.

The general conclusion on the effect of many professional production techniques is that they are not particularly associated with an increment in learning. Whereas some may avoid confusion, others may be distracting and inappropriate to learning. Typical news broadcasts illustrate a form of communication violating cuing, pacing, and redundancy principles found effective in educational television. Learning from the news is generally low because it is difficult to process rapidly paced information accompanied by a large number of brief visuals that may be weakly related to the verbal content. Studies of children's television indicate that attention and comprehension interact in ways that contradict a simple conception of viewers being reflexively controlled by the medium. Attention during normal broadcast television viewing is often discontinuous, and formal features of the medium, such as attention-getting devices, may serve to signal changes in program content. Viewers appear to monitor these cues along with other samples of information with a low level of engagement, deploying further attention and processing resources based on their interest and ability to comprehend the content.

Viewer preconceptions of television as an entertainment medium appear to have only a slight effect on learning from video. Exposure to commercial television may lead some viewers to have preconceptions that less mental effort is required to learn from video than text, but these vary among individuals and can be countered with appropriate instructional strategies that establish a disposition to learn. These strategies include clearly communicating the purpose of the video presentation and providing viewers with appropriate expectations regarding the content and the level of effort they will be required to exert. Although watching commercial television may compete with students' home studying, the evidence does not support the theory that extensive exposure to video, by itself, has a major effect on the ability of students to learn from video media.

VIDEO CAPABILITIES AND EFFECTIVENESS

The effectiveness of the video-based instruction we have been reviewing could itself be speculated to be subject to some preconceived beliefs. The fidelity offered by video fosters a kind of popular view or claim for a presumed effect on learning. The belief is supported by observations that many capabilities of video would be difficult to achieve in alternative media with fewer representational capabilities such as books, verbal narrative, and static graphics. A more conditional benefit of video is suggested by the range of research findings obtained. Positive examples are when video might provide additional visual forms of information to that available in descriptions given in text or by radio, and when learning procedural sequences might be benefited by conveying motion video compared to static or verbal descriptions. However, negative or equivocal examples include the possibility of video being less effective than actual hands-on experience, being detrimental when its pace exceeds what learners can tolerate, and yielding little difference in effectiveness when live and televised lectures carry essentially the same information. One might speculate that a belief in the effectiveness of video-based learning reflects perceived potential benefits arising from particularly memorable positive instances rather those that are equal or worse.

Two observations are worth reiterating with regard to these perceptions on the use of video-based media in instruction. First, video has the capability to convey many forms of representation—a wide range of symbol systems (Salomon, 1979). Thus, video conveys many other media and is itself characterized by the cluster of capabilities to combine motion, images, and auditory information in realistic ways. Second, the capabilities of video are potential capabilities; they offer an opportunity rather than a guarantee to benefit learning. This potential opportunity to affect learning depends on using those capabilities of video to best educational effect along with teaching methods that might be delivered by alternative media. The choice of a medium might make a difference in instructional effectiveness when a medium has the capability to present a particular kind of information or present it in a particular way and when this potential is used in a cognitively relevant way—then the medium might be more effective or efficient than others without this potential (Kozma, 1991; Levie, 1987).

References

Acker, S. R. (1983). Viewer's perceptions of velocity and distance in televised events. *Human Communication Research, 9,* 335–348.
Acker, S. R., & Klein, E. L. (1986). Visualizing spatial tasks: A comparison of computer graphic and full-band video displays. *Educational Communication and Technology Journal, 34,* 21–30.
Acker, S. R., & Levitt, S. R. (1987). Designing videoconference facilities for improved eye contact. *Journal of Broadcasting and Electronic Media, 31,* 181–191.
Adams, J. A. (1987). Historical review and appraisal of research on the learning, retention, and transfer of human motor skills. *Psychological Bulletin, 101,* 41–74.
Alesandrini, K. L. (1984). Pictures and adult learning. *Instructional Science, 13,* 63–77.
Alessi, S. M. (1988). Fidelity in the design of instructional simulations. *Journal of Computer-Based Instruction, 15,* 40–47.
Alessi, S. M., & Trollip, S. R. (1991). *Computer-based instruction methods and development* (2nd ed.). Englewood Cliffs, NJ: Prentice-Hall.
Allen, B. S. (1986). A theoretical framework for interactivating linear video. *Journal of Computer Based Instruction, 13,* 107–112.
Allen, J. A., Hays, R. T., & Buffardi, L. C. (1986). Maintenance training simulator fidelity and individual differences in transfer of training. *Human Factors, 28,* 497–509.
Allen, W. H. (1952). Readability of instructional film commentary. *Journal of Applied Psychology, 36,* 164–168.
Allen, W. H. (1957). Research on film use: Student participation. *AV Communication Review, 5,* 423–450.
Allen, W. H. (1960). Audio-visual communication. In C. W. Harris (Ed.), *Encyclopedia of educational research* (3rd ed., pp. 115–137). New York: Macmillan.
Allen, W. H. (1967). Media stimulus and types of learning. *Audiovisual Instruction, 12,* 27–31.
Allen, W. H. (1971). Instructional media research: Past, present and future. *AV Communication Review, 19,* 5–18.
Allen, W. H. (1973). Research in educational media. In J.W. Brown (Ed.), *Educational media yearbook, 1973* (pp. 113–121). New York: R. R. Bowker.
Allen, W. H. (1975). Intellectual abilities and instructional media design. *AV Communication Review, 23,* 139–170.
Allen, W. H., Cooney, S. M., & Weintraub, R. (1968). *Audio implementation of still and motion pictures: Final report* (USOE Final Report, Project No. 5-0741). Los Angeles: University of Southern California, Research Division, Department of Cinema. (ERIC Document Reproduction Service No. ED 021 462)
Allen, W. H., Daehling, W. A., Russell, J. J., IV, & Nielsen, T. G. (1970). *Effectiveness of different combinations of visual and verbal presentation modes in teaching different kinds of learning*

tasks. Final report (USOE Final Report, Project No. 6-1265). Los Angeles: University of Southern California, Research Division, Department of Cinema. (ERIC Document Reproduction Service No. ED 044 759)

Allen, W. H., & Weintraub, R. (1968). *The motion variables in film presentation* (OE Final Report, Project No. 5-1125). Los Angeles: University of Southern California, Department of Cinema. (ERIC Document Reproduction Service No. ED 027 750)

Alwitt, L. F., Anderson, D. R., Lorch, E. P., & Levin, S. R. (1980). Preschool children's visual attention to attributes of television. *Human Communication Research, 7,* 52–67.

Anderson, D., & Levin, S. (1976). Young children's attention to "Sesame Street." *Child Development, 47,* 806–811.

Anderson, D. R., Levin, S. R., & Lorch, E. P. (1977). The effects of TV program pacing on the behavior of pre-school children. *AV Communication Review, 25,* 159–166.

Anderson, D. R., & Lorch, E. P. (1983). Looking at television: Action or reaction? In J. Bryant & D. R. Anderson (Eds.), *Children's understanding of television: Research on attention and comprehension* (pp. 1–33). New York: Academic Press.

Anderson, G. H. (1984). *Video editing and post-production: A professional guide.* White Plains, NY: Knowledge Industry Publications.

Arnold, G. B. (1990). The teacher and nonverbal communication. *Political Science Teacher, 3,* pp. 1, 3–4.

Aylward, T. J. (1960). *A study of the effects of production techniques on a televised lecture.* Unpublished doctoral dissertation, University of Wisconsin, Madison.

Baek, Y., & Layne, B. (1988). Color, graphics and animation in computer-assisted learning tutorial lesson. *Journal of Computer-Based Instruction, 15,* 131–135.

Baggaley, J. (1973). Analyzing TV presentation techniques for educational effectiveness. *Educational Broadcasting International, 6,* 17–21.

Baggaley, J., & Duck, S. W. (1974). Experiments in ETV: Effects of adding background. *Educational Broadcasting International, 7,* 208–210.

Baggaley, J., & Duck, S. W. (1975a). *Communication effectiveness in the educational media: Three experiments.* London: Pitman.

Baggaley, J., & Duck, S. W. (1975b). Experiments in ETV: Effects of edited cut-aways. *Educational Broadcasting International, 8,* 36–38.

Baggaley, J., & Duck, S. W. (1975c). Experiments in ETV: Further effects of camera angle. *Educational Broadcasting International, 8,* 183–184.

Baggett, P. (1979). Structurally equivalent stories in movie and text and the effect of the medium on recall. *Journal of Verbal Learning and Verbal Behavior, 18,* 333–356.

Baggett, P. (1984). The role of temporal overlap of visual and auditory material in forming dual media associations. *Journal of Educational Psychology, 76,* 408–417.

Baggett, P. (1987). Learning procedures from multi-media instructions: The effect of film and practice. *Applied Cognitive Psychology, 1,* 183–197.

Baggett, P. (1988). The role of practice in videodisc-based procedural instructions. *IEEE Transactions on Systems, Man, and Cybernetics, 18,* 487–496.

Baggett, P. (1989a, August). *Designing and implementing an "intelligent" multimedia tutoring system for repair tasks: Final report* (Technical report for Office of Naval Research). Ann Arbor: University of Michigan School of Education. (ERIC Document Reproduction Service No. ED 316 217)

Baggett, P. (1989b). Understanding visual and verbal messages. In H. Mandl & J. R. Levin (Eds.), *Knowledge acquisition from text and pictures* (pp. 101–124). New York: North-Holland.

Baggett, P., & Ehrenfeucht, A. (1982). Information in content equivalent movie and text stories. *Discourse Processes, 5,* 73–99.

REFERENCES 213

Baggett, P., & Ehrenfeucht, A. (1983). Encoding and retaining information in the visuals and verbals of an educational movie. *Educational Communication and Technology Journal, 31*, 23–32.
Baggett, P., & Ehrenfeucht, A. (1988). Conceptualizing in assembly tasks. *Human Factors, 30*, 269–284.
Baggett, P., Ehrenfeucht, A., & Guzdial, M. (1989, August). *Sequencing and access in interactive graphics-based procedural instructions* (Technical report for Office of Naval Research). Ann Arbor: University of Michigan School of Education.
Bailey, S. S., Sheppe, M. L., Hodak, G. W., Kruger, R. L., & Smith, R. F. (1989, December). *Video teletraining and video teleconferencing: A review of the literature* (Tech. Rep. 89-036). Orlando, FL: Naval Training Systems Center.
Bailyn, L. (1959). Mass media and children: A study of exposure habits and cognitive effects. *Psychological Monographs: General and Applied, 73* (Whole No. 471).
Barker, B. O. (1985, October). *Maintaining and/or expanding curriculum offerings in small and rural high schools.* Paper presented at the Technology-Based Curriculum Systems Teleconference, Dallas, TX. (ERIC Document Reproduction Service No. ED 261 849)
Barker, B. O., & Platten, M. R. (1988). Student perceptions on the effectiveness of college credit courses taught via satellite. *The American Journal of Distance Education, 2*, 44–50.
Barnard, J. (1992–1993). Video-based instruction: Issues of effectiveness, interaction, and learner control. *Journal of Educational Technology Systems, 21*, 45–50.
Barrington, H. (1970). *An evaluation of the effectiveness of educational TV presentation variables.* Unpublished dissertation, University of Manchester, England.
Barrington, H. (1972). Instruction by television—two presentations compared. *Educational Research, 14*, 187–190.
Bates, A. W. (1980). Towards a better theoretical framework for studying learning from educational television. *Instructional Science, 9*, 393–415.
Bates, A. W. (1987). *Teaching, media choice and cost-effectiveness of alternative delivery systems* (I.E.T. Paper No. 264). Walton, Bletchley, Bucks, England: Institute of Educational Technology, Open University. (ERIC Document Reproduction Service No. ED 292 441)
Bates, A. W. (1988). Television, learning and distance education. *Journal of Educational Television, 14*, 213–225.
Beagles-Roos, J., & Gat, I. (1983). The specific impact of radio and television on children's story comprehension. *Journal of Educational Psychology, 75*, 128–137.
Beare, P. L. (1989). The comparative effectiveness of videotape, audiotape, and telelecture in delivering continuing teacher education. *American Journal of Distance Education, 3*, 57–66.
Beentjes, J. W. J. (1989). Learning from television and books: A Dutch replication study based on Salomon's model. *Educational Technology Research and Development, 37*, 47–58.
Beentjes, J. W. J., & Van Der Voort, T. H. A. (1988). Television's impact on children's reading skills: A review of research. *Reading Research Quarterly, 23*, 389–413.
Berry, C., & Unwin, D. (1975). A selected bibliography of production and audience variables in film and television. *Programmed Learning and Educational Technology, 12*, 54–70.
Berry, C., Gunter, B., & Clifford, B. R. (1981). Memory for televised information: A problem for applied and theoretical psychology. *Current Psychological Reviews, 1*, 171–192.
Biederman, I., Glass, A. L., & Stacy, E. W. (1973). Searching for objects in real-world scenes. *Journal of Experimental Psychology, 97*, 22–27.
Blaiwes, A. S., & Regan, J. J. (1986). Training devices: Concepts and progress. In J. A. Ellis (Ed.), *Military contributions to instructional technology* (pp. 83–170). New York: Praeger.
Blake, T. (1977). Motion in instructional media: Some subject-display mode interactions. *Perceptual and Motor Skills, 44*, 975–985.
Blinn, J. (1989). The making of The Mechanical Universe. In S. R. Ellis, M. K. Kaiser, & A. Grunwald (Eds.), *Spatial displays and spatial instruments: Proceedings of a conference*

sponsored by NASA Ames Research Center, and the School of Optometry, University of California, Asilomar, California, August 31 – September 3, 1987 (pp. 45-1—45-18). Springfield, VA: U.S. Department of Commerce, National Technical Information Service.
Bogart, L. (1965). The mass media and the blue-collar worker. In B. Shostak & W. Gomberg (Eds.), *Blue-collar world: Studies of the American worker* (pp. 416–428). Englewood Cliffs, NJ: Prentice-Hall.
Boltz, M., Schulkind, M., & Kantra, S. (1991). Effects of background music on the remembering of filmed events. *Memory and Cognition, 19,* 593–606.
Booher, H. R. (1975). Relative comprehensibility of pictorial information and printed words in proceduralized instructions. *Human Factors, 17,* 266–277.
Bordeaux, B. R., & Lange, G. (1991). Children's reported investment of mental effort when viewing television. *Communications Research, 18,* 617–635.
Borg, W. R., & Schuller C. F. (1979). Detail and background in audiovisual lessons and their effect on learners. *Educational Communication and Technology Journal, 27,* 31–38.
Bosco, J. (1986). An analysis of evaluations of interactive video. *Educational Technology, 26,* 7–17.
Braden, R. A. (1986). Visuals for interactive video: Images for a new technology (with some guidelines). *Educational Technology, 26,* 8–23.
Brandon, J. R. (1956). The relative effectiveness of the lecture, interview, and discussion methods of presenting factual information by television. *Speech Monographs, 23,* 272–283.
Breed, G. (1971). *Nonverbal behavior and teaching effectiveness. Final report.* Washington, DC: Department of Health, Education, and Welfare; Office of Education.
Breen, M. P. (1968). *A comparative study of the effect of the mosaic and didactic forms of TV presentation on the audience's fact retention and attitude toward the understandability of the program.* Unpublished doctoral dissertation, Wayne State University, Detroit.
Breen, M. P., & Ary, D. E. (1972). A nationwide survey to determine who chooses instructional films. *Audiovisual Instruction, 17,* 46–48.
Briggs, L. J., Campeau, P. L., Gagné, R. M., & May, M. A. (1967). *Instructional media: A procedure for the design of multi-media instruction, a critical review of research, and suggestions for future research.* Pittsburgh, PA: American Institutes for Research.
Brosius, H. B. (1989). Influence of presentation features and news content on learning from television news. *Journal of Broadcasting and Electronic Media, 33,* 1–14.
Brown, C. M., Brown, D. B., Burkleo, H. V., Mangelsdorf, J. E., Olsen, R. A., & Perkins, R. D. (1983). *Human factors engineering standards for information processing systems* (LMSC-D877141). Sunnyvale, CA: Lockheed Missiles and Space Company.
Brown, J. R., Cramond, J. K., & Wilde, R. J. (1974). Displacement effects of television and the child's functional orientation to media. In J. G. Blumler & E. Katz (Eds.), *The uses of mass communication: Current perspectives on gratifications research* (pp. 93–112). London: Sage.
Brown, S. (1983). *Videocassettes versus broadcasts* (I.E.T. Papers on Broadcasts No. 228). Walton, Bletchley, Bucks, England: Institute of Educational Technology, Open University. (ERIC Document Reproduction Service No. ED 298 953)
Brown, S., Nathenson, M., & Kirkup, G. (1982). Learning from evaluation at the Open University II. Helping students to learn from audio-visual media. *British Journal of Education Technology, 13,* 217–236.
Browne, S. E. (1989). *Videotape editing: A post-production primer.* Boston: Focal Press.
Bryant, J., Comisky, P. W., Crane, J., & Zillmann, D. (1979). *The relationship between college teachers' use of humor in the classroom and students' evaluation of their teachers.* Unpublished manuscript, University of Massachusetts, Amherst.
Bryant, J., & Zillmann, D. (1981). *Humor and audio-visual fireworks in educational television: Effects on learning.* Unpublished manuscript, Department of Communications, University of Evansville, Evansville, IN.

Bryant, J., Zillmann, D., & Brown, D. (1983). Entertainment features in childrens' educational television: Effects on attention and information acquisition. In J. Bryant & D. R. Anderson (Eds.), *Children's understanding of television: Research on attention and comprehension* (pp. 221–240). New York: Academic Press.

Bunker, L. K., Shearer, J. D., & Hall, E. G. (1976). Video-taped feedback and children's learning to flutter kick. *Perceptual and Motor Skills, 43,* 371–374.

Burkhard, D. G., Patterson, J., & Rapue, R. (1967). Effect of film feedback on learning the motor skills of karate. *Perceptual and Motor Skills, 25,* 65–69.

Burroughs, W. A. (1984). Visual simulation training of baseball batters. *International Journal of Sports Psychology, 15,* 117–126.

Burrows, T. D., Wood, D. N., & Gross, L. (1989). *Television production: Disciplines and techniques* (4th ed.). Dubuque, IA: Brown.

Burwell, L. B. (1991). The interaction of learning styles with learner control treatments in an interactive videodisc lesson. *Educational Technology, 31,* 37–43.

Calvert, S. L., & Gersh, T. L. (1987). The selective use of sound effects and visual inserts for children's comprehension of television content. *Journal of Applied Developmental Psychology, 8,* 363–375.

Calvert, S., Huston, A., Watkins, B., & Wright, J. (1982). The relation between selective attention to television forms and children's comprehension of content. *Child Development, 53,* 601–610.

Calvert, S. L., & Scott, M. C. (1989). Sound effects for children's temporal integration of fast-paced television content. *Journal of Broadcasting and Electronic Media, 33,* 233–246.

Campbell, A. J., Marchetti, F. M., & Mewhort, D. J. K. (1981). Reading speed and text production: A note on right justification techniques. *Ergonomics, 24,* 633–640.

Campeau, P. L. (1967). Selective review of literature on audiovisual media of instruction. In L. J Briggs, P. L. Campeau, R. M. Gagné, & M. A. May (Eds.), *Instructional media: A procedure for the design of multi-media instruction, a critical review of research, and suggestions for future research* (pp. 99–142). Pittsburgh, PA: American Institutes for Research.

Campeau, P. L. (1974). Selective review of results of research on the use of audio-visual media in teaching adults. *AV Communication Review, 22,* 5–40.

Caraballo, A. (1985). *An experimental study to investigate the effect of computer animation on the understanding and retention of selected levels of learning outcomes.* Unpublished doctoral dissertation, The Pennsylvania State University, University Park.

Caraballo, J. (1985). *The effect of various visual display modes of selected educational objectives.* Unpublished doctoral dissertation, The Pennsylvania State University, University Park.

Carnoy, M., & Levin, H. M. (1975). Evaluation of educational media: Some issues. *Instructional Science, 4,* 385–406.

Carpenter, C. R. (1972). Instructional film research—A brief review. *British Journal of Educational Technology, 2,* 229–246.

Carpenter, C. R., & Greenhill, L. P. (1956). *Instructional film research reports* (Vol. 2; Tech. Rep. 269-7-61, NAVEXOS P1543). Port Washington, NY: U.S. Naval Special Devices Center.

Carroll, J. M. (1980). *Toward a structural psychology of cinema.* The Hague: Mouton.

Carroll, W. R., & Bandura, A. (1982). The role of visual monitoring in observational learning of action patterns: Making the unobservable observable. *Journal of Motor Behavior, 14,* 153–167.

Cartwright, S. R. (1986). *Training with video.* White Plains, NY: Knowledge Industry Publications.

Cavanaugh, J. C. (1983). Comprehension and retention of television programs by 20- and 60-year olds. *Journal of Gerontology, 38,* 190–196.

Cavanaugh, J. C. (1984). Effects of presentation format on adult's retention of television programs. *Experimental Aging Research, 10,* 51–53.

Cennamo, K. S. (1989, February). *Factors influencing mental effort: A theoretical overview and review of the literature.* Paper presented at the annual meeting of the Association for Educational Communications and Technology, Dallas, TX. (ERIC Document Reproduction Service No. ED 308 810)

Cennamo, K. S., Savenye, W. C., & Smith, P. L. (1991). Mental effort and video-based learning: The relationship between preconceptions and the effects of interactive and covert practice. *Educational Technology Research and Development, 39,* 5–16.

Chaffee, S. H., & Schleuder, J. (1986). Measurement and effects of attention to media news. *Human Communication Research, 13,* 76–107.

Chapman, A. J., & Crompton, P. (1978). Humorous presentations of material and presentation of humorous material: A review of the humor literature and two experimental studies. In M. M. Gruneberg, P. E. Morris, & R. N. Sykes (Eds.), *Practical aspects of memory* (pp. 84–92). London: Academic Press.

Chu, G. C., & Schramm, W. (1967). *Learning from television: What the research says.* Washington, DC: National Association of Educational Broadcasters; Stanford, CA: Institute for Communication Research. (ERIC Document Reproduction Service No. ED 914 900)

Chu, C. G., & Schramm, W. (1975). *Learning from television: What the research says.* (ERIC Document Reproduction Service No. ED 109 985)

Chute, A. G. (1980). Effect of color and monochrome versions of a film on incidental and task-relevant learning. *Educational Communication and Technology Journal, 28,* 10–18.

Chute, A. G., Balthazar, L. B., & Poston, C. O. (1988). Learning from teletraining. *American Journal of Distance Education, 2,* 1–9.

Chute, A. G., Balthazar, L. B., & Poston, C. O. (1990). Learning from teletraining: What AT&T research says. In M. G. Moore (Ed.), *Contemporary issues in American distance education* (pp. 260–276). Oxford, England: Pergamon.

Clark, R. E. (1982). Antagonism between achievement and enjoyment in ATI studies. *Educational Psychologist, 17,* 92–101.

Clark, R. E. (1983). Reconsidering research on learning from media. *Review of Educational Research, 53,* 445–459.

Clark, R. E. (1984). A reply to Petkovich and Tennyson. *Educational Communication and Technology Journal, 33,* 238–241.

Clark, R. E. (1985). The importance of treatment explication: A reply to J. Kulik, C-L. Kulik and R. Bangert-Drowns. *Journal of Educational Computing Research, 1,* 389–394.

Clark, R. E., & Salomon, G. (1986). Media in teaching. In M. C. Wittrock (Ed.), *Handbook of research on teaching* (3rd ed., pp. 464–478). New York: Macmillan.

Clark, R. E., & Sugrue, B. M. (1988). Research on instructional media, 1978–1988. In D. Ely, B. Broadbent, & R. K. Wood (Eds.), *Educational media and technology yearbook 1988* (Vol. 14, pp. 19–36). Denver, CO: Libraries Unlimited.

Cohen, P. A., Ebeling, B. J., & Kulik, J. A. (1981). A meta-analysis of outcome studies of visual-based instruction. *Educational Communication and Technology Journal, 29,* 26–36.

Coldevin, G. O. (1975). Spaced, massed, and summary treatments as review strategies for ITV production. *AV Communication Review, 23,* 289–303.

Collins, A., Adams, M., & Pew, R. (1978). Effectiveness of an interactive map display in tutoring geography. *Journal of Educational Psychology, 70,* 1–7.

Collins, W. A. (1982). Cognitive processing in television viewing. In *Television and behavior: Ten years of scientific progress and implications for the eighties; Volume II technical reviews* (U.S. Department of Health and Human Services, National Institute of Mental Health, DHHS Publication No. (ADM) 82-1196). Washington, DC: U.S. Government Printing Office.

Compesi, R. J., & Sherriffs, R. E. (1990). *Small format television production* (2nd ed.). Boston: Allyn & Bacon.

REFERENCES 217

Cookson, P. S. (1990). Persistence in distance education: A review. In M. G. Moore (Ed.), *Contemporary issues in American distance education* (pp. 192–204). Oxford, England: Pergamon.

Corbin, M. T., & McIntyre, C. J. (1961). *The development and application of a new method to test the relative effectiveness of specific visual production techniques for instructional TV.* Urbana: University of Illinois Press.

Cornell, E. H., & Hay, D. H. (1984) Children's acquisition of a route via different media. *Environment and Behavior, 16,* 627–641.

Crane, V. (1984). *Student uses of the Annenberg / CPB telecourses in the fall of 1984* (Executive summary and final research report). Chestnut Hill, MA: Research Communications. (ERIC Document Reproduction Service No. ED 264 822)

Croynik, D. (1974). *Movie making.* Chicago: Loyola University Press.

Csikszentmihalyi, M., & Kubey, R. (1982). Television and the rest of life: A systematic comparison of subjective experience. In D. C. Whitney & E. Wartella (Eds.), *Mass communication review yearbook* (Vol. 3, pp. 385–396). Beverly Hills, CA: Sage.

Dalton, D. W. (1986). The efficacy of computer-assisted video instruction on rule learning and attitudes. *Journal of Computer Based Instruction, 13,* 122–125.

Dalton, D. W. (1990). The effects of cooperative learning strategies on achievement and attitudes during interactive video. *Journal of Computer Based Instruction, 17,* 8–16.

Dalton, D. W., & Hannafin, M. J. (1987). The effects of knowledge-versus context-based design strategies on information and application learning from interactive video. *Journal of Computer Based Instruction, 14,* 138–141.

Davis, D. (1966). *The grammar of television production.* London: Barrie & Rockliff.

Dayton, D. K., & Schwier, R. A. (1979). Effects of postquestions on learning and learning efficiency from fixed-pace, fixed-sequence media. *Educational Communication and Technology Journal, 27,* 103–113.

Decker, P. J. (1983). The effects of rehearsal group size and video feedback in behavior modeling training. *Personnel Psychology, 36,* 763–773.

Deighton, J., Romer, D., & McQueen, J. (1989). Using drama to persuade. *Journal of Consumer Research, 16,* 335–343.

Del Rey, P. (1971). The effects of video-taped feedback on form, accuracy, and latency in an open and closed environment. *Journal of Motor Behavior, 3,* 281–287.

De Meyer, G., Hendriks, A., & Fauconnier, G. (1987). Breaking TV addiction: An experimental panel study of television's impact upon everyday life. *Vrijetijd en Samenleving, 5,* 51–73.

Descy, D. E. (1992). First year elementary schoolteachers' utilization of instructional media. *International Journal of Instructional Media, 19,* 15–21.

Dille, B., & Mezack, M. (1991). Identifying predictors of high risk among community college telecourse students. *American Journal of Distance Education, 5,* 24–35.

DiSessa, A. A. (1982). Unlearning Aristotelian physics: A study of knowledge-based learning. *Cognitive Science, 6,* 37–75.

Dixon, D., & Saltz, E. (1977). The role of imagery on concept acquisition in lower-SES children. *Child Development, 48,* 288–291.

Donohew, L., Palmgreen, P., & Rayburn, J. D. (1987). Social and psychological origins of media use: A lifestyle analysis. *Journal of Broadcasting and Electronic Media, 31,* 255–278.

Dorr, A. (1986). *Television and children: A special medium for a special audience.* Beverly Hills, CA: Sage.

Drew, D. G., & Grimes, T. (1987). Audio-visual redundancy and TV news recall. *Communication Research, 14,* 452–461.

Dubin, R., & Hedley, R. A. (1969). *The medium may be related to the message: College instruction by TV.* Eugene: University of Oregon Press.

Duby, P. B., & Giltrow, D. R. (1978). Predicting student withdrawals in open learning courses. *Educational Technology, 18,* 43–47.

Duchnicky, R. L., & Kolers, P. A. (1983). Readability of text scrolled on visual display terminals as a function of window size. *Human Factors, 25,* 683–692.
Duck, S. W., & Baggaley, J. (1974). Research notes: ETV production methods versus educational intentions. *Educational Broadcasting International, 7,* 158–159.
Duck, S. W., & Baggaley, J. (1975). Research notes: Experiments in ETV: Effects of camera angle. *Educational Broadcasting International, 8,* 134.
Dukelow, J. D. (1979). *A comparison of the effects of three short delays of augmenting videotape feedback on the learning and retention of a novel motor skill.* Unpublished doctoral dissertation, Temple University, Philadelphia, PA.
Dwyer, F. M. (1969). The instructional effect of motion in varied visual illustrations. *Journal of Psychology, 73,* 167–172.
Dwyer, F. M. (1971). Color as an instructional variable. *AV Communication Review, 19,* 399–416.
Dwyer, F. M. (1972). *A guide for improving visualized instruction.* State College, PA: Learning Services.
Dwyer, F. M. (1976). The effect of IQ level on the instructional effectiveness of black-and-white and color illustrations. *AV Communication Review, 24,* 49–62.
Dwyer, F. M. (1978). *Strategies for improving visual learning.* State College, PA: Learning Services.
D'Ydewalle, G., Muylle, P., & Van Rensbergen, J. (1985). Attention shifts in partially redundant information situations. In R. Groner, G. W. McConkie, & C. Menz (Eds.), *Eye movements and human information processing* (pp. 375–384). Amsterdam: North-Holland.
D'Ydewalle, G., & Van Rensbergen, J. (1989). Developmental studies of text-picture interactions in the perception of animated cartoons with text. In H. Mandl & J. R. Levin (Eds.), *Knowledge acquisition from text and pictures* (pp. 233–248). New York: North-Holland.
D'Ydewalle, G., Van Rensbergen, J., & Pollet, J. (1987). Reading a message when the same message is available auditorily in a different language: The case of subtitling. In J. K. O'Regan & A. Levy-Schoen (Eds.), *Eye movements: From physiology to cognition* (pp. 313–321). Amsterdam: North-Holland.
Educational Policy Research Center. (1976, November). *Instructional television: A comparative study of satellites and other deliver systems* (Final Report [SRC-TR76-596] for The National Institute of Education). Syracuse, NY: Syracuse Research Corporation. (ERIC Document Reproduction Service No. ED 138 242)
Ellis, L., & Mathis, D. (1985). College student learning from televised versus conventional classroom lectures: A controlled experiment. *Higher Education, 14,* 165–173.
Engel, S. E., & Granda, R. E. (1975). *Guidelines for man/display interfaces* (Tech. Rep. TR 00.2720). Poughkeepsie, NY: IBM.
Feltz, D. L., & Landers, D. M. (1983). The effects of mental practice on motor skill learning and performance: A meta-analysis. *Journal of Sport Psychology, 5,* 25–57.
Findahl, O. (1971). *The effect of visual illustrations upon perception and retention of news programmes.* (ERIC Document Reproduction Service No. ED 054 631)
Findahl, O., & Hoijer, B. (1985). Some characteristics of news memory and comprehension. *Journal of Broadcasting and Electronic Media, 29,* 379–396.
Finn, J. D. (1953). Television and education: A review of research. *AV Communication Review, 1,* 106–126.
Fletcher, J. D. (1990, July). *Effectiveness and cost of interactive videodisc instruction in defense training and education* (IDA Paper P-2372). Alexandria, VA: Institute for Defense Analyses.
Fletcher, J. D., Hawley, D. E., & Piele, P. K. (1990). Costs, effects, and utility of microcomputer assisted instruction in the classroom. *American Educational Research Journal, 27,* 783–806.

Frager, A. M. (1985). Video technology and teacher training: A research perspective. *Educational Technology, 25,* 20–22.
Freeman, J., & Neidt, C. (1959). Effects of familiar background music upon film learning. *Journal of Educational Research, 53,* 91–96.
Frey, P. W., & Adesman, P. (1976). Recall memory for visually presented chess positions. *Memory and Cognition, 4,* 541–547.
Friederich, L. K., & Stein, A. H. (1973). Aggressive and pro-social television programs and the natural behavior of preschool children. *Monographs of the Society for Research in Child Development, 38,* 1–64.
Friedman, A. (1993). Designing graphics to support mental models. In J. M. Spector, M. C. Polson, & D. J. Muraida (Eds.), *Automating instructional design: Concepts and issues* (pp. 249–292). Englewood Cliffs, NJ: Educational Technology Publications.
Fuller, B. J., Kanaba, S., & Brisch-Kanaba, J. (1982). *Single-camera video production.* Englewood Cliffs, NJ: Prentice-Hall.
Fuller, F. F., & Manning, B. A. (1973). Self-confrontation reviewed: A conceptualization for video playback in teacher education. *Review of Educational Research, 43,* 469–528.
Furnham, A., & Gunter, B. (1987). Effects of time of day and medium of presentation on immediate recall of violent and non-violent news. *Applied Cognitive Psychology, 1,* 255–262.
Furnham, A., Gunter, B., & Green, A. (1990). Remembering science: The recall of factual information as a function of the presentation mode. *Applied Cognitive Psychology, 4,* 203–212.
Furnham, A., Proctor, E., & Gunter, B. (1988). Memory for material presented in the media: The superiority of written communication. *Psychological Reports, 63,* 935–938.
Furu, T. (1971). *Function of television for children and adolescents.* Tokyo: Sophia University.
Gadberry, S. (1980). Effects of restricting first graders' TV-viewing on leisure time use, IQ change, and cognitive style. *Journal of Applied Developmental Psychology, 1,* 45–57.
Gaddy, G. D. (1980). Television's impact on high school achievement. *Public Opinion Quarterly, 50,* 340–359.
Gagnon, D. (1985). Videogames and spatial skills: An exploratory study. *Educational Communication and Technology Journal, 33,* 263–275.
Gale, N., Golledge, R. G., Pellegrino, J. W., & Doherty, S. (1990). The acquisition and integration of route knowledge in an unfamiliar neighborhood. *Journal of Environmental Psychology, 10,* 3–25.
Gallez, D. (1976). *The effect upon cognitive learning of background music in instructional films.* Unpublished doctoral dissertation, University of California, Berkeley.
Gaver, W., Sellen, A., Heath, C., & Luff, P. (1993). One is not enough: Multiple views in a media space. In *Human factors in computing systems: INTERCHI '93 conference proceedings, bridges between worlds* (pp. 335–341). New York: Association for Computing Machinery Special Interest Group on Computer-Human Interaction [ACM SIGCHI].
Gay, G. (1986). Interaction of learner control and prior understanding in computer assisted video instruction. *Journal of Educational Psychology 78,* 225–227.
Geiger, S., & Reeves, B. (1993). We interrupt this program... Attention for television sequences. *Human Communication Research, 19,* 368–387.
Giannetti, L. D. (1987). *Understanding movies* (4th ed.). Englewood Cliffs, NJ: Prentice-Hall.
Gibbons, J., Anderson, D. R., Smith, R., Field, D. E., & Fischer, C. (1986). Young children's recall and reconstruction of audio and audiovisual narratives. *Child Development, 57,* 1014–1023.
Gibbons, J. F., Kincheloe, W. R., & Down, K. S. (1977). Tutored video tape instruction: A new use of electronics media in education. *Science, 195,* 1139–1146.
Gibson, J. J. (1947). *Motion picture testing and research* (Army Air Forces Aviation Psychology Program Research Report No. 7). Washington, DC: U.S. Government Printing Office.

Glenn, A. D., & Carrier, C. A. (1989). A perspective on teacher technology training. *Educational Technology, 29,* 7–11.

Gorman, D. A. (1973). Effects of varying pictorial detail and presentation strategy on concept formation. *AV Communication Review, 21,* 337–350.

Gould, G. M., Holosko, M. J., & Baggaley, J. P. (1981). Why teenagers watch television: Implications for ETV production. In J. Baggaley & P. Janega (Eds.), *Experimental research in TV instruction* (pp. 35–42). Montreal, Quebec, Canada: Concordia University, Department of Education. (ERIC Document Reproduction Service No. ED 264 833)

Gould, J. D., & Grischkowsky, N. (1984). Doing the same work with hard copy and with cathode ray tube (CRT) computer terminals. *Human Factors, 26,* 323–337.

Graber, D. A., (1990). Seeing is remembering: How visuals contribute to learning from television news. *Journal of Communication, 40,* 134–155.

Gray, S. W. (1990). Effect of visuomotor rehearsal with videotaped modeling on racquetball performance of beginning players. *Perceptual and Motor Skills, 70,* 379–385.

Greenberg, B. S. (1974). Gratifications of television viewing and their correlates for British children. In J. G. Blumler & E. Katz (Eds.), *The uses of mass communication: Current perspectives on gratifications research* (pp. 71–92). London: Sage.

Greenberg, B. S., & Reeves, B. (1976). Children and the perceived reality of television. *Journal of Social Issues, 32,* 86–97.

Greenwald, A. G., & Albert, S. M. (1968). Observational learning: A technique for elucidating S-R mediation processes. *Journal of Experimental Psychology, 76,* 267–272.

Gregory, M., & Poulton, E. C. (1970). Even versus uneven right hand margins and the rate of comprehension in reading. *Ergonomics, 13,* 427–434.

Griffin, R., & Dumestre, J. (1992–1993). An initial evaluation of the use of captioned television to improve the vocabulary and reading comprehension of Navy sailors. *Journal of Educational Technology Systems, 21,* 193–206.

Griffin, T. (1969). *An experimental study of the effectiveness of functional music in instructional television.* Unpublished doctoral dissertation, New York University, New York.

Grimes, T. (1990). Audio-video correspondence and its role in attention and memory. *Educational Technology Research and Development, 38,* 15–25.

Gropper, G. L. (1966). Learning from visuals: Some behavioral considerations. *AV Communication Review, 14,* 37–70.

Gropper, G. L. (1968). Programming visual presentations for procedural learning. *AV Communication Review, 16,* 33–56.

Grundin, H. U. (1983). *Audio-visual media in the Open University: Results of a survey of 93 courses* (I.E.T. Papers on Broadcasting No. 224). Walton, Bletchley, Bucks, England: Institute of Educational Technology, Open University. (ERIC Document Reproduction Service No. ED 253 199)

Grundin, H. U. (1985). *Report on the 1984 AV Media Survey* (I.E.T. Paper No. 261). Walton, Bletchley, Bucks, England: Institute of Educational Technology, Open University. (ERIC Document Reproduction Service No. ED 298 961)

Guba, E., Wolf, W., de Groot, S., Knemeyer, M., Van Atta, R., & Light, L. (1964). Eye movement and TV viewing in children. *AV Communication Review, 12,* 386–401.

Gunter, B. (1980). Remembering television news: Effects of picture content. *The Journal of General Psychology, 102,* 127–133.

Gunter, B., Berry, C., & Clifford, B. R. (1981). Proactive interference effects with television news items: Further evidence. *Journal of Experimental Psychology, 7,* 480–487.

Guri-Rosenblit, S. (1988). The interrelationships between diagrammatic representations and verbal explanations in learning from social science texts. *Instructional Science, 17,* 219–234.

Gutman, J. (1978). Television viewer types: A Q analysis. *Journal of Broadcasting, 22,* 505–515.

Haeghen, P. V. (1981). Independent study courses can be very cost effective. *Technological Horizons in Education (THE) Journal, 8*(4), 52–53, 59.
Hamilton, H. B. (1975). The relationship between televiewing and reading interests of seventh-grade pupils. *Dissertation Abstracts International, 35,* 100–A. (University Microfilms No. 74-14,232)
Hannafin, M. J. (1985). Empirical issues in the study of computer-assisted interactive video. *Educational Communication and Technology Journal, 33,* 235–247.
Hannafin, M. J., & Colamaio, M. E. (1987). The effects of variations in lesson control and practice on learning from interactive video. *Educational Communication and Technology Journal, 35,* 203–212.
Hannafin, M. J., & Hughes, C. W. (1986). A frame work for incorporating orienting activities in computer-based interactive video. *Instructional Science, 15,* 239–255.
Hannafin, M. J., & Phillips, T. L. (1987). Perspectives in the design of interactive video: Beyond tape versus disc. *Journal of Research and Development in Education, 21,* 44–60.
Hannafin, M. J., Phillips, T. L., & Tripp, S. D. (1986). The effects of orienting, processing, and practicing activities on learning from interactive video. *Journal of Computer Based Instruction, 13,* 134–139.
Hansford, B. C., & Baker, R. A. (1990). Evaluation of a cross-campus interactive video teaching trial. *Distance Education, 11,* 287–307.
Hanson, L. (1989). Multichannel learning research applied to principles of television production: A review and synthesis of the literature. *Educational Technology, 29,* 15–19.
Hanson, L. (1992). The concept of redundancy in television learning research: Questions of meaning. *International Journal of Instructional Media, 19,* 7–13.
Haring, M. J., & Fry, M. A. (1979). Effect of pictures on children's comprehension of written text. *Educational Communication and Technology Journal, 27,* 185–190.
Harless, W. G., Duncan, R. C., Zier, M. A., Ayers, W. R., Berman, J. R., & Pohl, H. S. (1990). A field test of the TIME patient simulation model. *Academic Medicine, 65,* 327–333.
Hartley, J. (1992). A postscript to Wainer's "Understanding graphs and tables." *Educational Researcher, 21*(5), 25–26.
Hartman, F. R. (1961). Single and multiple channel communication: A review of research and a proposed model. *AV Communication Review, 9,* 235–262.
Haskins, M. J. (1965). Development of a response-recognition training film in tennis. *Perceptual and Motor Skills, 21,* 207–211.
Hawkridge, D. (1987). *General operational review of distance education* (Sponsored by International Bank for Reconstruction and Development, Washington, DC). Walton, Bletchley, Bucks, England: Institute of Educational Technology, Open University (ERIC Document Reproduction Service No . ED 304 123)
Hayes, D. S., & Kelly, S. B. (1984). Young children's processing of television: Modality differences in the retention of temporal relations. *Journal of Experimental Child Psychology, 38,* 505–514.
Hayes, D. S., Kelly, S. B., & Mandel, M. (1986). Media differences in children's story synopses: Radio and television contrasted. *Journal of Educational Psychology, 78,* 341–346.
Hays, R. T., & Singer, M. J. (1989). *Simulation fidelity in training system design.* New York: Springer-Verlag.
Head, G. E., & Buchanan, C. C. (1981). Cost/benefit analysis of training: A foundation for change. *Performance and Instruction, 20,* 25–27.
Heestand, D. E. (1980). The use of inserted questions in videotape programs. *International Journal of Instructional Media, 7,* 149–158.
Hegarty, M., Carpenter, P. A., & Just, M. A. (1991). Diagrams in the comprehension of scientific texts. In R. Barr, M. Kamil, P. Mosenthal, & P. D. Pearson (Eds.), *Handbook of reading research* (Vol. II, pp. 641–668). New York: Longman.

Hegarty, M., & Just, M. A. (1989). Understanding machine from text and diagrams. In H. Mandl & J. R. Levin (Eds.), *Knowledge acquisition from text and pictures* (pp. 171–194). New York: North-Holland.

Herx, H. (1986). The video-cassette classroom. *Momentum, 17*(1), 20–21.

Hill, R. D., Crook, T. H., Zadek, A., Sheikh, J., & Yesavage, J. (1989). The effects of age on recall of information from a simulated television news broadcast. *Educational Gerontology, 15,* 607–613.

Himmelweit, H. T., Oppenheim, A. N., & Vince, P. (1958). *Television and the child.* London: Oxford University Press.

Himmelweit, H., & Swift, B. (1976). Continuities and discontinuities in media usage and taste: A longitudinal study. *Journal of Social Issues, 32,* 133–156.

Ho, C. P., Savenye, W., & Haas, N. (1986). The effects of orienting objectives and review on learning from interactive video. *Journal of Computer Based Instruction, 13,* 126–129.

Hoban, C. F. (1953). Determinants of audience reaction to a training film. *AV Communication Review, 1,* 30–37.

Hoban, C. F., & Van Ormer, E. B. (1950). *Instructional film research, 1918–1950* (Tech. Rep. No. SDC 269-7-19). Port Washington, NY: U.S. Naval Special Devices Center. (ERIC Document Reproduction Service No. ED 647 255)

Hochberg, J., & Brooks, V. (1978). The perception of motion pictures. In E. C. Carterette & M. P. Friedman (Eds.), *Handbook of perception: Vol. 10. Perceptual ecology* (pp. 35–68). New York: Academic Press.

Holliday, W. G. (1973). Critical analysis of pictorial research related to science education. *Science Education, 57*(2), 201–214.

Horn, G. (1972, December). Laughter ... A saving grace. *Today's Education,* 37–38.

Hornik, R. (1981). Out-of-school television and schooling: Hypotheses and methods. *Review of Educational Research, 51,* 193–214.

Hosford, R. E., & Johnson, M. E. (1983). A comparison of self-observation, self-modeling, and practice without video feedback for improving counselor interviewing behaviors. *Counselor Education and Supervision, 23,* 62–70.

Hosie, P. J. (1985). A window on the world. *British Journal of Educational Technology, 16,* 145–163.

Houser, R. L., Houser, E. J., & Van Mondfrans, A. P. (1970). Learning a motion and nonmotion concept by motion picture versus slide presentation. *AV Communication Review, 18,* 425–430.

Hoyt, D. B., Shackford, S. R., Fridland, P. H., Mackersie, R. C., Hansbrough, J. F., Wachtel, T. L., & Fortune, J. B. (1988). Video recording trauma resuscitations: An effective teaching technique. *The Journal of Trauma, 28,* 435–440.

Huddleston, B. M. (1985, February). *An examination of behavioral responses to stereotypical deceptive displays.* Paper presented at the annual meeting of the Western Speech Communication Association, Fresno, CA.

Hunter, B., Crismore, A., & Pearson, P.D. (1987). Visual displays in basal readers and social studies textbooks. In H. A. Houghton & D. M. Willows (Eds.), *The psychology of illustration: Vol. 2: Instructional issues* (pp. 116–135). New York: Springer-Verlag.

Huston, A., & Wright, J. (1983). Children's processing of television: The informative functions of formal features. In J. Bryant & D. R. Anderson (Eds.), *Children's understanding of television: Research on attention and comprehension* (pp. 35–68). New York: Academic Press.

Isenhour, J. P. (1975). The effects of context and order in film editing. *AV Communication Review, 23,* 69–80.

Jackson, R. (1955). *Visual principles for training by television* (Human Engineering Report SDC 20-TV-2). Port Washington, NY: Office of Naval Research, Human Engineering Division, U.S. Naval Special Devices Center. (ERIC Document Reproduction Service No. ED 901 61)

Jackson-Beeck, M. (1977). The non-viewers: Who are they? *Journal of Communication, 27,* 65–72.

Jamison, D. T., & Klees, S. J. (1975). The cost of instructional radio and television for developing countries. *Instructional Science, 4,* 333–384.

Jamison, D. T., Klees, S. J., & Wells, S. J. (1976). *Cost analysis for educational planning and evaluation: Methodology and application to instructional technology.* Princeton, NJ: Educational Testing Service. (ERIC Document Reproduction Service No. ED 127 918)

Jamison, D. T., Klees, S. J., & Wells, S. J. (1978). *The cost of educational media.* Beverly Hills, CA: Sage.

Jamison, D., Suppes, P., & Wells, S. (1974). The effectiveness of alternative instructional media: A survey. *Review of Educational Research, 44,* 1–67.

Jensen, L. C., & Young, J. I. (1972). Effect of televised simulated instruction on subsequent teaching. *Journal of Educational Psychology, 63,* 368–373.

Jeon, U. H., & Branson R. K. (1981–1982). Performance and simulated performance test results as a function of instruction by still and motion visuals. *Journal of Educational Technology Systems, 10,* 33–44.

Jonassen, D. H. (1988). Interactive designs for courseware. In D. H. Jonassen (Ed.), *Instructional designs for microcomputer courseware* (pp. 97–102). Hillsdale, NJ: Lawrence Erlbaum Associates.

Jonassen, D. H., & Hannum, W. H. (1987). Research-based principles for designing computer software. *Educational Technology, 27,* 7–14.

Jorgensen, E. S. (1955). *The relative effectiveness of three methods of TV newscasting.* Unpublished doctoral dissertation, University of Wisconsin, Madison.

Kagan, J. (1965). Impulsive and reflective children: Significance of conceptual tempo. In J. D. Krumboltz (Ed.), *Learning and the educational process* (pp. 133–161). Chicago: Rand McNally.

Kanner, J. H. (1968). *The instructional effectiveness of color in television: A review of the evidence.* Washington, DC: Department of the Army, Office of the Assistant Chief of Staff for Communications-Electronics. (ERIC Document Reproduction Service No. ED 015 675)

Kanner, J. H., & Rosenstein, A. J. (1960). Television in army training: Color versus black and white. *AV Communication Review, 8,* 243–252.

Kantor, B. R. (1960) Effectiveness of inserted questions in instructional films. *AV Communication Review, 8,* 104–108.

Kaplan, R. M., & Pascoe, G. C. (1977). Humorous lectures and humorous examples: Some effects upon comprehension and retention. *Journal of Educational Psychology, 69,* 61–65.

Karasar, N. (1970). *Impact of video feedback on teachers' eye-contact mannerisms in microteaching.* Unpublished doctoral dissertation, Ohio State University, Columbus.

Katz, E., Adoni, H., & Parness, P. (1977). Remembering the news: What the picture adds to recall. *Journalism Quarterly, 54,* 231–239.

Katz, E., Blumler, J. G., & Gurevitch, M. (1974). Utilization of mass media by the individual. In J. G. Blumler & E. Katz (Eds.), . *The uses of mass communication: Current perspectives on gratifications research* (pp. 19–32). London: Sage.

Katzman, N., & Nyenhuis, J. (1972). Color versus black and white effects on learning, opinion, and attention. *AV Communication Review, 20,* 16–28.

Kaye, A. R. (1973). The design and evaluation of science courses at the Open University. *Instructional Science, 2,* 119–192.

Kazem, A. K. M. (1960). *An experimental study of the contribution of certain instructional films to the understanding of the elements of scientific method, by tenth-grade biology students.* Unpublished doctoral dissertation, University of Michigan, Ann Arbor.

Kearsley, G. P., & Frost, J. (1985). Design factors for successful videodisc-based instruction. *Educational Technology, 25,* 7–13.

Kernodle, M. W., & Carlton, L. G. (1992). Information feedback and the learning of multiple-degree-of-freedom activities. *Journal of Motor Behavior, 24*, 187–196.

Kiesling, H. (1979). Economic cost analysis in higher education: The University of Mid-America and traditional institutions compared. *Educational Communication and Technology Journal, 27*, 9–24.

King, W. A. (1975). *A comparison of three combinations of text and graphics for concept learning* (NPRDC-TR-76-16). San Diego, CA: Navy Personnel Research and Development Center. (AD-A016 805)

Kintsch, W., & Van Dijk, T. (1978). Toward a theory of text comprehension and production. *Psychological Review, 85*, 363–394.

Kipper, P. (1986). Television camera movement as a source of perceptual information. *Journal of Broadcasting and Electronic Media, 30*, 295–307.

Kipper, P. (1988). *Judging presidential debaters: The power of the TV factor.* (ERIC Document Reproduction Service No. ED 305 694)

Konoske, P. J., & Ellis, J. A. (1986, December). *Cognitive factors in learning and retention of procedural tasks* (NPRDC-TR-87-14). San Diego, CA: Navy Personnel Research and Development Center. (AD-A176 105)

Koran, M. L., Snow, R. E., & McDonald, F. J. (1971). Teacher aptitude and observational learning of a teaching skill. *Journal of Educational Psychology, 62*, 219–228.

Kozma, R. B. (1986). Implications of instructional psychology for the design of educational television. *Educational Communication and Technology Journal, 34*, 11–19.

Kozma, R. B. (1991). Learning with media. *Review of Educational Research, 61*, 179–211.

Kraft, R. N. (1986). The role of cutting in the evaluation and retention of film. *Journal of Experimental Psychology: Learning, Memory, and Cognition, 12*, 155–162.

Kraft, R. N. (1987). Rules and strategies for visual narratives. *Perceptual and Motor Skills, 64*, 3–14.

Kraft, R. N., Cantor, P., & Gottdiener, C. (1991). The coherence of visual narrative. *Communication Research, 18*, 601–616.

Krendl, K. A. (1986). Media influence on learning: Examining the role of preconceptions. *Educational Communication and Technology Journal, 34*, 223–234.

Krendl, K. A., Clark, G., Dawson, R., & Troiano, C. (1993). Preschoolers and VCRs in the home: A multiple methods approach. *Journal of Broadcasting and Electronic Media, 37*, 293–312.

Krendl, K. A., & Watkins, B. (1983). Understanding television: An exploratory inquiry into the reconstruction of narrative content. *Educational Communication and Technology Journal, 31*, 201–212.

Ksobiech, K. J. (1976). The importance of perceived task and type of presentation in student response to instructional television. *AV Communication Review, 24*, 401–412.

Kulik, C. C., Kulik, J. A., & Shwalb, B. J. (1986). The effectiveness of computer-based adult education: A meta-analysis. *Journal of Educational Computing Research, 2*, 235–252.

Kulik, C-L. C., & Kulik, J. A. (1986). Effectiveness of computer based education in colleges. *AEDS Journal, 19*, 81–108.

Kulik, J. A., & Kulik, C. C. (1987). Review of recent research literature on computer-based instruction. *Contemporary Educational Psychology, 12*, 222–230.

La Blonde, J. A. (1966). A study of the relationship between the television viewing habits and scholastic achievement of fifth grade children. *Dissertation Abstracts, 27*, 2284-A. (University Microfilms No. 67-19)

Laesecke, A. (1990). Computer animation as a teaching aid: The Sterling cycle. *Cryogenics, 30*, 367–370.

Laidlaw, B., & Layard, R. (1974). Traditional versus Open University teaching methods: A cost comparison. *Higher Education, 3*, 439–468.

REFERENCES   225

Lamberski, R. J., & Dwyer, F. M. (1983). The instructional effect of coding (color and black and white) on information acquisition and retrieval. *Educational Communication and Technology Journal, 31,* 9–21.

Laner, S. (1954). The impact of visual aid displays showing a manipulative task. *Quarterly Journal of Experimental Psychology, 6,* 95–106.

Laner, S. (1955). Some factors influencing the effectiveness of a training film. *British Journal of Psychology, 46,* 280–292.

Langer, E. J., Blank, A., & Chanowitz, B. (1978). The mindlessness of ostensibly thoughtful action: The role of "placebic" information in interpersonal interaction. *Journal of Personality and Social Psychology, 36,* 635–642.

Langer, E., & Imber, L. G. (1979) When practice makes imperfect: Debilitating effects of overlearning. *Journal of Personality and Social Psychology, 37,* 2014–2024.

Lepper, M. R., & Greene, D. (1978). Overjustification research and beyond: Toward a means-ends analysis of intrinsic and extrinsic motivation. In M. R. Lepper & D. Greene (Eds.), *The hidden costs of reward: New perspectives on the psychology of human motivation* (pp. 109–148). Hillsdale, NJ: Lawrence Erlbaum Associates.

Lesser, G. S. (1972). Assumptions behind the production and writing methods in "Sesame Street." In W. Schramm (Ed.), *Quality in instructional television* (pp. 108–164). Honolulu: University Press of Hawaii.

Lesser, G. S. (1974). *Children and television: Lessons from Sesame Street.* New York: Random House.

Levenson, P. M., Morrow, J. R., & Signer, B. (1985–1986). A comparison of noninteractive and interactive video instruction about smokeless tobacco. *Journal of Educational Technology Systems, 14,* 193–202.

Levie, W. H. (1987). Research on pictures: A guide to the literature. In D. M. Willows & H. A. Houghton (Eds.), *The psychology of illustration: Vol. 1. Basic research* (pp. 1–50). New York: Springer-Verlag.

Levie, W. H., & Dickie, K. (1973). The analysis and application of media. In R. M. W. Travers (Ed.), *Second handbook of research on teaching* (pp. 858–882). Chicago: Rand McNally.

Levie, W. H., & Lentz, R. (1982). Effects of text illustrations: A review of research. *Educational Communication and Technology Journal, 30,* 195–232.

Levin, H. M. (1988). Cost-effectiveness and educational policy. *Educational Evaluation and Policy Analysis, 10,* 51–69.

Levin, J. R., Anglin, G. J., & Carney, R. N. (1987). On empirically validating functions of pictures in prose. In D. M. Willows & H. A. Houghton (Eds.), *The psychology of illustration: Vol. 1. Basic research* (pp. 51–85). New York: Springer-Verlag.

Lin, C. A., & Cresswell, K. W. (1989). Effects of televised lecture presentation styles on student learning. *Journal of Educational Television, 15,* 37–52.

Link, J. D. (1961). A comparison of the effects on learning of viewing films in color on a screen and in black and white on a closed-circuit TV. *Ontario Journal of Educational Research, 3,* 111–115.

Lipsey, M. W., & Wilson, D. B. (1993). The efficacy of psychological educational, and behavioral treatment: Confirmation from meta-analysis. *American Psychologist, 48,* 1181–1209.

Loftus, G. R., & Bell, S. M. (1975). Two types of information in picture memory. *Journal of Experimental Psychology: Human Learning and Memory, 1/104,* 103–113.

Lumsdaine, A. A. (Ed.). (1961). *Student response in programmed instruction.* Washington, DC: National Academy of Sciences, National Research Council. (AD-281 936)

Lumsdaine, A. A. (1963). Instruments and media of instruction. In N. L. Gage (Ed.), *Handbook of research on teaching* (pp. 583–682). Chicago: Rand-McNally.

Lumsdaine, A. A., & May, M. A. (1965). Mass communication and educational media. *Annual Review of Psychology, 16,* 475–534.

REFERENCES

Lumsdaine, A. A., Sulzer, R. L., & Kopstein, F. F. (1961). The effect of animation cues and repetition of examples on learning from and instructional film. In A. A. Lumsdaine (Ed.), *Student response in programmed instruction* (pp. 241–269). Washington, DC: National Academy of Sciences, National Research Council. (AD-281 936)

Lumsden, K. G., & Ritchie, C. (1975). The Open University: A survey and economic analysis. *Instructional Science, 4*, 237–291.

Lyle, J., & Hoffman, H. R. (1972). Children's use of television and other media. In E. A. Rubinstein, G. A. Comstock, & J. P. Murray (Eds.), *Television and social behavior* (Vol. 4, pp. 129–256). Rockville, MD: The National Institute of Mental Health.

Mace, J. (1978). Mythology in the making: Is the Open University really cost-effective? *Higher Education, 7*, 295–309.

Mace, J. (1982). Educational media and economic analysis. *Media in Education and Development, 15*(2), 91–93.

Magne, O., & Parknas, L. (1963). The learning effects of pictures. *British Journal of Educational Psychology, 33*, 265–275.

Maher, T. G. (1982). *Television-centered, instructional delivery systems: Costs and case studies. A review of research.* Alta Loma, CA: Chaffey Community College. (ERIC Document Reproduction Service No. ED 292 467)

Mandell, L. M. (1973). Judging people in the news—unconsciously: Effect of camera angle and bodily activity. *Journal of Broadcasting, 17*, 353–362.

Mann, R. (1979). *The effect of music and sound effects on the listening comprehension of fourth grade students.* Unpublished doctoral dissertation, North Texas State University, Denton.

Markham, P. L. (1989). Effects of contextual versus definitional computer-assisted vocabulary instruction in immediate and long-term vocabulary retention of advanced ESL students. *Educational Psychology, 9*, 121–126.

Mascelli, J. (1965). *The five C's of cinematography.* Hollywood, CA: Cine/Graphic.

Mason, R., & Kaye, A. (1989). *Mindweave: Communication, computers and distance education.* Oxford, England: Pergamon.

Masterson, J. W. (1976). Compressed motion-picture effects on psychomotor performance. *Journal of Industrial Teacher Education, 14*, 72–79.

Mathias, H., & Patterson, R. (1985). *Electronic cinematography.* Belmont, CA: Wadsworth.

May, M. A., & Lumsdaine, A. A. (1958). *Learning from films.* New Haven, CT: Yale University Press.

Mayer, R. E. (1989a). Models for understanding. *Review of Educational Research, 59*, 43–64.

Mayer, R. E. (1989b). Systematic thinking fostered by illustrations in scientific text. *Journal of Educational Psychology, 81*, 240–264.

Mayer, R. E., & Gallini, J. K. (1990). When is an illustration worth ten thousand words? *Journal of Educational Psychology, 82*, 715–726.

Mayton, G. B. (1991). Learning dynamic processes from animated visuals in microcomputer-based instruction. In *Proceedings of Selected Research Presentations at the Annual Convention of the Association for Educational Communications and Technology.* (ERIC Document Reproduction Service No. ED 334 999)

McArthur, L. Z., & Post, D. L. (1977). Figural emphasis and person perception. *Journal of Experimental Social Psychology, 13*, 520–535.

McCabe, R. H. (1979). The economics of television-centered courses. In R. Yarrington (Ed.), *Using mass media for learning* (pp. 29–36). Washington DC: American Association of Community and Junior Colleges (AACJC). (ERIC Document Reproduction Service No. ED 165 856)

McCain, T. A., Chilberg, J., & Wakshlag, J. (1977). The effect of camera angle on source credibility and attraction. *Journal of Broadcasting, 21*, 35–46.

McCullagh, P. (1986). Model status as a determinant of observational learning and performance. *Journal of Sport Psychology, 8*, 319–331.

McGhee, P. E. (1980). Toward the integration of entertainment and educational functions of television. In P. H. Tannenbaum (Ed.), *The entertainment functions of television* (pp. 183–208). Hillsdale, NJ: Lawrence Erlbaum Associates.

McIntyre, C. J. (1954). *Training film evaluation—cold weather uniforms* (Instructional Film Research Rep. No. 24). Port Washington, NY: U.S. Naval Special Devices Center.

McNeil, B. J., & Nelson, K. R. (1991). Meta-analysis of interactive video instruction: A 10 year review of achievement effects. *Journal of Computer Based Instruction, 18,* 1–6.

Mechanic, D. (1962). *Students under stress: A study of the social psychology of adaptation.* New York: The Free Press.

Mercer, J. (1952). *Relationships of optical effects and film literacy to learning from instructional films* (Instructional Film Research Rep. No. SDC 269-7-34). Port Washington, NY: U.S. Naval Special Devices Center.

Meringoff, L. K. (1980). Influence of the medium on children's story apprehension. *Journal of Educational Psychology, 72,* 240–249.

Merritt, B. D. (1984, November). *Jesse Jackson and television: Black image presentation and affect in the 1984 Democratic campaign debates.* Paper presented at the 70th Annual Meeting of the Speech Communication Association, Chicago, IL.

Metallinos, N., & Tiemans, R. K. (1977). Asymmetry of screen—Effect of left versus right placement of television images. *Journal of Broadcasting, 21,* 21–33.

Meyer, G. E., Rocheleau, D. J., McMullen, J., & Ritter, B. E. (1991). The use of Macintosh 24-bit color and animation programs in undergraduate research and visual perception courses. *Behavior Research Methods, Instruments and Computers, 23,* 166–182.

Michael, D. N., & Maccoby, N. (1953). Factors influencing verbal learning from films under varying conditions of audience participation. *Journal of Experimental Psychology, 46,* 411–418.

Millerson, G. (1985). *The technique of television production.* London: Focal Press.

Monson, D. (1968). Children's test responses to seven humorous stories. *Elementary School Journal, 58,* 334–339.

Moore, M. V., & Nawrocki, L. H. (1978). *The educational effectiveness of graphic displays for computer assisted instruction* (Tech. Paper No. 332). Arlington, VA: Army Research Institute for the Behavioral and Social Sciences. (ERIC Document Reproduction Service No. ED 169 917)

Moore, M. V., Nawrocki, L. H., & Simutis, Z. M. (1979). *The instructional effectiveness of three levels of graphic displays for computer assisted instruction* (Tech. Paper No. 359). Arlington, VA: Army Research Institute for the Behavioral and Social Sciences. (ERIC Document Reproduction Service No. ED 178 057)

Moore, P. J., & Skinner, M. J. (1985). The effects of illustrations on children's comprehension of abstract and concrete passages. *Journal of Research in Reading, 8,* 45–56.

Morgan, M. (1980). Television viewing and reading: Does more equal better? *Journal of Communication, 30,* 159–165.

Morgan, M., & Gross, L. (1980). Television and academic achievement. *Journal of Broadcasting, 24,* 117–232.

Morgan, M., & Gross, L. (1982). Television and educational achievement and aspiration. In D. Pearl, L. Bouthilet, & J. Lazar (Eds.), *Television and behavior: Ten years of scientific progress and implications for the eighties* (Vol. 2, pp. 78–91). Washington, DC: U.S. Government Printing Office.

Morris, J. D. (1984). The Florida study: Improving achievement through the use of more dynamics in TV production. *T.H.E. Journal, 12,* 104–107.

Morris, J. D. (1988a). A review of literature on the effects of production techniques in instructional television. *International Journal of Instructional Media, 15,* 41–48.

Morris, J. D. (1988b). The use of television production techniques to facilitate the learning process: An experiment. *International Journal of Instructional Media, 15,* 244–256.

Murphy, R. T. (1991, October). *Educational effectiveness of Sesame Street: A review of the first twenty years of research 1969–1989* (RR-91-55). Princeton, NJ: Educational Testing Service.

Murray, J. P., & Kippax, S. (1978). Children's social behavior in three towns with differing television experience. *Journal of Communication, 28,* 19–29.

Muta, H., & Sakamoto, T. (1989). The economics of the University of the Air of Japan revisited. *Higher Education, 18*(5), 585–611.

Muter, P., Latremouille, S. A., Treurniet, W. C., & Beam, P. (1982). Extended readings of continuous text on television screens. *Human Factors, 24,* 501–508.

Neu, D. M. (1951). The effect of attention gaining devices on film-mediated learning. *Journal of Educational Psychology, 42,* 479–490.

Neuman, S. B. (1988). The displacement effect: Assessing the relation between television viewing and reading performance. *Reading Research Quarterly, 23,* 414–440.

Neuman, S. B., & Prowda, P. (1982). Television and reading achievement. *Journal of Reading, 25,* 666–670.

Neuman, W. R. (1976). Patterns of recall among television news viewers. *Public Opinion Quarterly, 40,* 115–123.

Nugent, G. C. (1982). Pictures, audio, and print: Symbolic representation and effect on learning. *Education Communication and Technology Journal, 30,* 163–174.

Nugent, G. C., Tipton, T. J., & Brooks, D. W. (1980). Task, learner, and presentation interactions in television production. *Educational Communication and Technology Journal, 28,* 30–38.

O'Bryan, K. G. (1976). *Cues and attention to the visual display in children's television.* (ERIC Document Reproduction Service No. ED 122 810)

Orlansky, J., & String, J. (1977). *Cost effectiveness of computer-based instruction in military training* (IDA Paper P-1375). Arlington, VA: Institute for Defense Analyses.

Orlansky, J., & String, J. (1981). Computer-based instruction for military training. *Defense Management Journal* (2nd quarter), 46–54.

Palmer, E. (1978, June). *A pedagogical analysis of recurrent formats on Sesame Street and Electric Company.* Paper presented at the International Conference on Children's Educational Television, Amsterdam.

Palmiter, S., & Elkerton, J. (1991). An evaluation of animated demonstrations for learning computer-based tasks. In *Conference Proceedings of CHI'91: Human Factors in Computer Systems* (pp. 257–263). New York: Association for Computing Machinery Special Interest Group on Computer-Human Interaction [ACM SIGCHI].

Palmiter, S., Elkerton, J., & Baggett, P. (1991). Animated demonstrations versus written instructions for learning procedural tasks: A preliminary investigation. *International Journal of Man-Machine Studies, 34,* 687–701.

Park, O., & Gittelman, S. S. (1992). Selective use of animation and feedback in computer-based instruction. *Educational Technology Research and Development, 40,* 27–38.

Parkhurst, P. E., & Dwyer, F. M. (1983). An experimental assessment of students' IQ level and their ability to profit from visualized instruction. *Journal of Instructional Psychology, 10,* 9–20.

Pavio, A. (1971). *Imagery and verbal processes.* New York: Holt, Rinehart, & Winston.

Peeck, J. (1987). The role of illustrations in processing and remembering illustrated text. In D. M. Willows & H. A. Houghton (Eds.), *The psychology of illustration: Vol. 1. Basic research* (pp. 115–151). New York: Springer-Verlag.

Penn, R. (1971). Effects of motion and cutting rate in motion pictures. *AV Communication Review, 19,* 29–30.

Peters, H. J., & Daiker, K. C. (1982). Graphics and animation as an instructional tool: A case study. *Pipeline, 7,* 11–13, 57.

Peters, O. (1992). Some observations on dropping out in distance education. *Distance Education, 13,* 234–269.

Petkovich, M. D., & Tennyson, R. D. (1984). Clark's "learning from media": A critique. *Educational Communication and Technology Journal, 32,* 233–241.

Petkovich, M. D., & Tennyson, R. D. (1985). A few more thoughts on Clark's "learning from media". *Educational Communication and Technology Journal, 33,* 146.

Pezdek, K., & Hartman, E. F. (1983). Children's television viewing: Attention and comprehension of auditory versus visual information. *Child Development, 54,* 1015–1023.

Pezdek, K., Lehrer, A., & Simon, S. (1984). The relationship between reading and cognitive processing of television and radio. *Child Development, 55,* 2072–2082.

Pezdek, K., Simon, S., Stoeckert, J., & Kiely, J. (1987). Individual differences in television comprehension. *Memory and Cognition, 15,* 428–435.

Pezdek, K., & Stevens, E. (1984). Children's memory of auditory and visual information on television. *Developmental Psychology, 20,* 212–218.

Phillips, T. L., Hannafin, M. J., & Tripp, S. D. (1988). The effects of practice and orienting activities on learning from interactive video. *Educational Communication and Technology Journal, 36,* 93–102.

Pintrich, P. R., Cross, D. R., Kozma, R. B., & McKeachie, W. J. (1986). Instructional psychology. *Annual Review of Psychology, 37,* 611–651.

Pirrong, G. D., & Lathen, W. C. (1990). The use of interactive television in business education. *Educational Technology, 30,* 49–54.

Poole, R., & Wade, B. (1985). Pupils' perception of topics in educational broadcasts: A case study. *Educational Studies, 11,* 119–125.

Postman, N. (1986). *Amusing ourselves to death: Public discourse in the age of show business.* London: Heinemann.

Pressley, M. (1977). Imagery and children's learning: Putting the picture in developmental perspective. *Review of Educational Research, 47,* 585–622.

Pressley, M., & Miller, G. E. (1987). Children's listening comprehension and oral prose memory. In D. M. Willows & H. A. Houghton (Eds.), *The psychology of illustration: Vol. 1. Basic research* (pp. 87–114). New York: Springer-Verlag.

Price, V., Richie, D., Roberts, D. F., & Lieberman, D. (1986). *The Stanford reading and television study: A progress report.* Stanford, CA: Institute for Communications Research. (ERIC Document Reproduction Service No. ED 277 064)

Pudovkin, V.I. (1958). *Film technique and film acting.* London: Vision Press.

Pugh, H. L., Parchman, S. W., & Simpson, H. (1991). *Field survey of videoteletraining systems in public education, industry and the military* (NPRDC-TR-91-7). San Diego, CA: Navy Personnel Research and Development Center. (AD-A234 875)

Pugh, H. L., Parchman, S. W., & Simpson, H. (1992). Video telecommunications for distance education: A field survey of systems in U.S. public education, industry and the military. *Distance Education, 13,* 46–64.

Radtke, P. H., & Ulozas, B. (1991). *Choices in media survey results: How Navy trainers use media.* Unpublished manuscript, Navy Personnel Research and Development Center, San Diego, CA.

Randel, J. M., Morris, B. A., Wetzel, C. D., & Whitehill, B. V. (1992). The effectiveness of games for educational purposes: A review of recent research. *Simulation & Gaming, 23,* 261–276.

Reed, S. (1985). Effect of computer graphics on improving estimates to algebra word problems. *Journal of Educational Psychology, 77,* 285–298.

Reese, S. D. (1983). *Improving audience learning from television news through between-channel redundancy.* (ERIC Document Reproduction Service No. ED 229 777)

Reeves, T. C. (1986). Research and evaluation models for the study of interactive video. *Journal of Computer Based Instruction, 13,* 102–106.

Reid, J. C., & MacLennan, D. W. (1967). *Research in instructional television and film: Summaries of studies.* Washington, DC: U.S. Office of Education, U.S. Government Printing Office.
Reider, W. L. (1984). Videocassette technology in education: A quiet revolution in progress. *Educational Technology, 24*(10), 12–15.
Reider, W. L. (1985). VCRs silently take over the classroom. *TechTrends, 30*(8), 14–18.
Reider, W. L. (1987a). The VCR as high tech: The most significant educational tool since the textbook. *Wilson Library Bulletin, 61*(9), 16–18.
Reider, W. L. (1987b). We put V.C.R.s and a videotape library in every school; you can, too. *The American School Board Journal, 173,* 38, 41.
Reiser, R. A., & Gagné, R. M. (1982). Characteristics of media selection models. *Review of Educational Research, 52,* 499–512.
Richardson, A. (1967a). Mental practice: A review and discussion (Part 1). *Research Quarterly, 38,* 95–107.
Richardson, A. (1967b). Mental practice: A review and discussion (Part 2). *Research Quarterly, 38,* 263–273.
Riches, B. (1990). Electric circuit theory—Computer illustrated text. *Collegiate Microcomputer, 8,* 29–33.
Rieber, L. P. (1989a). The effect of computer animated elaboration strategies and practice on factual and application learning in an elementary science lesson. *Journal of Educational Computing Research, 5,* 431–444.
Rieber, L. P. (1989b, November). *The effect of computer animation on intentional and incidental learning and motivation.* Paper presented at the annual meeting of the Association for the Development of Computer-Based Instruction Systems, Washington, DC.
Rieber, L. P. (1990a). Animation in computer-based instruction. *Educational Technology Research and Development, 38,* 77–86.
Rieber, L. P. (1990b). Using computer animated graphics in science instruction with children. *Journal of Educational Psychology, 82,* 135–140.
Rieber, L. P. (1991a). Animation, incidental learning, and continuing motivation. *Journal of Educational Psychology, 83,* 318–328.
Rieber, L. P. (1991b). The effects of visual grouping on learning from computer animated presentations. In *Proceedings of selected research presentations at the Annual Convention of the Association for Educational Communications and Technology* (pp. 695–703). (ERIC Document Reproduction Service No. ED 335 006)
Rieber, L. P., Boyce, M. J., & Assad, C. (1990). The effect of computer animation on adult learning and retrieval tasks. *Journal of Computer Based Instruction, 17,* 46–52.
Rieber, L. P., & Kini, A. S. (1991). Theoretical foundations of instructional applications of computer-generated animated visuals. *Journal of Computer-Based Instruction, 18,* 83–88.
Rigney, J., & Lutz, K. (1975). *The effects of interactive graphic analogies of recall of concepts in chemistry* (Tech. Rep. No. 75). Washington, DC: Office of Naval Research.
Rikli, R., & Smith, G. (1980). Videotape feedback effects on tennis serving form. *Perceptual and Motor Skills, 50,* 895–901.
Rink, O. (1975). Background music in dramatic television: Will it increase learning for American university students? *International Journal of Instructional Media, 3,* 193–203.
Ritchie, H., & Newby, T. J. (1989). Classroom lecture/discussion vs. live televised instruction: A comparison of effects on student performance, attitude and interaction. *The American Journal of Distance Education, 3,* 36–45.
Robinson, D. C. (1975). Television/film attitudes of upper-middle class professionals. *Journal of Broadcasting, 21,* 195–209.
Rohwer, W. D., Jr., & Harris, W. J. (1975). Media effects on prose learning in two populations of children. *Journal of Educational Psychology, 67,* 651–657.

Rolandelli, D. R. (1989). Children and television: The visual superiority effect reconsidered. *Journal of Broadcasting and Electronic Media, 33,* 69–81.

Rolandelli, D. R., Wright, J. C., Huston, A. C., & Eakins, D. (1991). Children's auditory and visual processing of narrated and nonnarrated television programming. *Journal of Experimental Child Psychology, 51,* 90–122.

Roper, B. W. (1978). Changing public attitudes toward television and other media: 1959–1976. *Communications, 4,* 220–238.

Rosengren, K. E., & Windahl, S. (1972). Mass media consumption as a functional alternative. In D. McQuail (Ed.), *Sociology of mass communications* (pp. 166–194). Harmondsworth, England: Penguin.

Rosenkoetter, J. S. (1984). Teaching psychology to large classes: Videotapes, PSI, and lecturing. *Teaching of Psychology, 11,* 85–87.

Roshal, S. M. (1949). *Effects of learner representation in film-mediated perceptual-motor learning* (Tech. Rep. SDC 269-7-5). Port Washington, NY: U.S. Naval Special Devices Center.

Roshal, S. M. (1961). Film-mediated learning with varying representation of the task: Viewing angle, portrayal of demonstration, motion and student participation. In A. A. Lumsdaine (Ed.), *Student response in programmed instruction* (pp. 155–175). Washington, DC: National Academy of Sciences, National Research Council. (AD-281 936)

Rothkopf, E. Z., Dixon, P., & Billington, M. J. (1986). Effects of enhanced spatial context on television message retention. *Communication Research, 13,* 55–69.

Rothstein, A. L., & Arnold, R. K. (1976). Briding the gap: Application of research on video-tape feedback and bowling. *Motor Skills: Theory into Practice, 1,* 35–62.

Royer, J. M., & Cable, G. W. (1976). Illustrations, analogies, and facilitative transfer in prose learning. *Journal of Educational Psychology, 68,* 205–209.

Rubin, A. M. (1977). Television usage, attitudes and viewing behaviors of children and adolescents. *Journal of Broadcasting, 21,* 355–369.

Rule, S., DeWulf, M. J., & Stowitschek, J. J. (1988). An economic analysis of inservice teacher training. *American Journal of Distance Education, 2,* 12–22.

Rumble, G. (1982). The cost analysis of learning at a distance: Venezuela's Universidad Nacional Abierta. *Distance Education, 3,* 116–140.

Rumble, G. (1987). Why distance education can be cheaper than conventional education. *Distance Education, 8,* 72–94.

Rupinski, T. E. (1991). *Analyses of video teletraining utilization, effectiveness, and acceptance* (CRM Research Memo. 91–159). Alexandria, VA: Center for Naval Analyses.

Rupinski, T. E., & Stoloff, P. H. (1990). *An evaluation of Navy video teletraining (VTT)* (CRM Research Memo. 90-36). Alexandria, VA: Center for Naval Analyses.

Rusted, R., & Coltheart, V. (1979). The effect of pictures on the retention of novel words and prose passages. *Journal of Experimental Child Psychology, 28,* 516–524.

Saettler, P. A. (1968). *A history of instructional technology.* New York: McGraw Hill.

Salomon, G. (1974). Internalization of filmic schematic operations in interaction with learners' aptitudes. *Journal of Educational Psychology, 66,* 499–511.

Salomon, G. (1979). *Interaction of media, cognition, and learning.* San Francisco: Jossey-Bass.

Salomon, G. (1983). Television watching and mental effort: A social psychological view. In J. Bryant & D. R. Anderson (Eds.), *Children's understanding of television* (pp. 181–198). New York: Academic Press.

Salomon, G. (1984). Television is "easy" and print is "tough": The differential investment of mental effort in learning as a function of perceptions and attributions. *Journal of Educational Psychology, 76,* 647–658.

Salomon, G., & Clark, R. E. (1977). Reexamining the methodology of research on media and technology in education. *Review of Educational Research, 47,* 99–120.

Salomon, G., & Cohen, A. A. (1977). Television formats, mastery of mental skills, and the acquisition of knowledge. *Journal of Educational Psychology, 69,* 612–619.

Salomon, G., & Leigh, T. (1984). Predispositions about learning from print and television. *Journal of Communication, 34,* 119–135.

Samuels, S. (1970). Effects of pictures on learning to read, comprehension, and attitudes. *Review of Educational Research, 40,* 397–407.

Schaffer, L. C., & Hannafin, M. J. (1986). The effects of progressive interactivity on learning from interactive video. *Educational Communication and Technology Journal, 34,* 89–96.

Schallert, D. L. (1980). The role of illustrations in reading comprehension. In R. J. Spiro, B. C. Bruce, & W. F. Brewer (Eds.), *Theoretical issues in reading comprehension* (pp. 503–524). Hillsdale, NJ: Lawrence Erlbaum Associates.

Schank, R. C., & Abelson, R. P. (1977) *Scripts, plans, goals, and understanding.* Hillsdale, NJ: Lawrence Erlbaum Associates.

Schneider, S. L., & Laurion, S. K. (1993). Do we know what we've learned from listening to the news? *Memory and Cognition, 21,* 198–209.

Schramm, W. (1962). Learning from instructional television. *Review of Educational Research, 32,* 156–167.

Schramm, W. (1972). What the research says. In W. Schramm (Ed.), *Quality in instructional television* (pp. 44–79). Honolulu: University of Hawaii Press.

Schramm, W. (1973). *Men, messages, and media: A look at human communication.* New York: Harper & Row.

Schramm, W. (1977). *Big media, little media.* Beverly Hills CA: Sage.

Schramm, W., Lyle, J., & Parker, E. (1961). *Television in the lives of our children.* Stanford, CA: Stanford University Press.

Schwab, R., & Harris, T. (1984). Effects of audio and video recordings on evaluation of counseling interviews. *Educational and Psychological Research, 4,* 57–65.

Scott, D. (1956). Television and school achievement. *Phi Delta Kappan, 38,* 25–28.

Seidman, S. (1981). On the contribution of music to media productions. *Educational Communication and Technology Journal, 19,* 49–61.

Seidman, S. A. (1986). A survey of schoolteachers' utilization of media. *Educational Technology, 26*(10), 19–23.

Sheffield, F. D., Margolius, G. J., & Hoehn, A. J. (1961). Experiments on perceptual mediation in the learning of organizable sequences. In A. A. Lumsdaine (Ed.), *Student response in programmed instruction* (pp. 107–116). Washington, DC: National Academy of Sciences, National Research Council. (AD-281 936)

Shyu, H., & Brown, S. W. (1992). Learner control versus program control in interactive videodisc instruction: What are the effects in procedural learning? *International Journal of Instructional Media, 19,* 85–96.

Siepmann, C. A. (1973). Mass media and communication. In *Audio-visual technology and learning, The educational technology review series, No. 6.* Englewood Cliffs, NJ: Educational Technology Publications.

Silvernail, D. L., & Johnson, J. L. (1990). The impact of interactive televised instruction on college student achievement and attitudes: A controlled experiment. *International Journal of Instructional Media, 17,* 1–8.

Simonson, M. R. (1980). Media and attitudes: A bibliography, Part 2. *Educational Communication and Technology Journal, 28,* 47–61.

Simonson, M., Thies, P., & Burch, G. (1979). Media and attitudes: A bibliography, Part 1 —Articles published in AV Communication Review (1953–1977). *Educational Communication and Technology Journal, 27,* 217–236.

Simpson, H. (1993). *Conversion of live instruction for videoteletraining: Training and classroom design considerations* (TN-93-04). San Diego, CA: Navy Personnel Research and Development Center. (AD-A261 051)

Simpson, H., Pugh, H. L., & Parchman, S. W. (1990). *A two-point videoteletraining system: Design, development, and evaluation* (NPRDC-TR-90-05). San Diego, CA: Navy Personnel Research and Development Center. (AD-A226 734)

Simpson, H., Pugh, H. L., & Parchman, S. W. (1991a). An experimental two-way video teletraining system: Design, development and evaluation. *Distance Education, 12,* 209–231.

Simpson, H., Pugh, H. L., & Parchman, S. W. (1991b). *Empirical comparison of alternative video teletraining technologies* (NPRDC-TR-92-3). San Diego, CA: Navy Personnel Research and Development Center. (AD-A242 200)

Simpson, H., Pugh, H. L., & Parchman, S. W. (1992). *The use of videoteletraining to deliver hands-on training: Concept test and evaluation* (NPRDC-TN-92-14). San Diego, CA: Navy Personnel Research and Development Center. (AD-A250 708)

Simpson, H., Pugh, H. L., & Parchman, S. W. (1993). Empirical comparison of alternative instructional TV technologies. *Distance Education, 14,* 147–164.

Singer, D. G. (1983). A time to reexamine the role of television in our lives. *American Psychologist, 38,* 815–816.

Singer, J. L. (1980). The powers and limitations of television: A cognitive-affective analysis. In P. H. Tannenbaum (Ed.), *The entertainment functions of television* (pp. 31–66). Hillsdale, NJ: Lawrence Erlbaum Associates.

Singer, J. L., & Singer, D. G. (1979, March). Come back, Mister Rogers, come back. *Psychology Today, 56,* 59–60.

Singer, J. L., & Singer, D. G. (1983). Psychologists look at television: Cognitive, developmental, personality, and social policy implications. *American Psychologist, 38,* 826–834.

Smeltzer, D. K. (1988). Media utilization and the student-content teaching inventory: A correlational study of community college instructors. *International Journal of Instructional Media, 15,* 222–233.

Smith, C. B., & Ingersoll, G. M. (1984). Audiovisual materials in U.S. schools: A national survey on availability and use. *Educational Technology, 24*(9), 36–38.

Smith, D. (1971). Some uses of mass media by 14 year olds. *Journal of Broadcasting, 16,* 37–50.

Smith, E. E. (1987). Interactive video: An examination of use and effectiveness. *Journal of Instructional Development, 10,* 2–10.

Smith, J. R., & McEwen, W. J. (1973–1974). Effects of newscast delivery rate on recall and judgement of sources. *Journal of Broadcasting, 18,* 73–78.

Smith, S. G., Jones, L. L., & Waugh, M. L. (1986). Production and evaluation of interactive videodisc lessons in laboratory instruction. *Journal of Computer Based Instruction, 13,* 117–121.

Smith, S. L., & Mosier, J. N. (1986). *Guidelines for designing user interface software* (MTR-10090, ESD-TR-86-278). Bedford, MA: The MITRE Corporation. (AD-A177 198)

Son, J., Reese, S. D., & Davie, W. R. (1987). Effects of visual-verbal redundancy and recaps on television news learning. *Journal of Broadcasting and Electronic Media, 31,* 207–216.

Spangenberg, R. W. (1973). The motion variable in procedural learning. *AV Communication Review, 21,* 419–436.

Splaine, J. (1978). Television and its influence on reading. *Educational Technology, 18,* 15–19.

Stauffer, J., Frost, R., & Rybolt, W. (1983). The attention factor in recalling network television news. *Journal of Communication, 33,* 29–37.

Steinberg, E. R. (1989). Cognition and learner control: A literature review, 1977–1988. *Journal of Computer Based Instruction, 16,* 117–121.

Steiner, G. A. (1963). *The people look at television.* New York: Knopf.

Stickell, D. W. (1963). *A critical review of the methodology and results of research comparing televised and face-to-face instruction.* Unpublished doctoral dissertation, Pennsylvania State University, University Park.

Stine, E. A. L., Wingfield, A., & Myers, S. D. (1990). Age differences in processing information from television news: The effects of bisensory augmentation. *Journal of Gerontology, 45,* 1–8.

Stoloff, P. H. (1991). *Cost-effectiveness of U.S. Navy video teletraining system alternatives.* (CRM Research Memo. 91–165). Alexandria, VA: Center for Naval Analyses.

Stone, D. E., & Glock, M. D. (1981). How do young adults read directions with and without pictures? *Journal of Educational Psychology, 73,* 419–426.

Stone, H. R. (1990). Economic development and technology transfer: Implications for video-based distance education. In M. G. Moore (Ed.), *Contemporary issues in American distance education* (pp. 231–242). Oxford, England: Pergamon.

Suber, J. R., & Leeded, J. A. (1988). The effect of graphic feedback on student motivation. *Journal of Computer-Based Instruction, 15,* 14–17.

Suedfeld, P., Little, B. R., Rank, A. D., Rank, D. S., & Ballard, E. (1986). Television and adults: Thinking, personality, and attitudes. In T. M. Williams (Ed.), *The impact of television: A natural experiment in three communities* (pp. 361–393). Orlando, FL: Academic Press.

Swann, W. B., & Miller, L. C. (1982). Why never forgetting a face matters: Visual imagery and social memory. *Journal of Personality and Social Psychology, 43,* 475–480.

Swezey, R. W., Perez, R. S., & Allen, J. A. (1988). Effects of instructional delivery system and training parameter manipulations on electromechanical maintenance performance. *Human Factors, 30,* 751–762.

Swezey, R. W., Perez, R. S., & Allen, J. A. (1991). Effects of instructional strategy and motion presentation conditions on the acquisition and transfer of electromechanical troubleshooting skill. *Human Factors, 33,* 309–323.

Tamborini, R., & Zillmann, D. (1985). Effects of questions, personalized communication style, and pauses for reflection in children's educational programs. *Journal of Educational Research, 79,* 19–26.

Tar, R. W. (1986). Task analysis for training development. In J. A. Ellis (Ed.), *Military contributions to instructional technology* (pp. 20–41). New York: Praeger.

Teather, D. C. B., & Marchant, H. (1974). Learning from film with particular reference to the effects of cueing, questioning, and knowledge of results. *Programmed Learning and Educational Technology, 11,* 317–327.

Texas Higher Education Coordinating Board. (1986). *Instructional television: A research review and status report.* Austin, TX: Texas College and University System, Division of Universities and Research. (ERIC Document Reproduction Service No. ED 276 422)

Thompson, G. (1964). Children's acceptance of television advertising and the relation of televiewing to school achievement. *Journal of Educational Research, 58,* 171–174.

Thompson, S. V., & Riding, R. J. (1990). The effect of animated diagrams on the understanding of a mathematical demonstration in 11- to 14-year-old pupils. *British Journal of Educational Psychology, 60,* 93–98.

Tiemans, R. (1970). Some relationships of camera-angle to communication credibility. *Journal of Broadcasting, 14,* 483–490.

Tolliver, D. L. (1970). *A study of color in instructional materials and its effects upon learning.* Unpublished doctoral dissertation, Purdue University, Audio-Visual Center, West Lafayette, IN.

Torres, J. (1984, April). *The impact of overt response and feedback on learning during children's viewing of Electric Company.* Paper presented at the American Educational Research Association (AERA) national meeting, New Orleans.

Torres-Rodriguez, J., & Dwyer, F. M. (1991). The effect of time on the instructional effectiveness of varied visual enhancement strategies. *International Journal of Instructional Media, 18,* 85–93.

Travers, R. M. (1967). *Research and theory related to audiovisual information transmission* (U.S. Office of Education contract No. OES-16-006). Kalamazoo: Western Michigan University. (ERIC Document Reproduction Service No. ED 081 245)

Trenaman, J. M. (1967). *Communications and comprehension.* London: Longman.

Tritz, G. J. (1987). Computer modeling of microbiological experiments in the teaching laboratory: Animation techniques. *Journal of Computers in Mathematics and Science Teaching, 5,* 52–53.

Trollip, S. R., & Sales, G. (1986). Readability of computer-generated fill-justified text. *Human Factors, 28,* 159–163.

Unwin, D. (1979). Production and audience variables in film and television: A second selected bibliography. *Programmed Learning and Educational Technology, 16,* 232–239.

U. S. Department of Health and Human Services, National Institute of Mental Health. (1982a). *Television and behavior: Ten years of scientific progress and implications for the eighties: Vol. I. Summary report* (DHHS Publication No. (ADM) 82-1195). Washington, DC: U. S. Government Printing Office.

U. S. Department of Health and Human Services, National Institute of Mental Health. (1982b). *Television and behavior: Ten years of scientific progress and implications for the eighties: Vol. II. Technical reviews* (DHHS Publication No. (ADM) 82-1196). Washington, DC: U. S. Government Printing Office.

U. S. Office of Technology Assessment. (1989, November). *Linking for learning: A new course for education* (OTA-SET-430). Washington, DC: U. S. Government Printing Office.

Utz, P. (1980). *Video user's handbook.* Englewood Cliffs, NJ: Prentice-Hall.

Utz, P. (1992). *Today's video: Equipment, setup, and production* (2nd ed.). Englewood Cliffs, NJ: Prentice-Hall.

Van Der Drift, K. D. J. M. (1980). Cost-effectiveness of audiovisual media in higher education. *Instructional Science, 9,* 355–364.

Vandermeer, A. W. (1953). *Training film evaluation—Comparison of two films on personal hygiene* (Tech. Rep. No. SDC 269-7-50). Washington, DC: U. S. Army.

Vandermeer, A. W. (1954). Color versus black and white in instructional films. *AV Communication Review, 2,* 121–134.

Velthuijsen, A., Hooijkaas, C., & Koomen, W. (1987). Image size in interactive television and evaluation of the interaction. *Social Behavior, 2,* 113–118.

Vernon, M. D. (1953). Perception and understanding of instructional TV programmes. *British Journal of Psychology, 44,* 116–126.

Vital stats: Tale of the tube. (1993, August 2). *Newsweek,* p. 6.

Wagley, M. (1978). *The effect of music on affective and cognitive development of sound-symbol recognition among preschool children.* Unpublished doctoral dissertation, Texas Women's University, Denton.

Wagner, L. (1972). The economics of the Open University. *Higher Education, 1,* 159–183.

Wagner, L. (1975). Television video-tape systems for off-campus education: A cost analysis of SURGE. *Instructional Science, 4,* 315–332.

Wagner, L. (1977). The economics of the Open University revisited. *Higher Education, 6,* 359–381.

Wainer, H. (1992). Understanding graphs and tables. *Educational Researcher, 21*(1), 14–23.

Wakshlag, J., Day, K. D., & Zillmann, D. (1981). Selective exposure to educational television as a function of differently paced humorous inserts. *Journal of Educational Psychology, 73,* 27–32.

Wakshlag, J., Reitz, R., & Zillmann, D. (1982). Selective exposure to and acquisition of information from educational television programs as a function of appeal and tempo of background music. *Journal of Educational Psychology, 74,* 666–677.

Walberg, H. J., & Tsai, S. L. (1985). Correlates of reading achievement and attitude: A national assessment study. *Journal of Educational Research, 78,* 159–167.

Watt, J. H., & Welch, A. J. (1983). Effects of static and dynamic complexity on children's attention and recall of television instruction. In J. Bryant & D. R. Anderson (Eds.), *Children's understanding of television: Research on attention and comprehension* (pp. 69–102). New York: Academic Press.

Weaver, J., Zillmann, D., & Bryant, J. (1988). Effects of humorous distortions on children's learning from educational television: Further evidence. *Communication Education, 37,* 181–187.

Weiner, B. (1979) A theory of motivation for some classroom experiences. *Journal of Educational Psychology, 71,* 3–25.

Welch, A. J., & Watt, J. H. (1982). Visual complexity and young children's learning from television. *Human Communication Research, 8,* 133–145.

Wells, R. A. (1990, September). *Computer-mediated communications for distance education and training: Literature review and international resources* (Contractor Technical Report for U.S. Army Research Institute (ARI) for the Behavioral and Social Sciences). Boise, ID: Boise State University.

Wells, S. (1976). Evaluation criteria and the effectiveness of instructional technology in higher education. *Higher Education, 5,* 253–275.

Wetzel, C. D., Van Kekerix, D. L., & Wulfeck, W. H. (1987a, May). *Characteristics of Navy training courses and potential for computer support* (NPRDC-TR-87-25). San Diego, CA: Navy Personnel Research and Development Center. (AD-A180 609)

Wetzel, C. D., Van Kekerix, D. L., & Wulfeck, W. H. (1987b, October). *Analysis of Navy technical school training objectives for microcomputer based training systems* (NPRDC-TR-88-3). San Diego, CA: Navy Personnel Research and Development Center. (AD-A187 666)

White, B. (1984). Designing computer games to help physics students understand Newton's laws of motion. *Cognition and Instruction, 1,* 69–108.

White, S. E. (1982). *The effect of the form complexity of television on the identification/recognition process: An examination of the symbol system of television.* Unpublished doctoral dissertation, Ohio State University, Columbus.

White, S. E., Evans, S. A., & Murray, M. J. (1986, August). *The effect of six production variables on recall of television commercials during fast-forward "zapping."* Paper presented to the AEJMC 1986 Conference, University of Oklahoma, Norman.

Whiting, H. T. A., Bijlard, M. J., & den Brinker, B. P. L. M. (1987). The effect of the availability of a dynamic model on the acquisition of a complex cyclical action. *Quarterly Journal of Experimental Psychology, 39,* 43–59.

Whittington, N. (1987). Is instructional television educationally effective? A research review. *The American Journal of Distance Education, 1,* 47–57.

Wickstrom, A. (1992, March 12). For first time, camcorder sales down last year. *San Diego Union-Tribune* "Night & Day" Weekend guide section, p. 11.

Wilkinson, G. L. (1982). Economics of school media programs. *Journal of Research and Development in Education, 16,* 37–43.

Williams, J. G. (1987a). Visual demonstration and movement production: Effects of motoric mediation during observation of a model. *Perceptual and Motor Skills, 65,* 825–826.

Williams, J. G. (1987b). Visual demonstration and movement sequencing: Effects of instructional control of the eyes. *Perceptual and Motor Skills, 65,* 366.

Williams, J. G. (1988). Perception of a throwing action from point-light demonstrations. *Perceptual and Motor Skills, 67,* 273–274.

Williams, J. G. (1989a). Throwing action from full-cue and motion-only video-models of an arm movement sequence. *Perceptual and Motor Skills, 68,* 259–266.

Williams, J. G. (1989b). Visual demonstration and movement production: Effects of timing variations in a model's action. *Perceptual and Motor Skills, 68,* 891–896.

Williams, P. A., Haertel, E. H., Haertel, G. D., & Walberg, H. J. (1982). The impact of leisure-time television on school learning: A research synthesis. *American Educational Research Journal, 19,* 19–50.

Williams, R. (1965). On the value of varying television shots. *Journal of Broadcasting, 9,* 33–43.

Williams, R. (1968). The value of varying film shot on interest level. *Speech Monographs, 35,* 166–169.

Winn, B. (1987a). Are media merely vehicles for instruction? In M. R. Simonson (Ed.), *"...Mere vehicles..." A symposium on the status of research in instructional technology* (pp. 35–43). (ERIC Document Reproduction Service No. ED 285 519)

Winn, B. (1987b). Charts, graphs, and diagrams in educational materials. In D. M. Willows & H. A. Houghton (Eds.), *The psychology of illustration: Vol. 1. Basic research* (pp. 152–198). New York: Springer-Verlag.

Winn, M. (1985). *The plug-in drug: Television, children and the family.* New York: Viking.

Winn, W. (1989). The design and use of instructional graphics. In H. Mandl & J. R. Levin (Eds.), *Knowledge acquisition from text and pictures* (pp. 125–144). Amsterdam: North-Holland.

Woodley, A., & Parlett, M. (1983). Student drop-out. *Teaching at a Distance, 24,* 2–23.

Wright, J. C., Huston, A. C., Ross, R. P., Calvert, S. L., Rolandelli, D., Weeks, L. A., Raeissi, P., & Potts, R. (1984). Pace and continuity of television programs: Effects on children's attention and comprehension. *Developmental Psychology, 20,* 653–666.

Wright, P. (1977). Presenting technical information: A survey of research findings. *Instructional Science, 6,* 93–134.

Wright, P., & Reid, F. (1973). Written information: Some alternatives to prose for expressing the outcomes of complex contingencies. *Journal of Applied Psychology, 57,* 160–166.

Zavotka, S. L. (1987). Three-dimensional computer animated graphics: A tool for spatial skill instruction. *Educational Communication and Technology Journal, 35,* 133–144.

Zettl, H. (1973). *Sight sound motion: Applied media aesthetics.* Belmont, CA: Wadsworth.

Zettl, H. (1984). *Television production handbook.* Belmont, CA: Wadsworth.

Zettl, H. (1990). *Sight, sound, motion: Applied media aesthetics* (2nd ed.). Belmont, CA: Wadsworth.

Ziegler, S. K. (1969). *Attention factors in televised messages: Effects on looking behavior and recall.* Unpublished doctoral dissertation, Michigan State University, East Lansing.

Zigerell, J. J. (1979). A brief historical survey. In R. Yarrington (Ed.), *Using mass media for learning* (pp. 1–12). Washington DC: American Association of Community and Junior Colleges (AACJC). (ERIC Document Reproduction Service No. ED 165 856)

Zigerell, J. J. (1986). *A guide to telecourses and their uses.* Costa Mesa, CA: Coast Community College District. (ERIC Document Reproduction Service No. ED 280 439)

Zigerell, J. J. (1991). *The uses of television in American higher education.* New York: Praeger.

Zillmann, D. (1977). Humor and communication. In A. J. Chapman & H. C. Foot (Eds.), *It's a funny thing, humor* (pp. 291–301). Oxford, England: Pergamon.

Zillmann, D., & Bryant, J. (1983). Uses and effects of humor in educational ventures. In P. E. McGhee & J. H. Goldstein (Eds.), *The handbook of humor research: Applied studies of humor* (pp. 173–193). New York: Springer-Verlag.

Zillmann, D., & Bryant, J. (1988). Guidelines for the effective use of humor in children's educational television programs. *Journal of Children in Contemporary Society, 20,* 201–221.

Zillmann, D., Masland, J. L., Weaver, J. B., Lacey, L. A., Jacobs, N. E., Dow, J. H., Klein, C. A., & Banker, S. R. (1984). Effects of humorous distortions on childrens' learning from educational television. *Journal of Educational Psychology, 76,* 802–812.

Zillmann, D., Williams, B., Bryant, J., Boynton, K., & Wolf, M. (1980). Acquisition of information from educational television programs as a function of differently paced humorous inserts. *Journal of Educational Psychology, 72,* 170–180.

Zuckerman, D. M., Singer, D., & Singer, J. (1980). Television viewing, children's reading, and related classroom behavior. *Journal of Communication, 30,* 166–174.

Zuckerman, J. (1949). *Music in motion pictures: A review of the literature with implications for instructional films.* Philadelphia: Pennsylvania State College. (ERIC Document Reproduction Service No. ED 002 434)

Author Index

A

Abelson, R. P., 59, 168, 169
Acker, S. R., 94, 96, 149, 150
Adams, J. A., 85
Adams, M., 94, 95
Adesman, P., 76
Adoni, H., 52, 54
Albert, S. M., 150
Alesandrini, K. L., 61, 66
Alessi, S. M., 101, 110, 153
Allen, B. S., 110
Allen, J. A., 73, 77, 78, 80, 101, 102
Allen, W. H., 6, 7, 10, 11, 22, 27, 47, 49, 50, 61, 71, 73, 74, 75, 76, 77, 78, 80, 100, 102, 103, 134, 138, 139, 140, 156, 157, 188, 190
Alwitt, L. F., 142
Anderson, D. R., 40, 45, 57, 58, 59, 60, 135, 142, 160, 168, 189, 196
Anderson, G. H., 114, 117, 126, 127, 128, 130
Anglin, G. J., 66
Arnold, G. B., 150
Arnold, R. K., 84, 86, 87
Ary, D. E., 23
Assad, C., 92, 93
Ayers, W. R., 136
Aylward, T. J., 142, 148

B

Baek, Y., 94
Baggaley, J. P., 139, 142, 147, 150, 151, 152, 153, 156, 164, 165
Baggett, P., 41, 42, 43, 51, 78, 81, 82, 83, 92, 93, 109, 157, 183
Bailey, S. S., 19, 35
Bailyn, L., 161, 162
Baker, R. A., 21
Ballard, E., 160

Balthazar, L. B., 20
Bandura, A., 85, 87
Banker, S. R., 145
Barker, B. O., 21, 25
Barnard, J., 20
Barrington, H., 142, 143, 155, 156
Bates, A. W., 16, 17, 28, 29, 31, 33, 38, 181
Beagles-Roos, J., 45
Beam, P., 154
Beare, P. L., 20, 21
Beentjes, J. W. J., 159, 160, 161, 178
Bell, S. M., 64
Berman, J. R., 136
Berry, C., 52, 53, 54, 57, 134, 139
Biederman, I., 64
Bijlard, M. J., 86
Billington, M. J., 149
Blaiwes, A. S., 101
Blake, T., 49, 73, 74, 76, 78, 92, 93, 102, 103, 192, 193
Blank, A., 168, 169
Blinn, J., 130
Blumler, J. G., 163
Bogart, L., 163
Boltz, M., 143
Booher, H. R., 68
Bordeaux, B. R., 179
Borg, W. R., 63, 100, 103
Bosco, J., 106, 108
Boyce, M. J., 92, 93
Boynton, K., 138, 145
Braden, R. A., 110, 139
Brandon, J. R., 137
Branson R. K., 73, 77, 78, 80
Breed, G., 150
Breen, M. P., 23, 137
Briggs, L. J., 191
Brisch-Kanaba, J., 114, 116, 117, 119, 120, 121, 122, 125, 126, 127, 130
Brooks, D. W., 136

Brooks, V., 73, 74, 75, 102, 126, 127
Brosius, H. B., 55, 57
Brown, C. M., 154
Brown, D., 143
Brown, D. B., 154
Brown, J. R., 160
Brown, S., 16, 17, 25, 26, 31, 36, 37, 38
Brown, S. W., 83
Browne, S. E., 114, 115, 117, 121, 125, 126, 127
Bryant, J., 138, 142, 143, 144, 145
Buchanan, C. C., 28
Buffardi, L. C., 101
Bunker, L. K., 86
Burch, G., 13, 191
Burkhard, D. G., 86
Burkleo, H. V., 154
Burroughs, W. A., 85
Burrows, T. D., 114, 115, 116, 117, 118, 119, 123, 126, 127, 128, 129
Burwell, L. B., 110

C

Cable, G. W., 61, 69
Calvert, S. L., 40, 52, 136, 138, 139, 143
Campbell, A. J., 154
Campeau, P. L., 6, 7, 10, 22, 140, 191, 192
Cantor, P., 152
Caraballo, A., 92, 93
Caraballo, J., 92, 93
Carlton, L. G., 86, 87
Carney, R. N., 66
Carnoy, M., 27
Carpenter, C. R., 134, 140
Carpenter, P. A., 62, 64, 68
Carrier, C. A., 22
Carroll, J. M., 126, 127
Carroll, W. R., 85, 87
Cartwright, S. R., 120, 121, 122, 125, 126, 130, 149
Cavanaugh, J. C., 53, 56
Cennamo, K. S., 163, 167, 168, 169, 177
Chaffee, S. H., 52
Chanowitz, B., 168, 169
Chapman, A. J., 144, 145
Chilberg, J., 150
Chu, G. C., 6, 7, 9, 10, 11, 12, 22, 25, 27, 102, 103, 134, 136, 137, 138, 139, 140, 141, 144, 145, 150, 153, 190, 203
Chute, A. G., 20, 49, 101, 146
Clark, G., 24
Clark, R. E., 4, 10, 51, 103, 104, 135, 137, 167, 181, 189, 190, 191, 193, 194, 197, 198

Clifford, B. R., 52, 53, 54, 57, 139
Cohen, A. A., 48, 147, 186
Cohen, P. A., 6, 8, 9, 13, 88, 107, 191
Colamaio, M. E., 109
Coldevin, G. O., 138, 139
Collins, A., 94, 95
Collins, W. A., 57
Coltheart, V., 68
Comisky, P. W., 144
Compesi, R. J., 114, 115, 116, 117, 119, 120, 122, 128
Cookson, P. S., 16
Cooney, S. M., 49, 75, 77, 102, 140, 156
Corbin, M. T., 136, 149
Cornell, E. H., 77, 81
Cramond, J. K., 160
Crane, J., 144
Crane, V., 16
Cresswell, K. W., 150
Crismore, A., 99
Crompton, P., 144, 145
Crook, T. H., 56
Cross, D. R., 194
Croynik, D., 126, 127
Csikszentmihalyi, M., 164

D

Daehling, W. A., 49, 75, 77, 102
Daiker, K. C., 92, 93, 94
Dalton, D. W., 108, 109, 110
Davie, W. R., 53, 55
Davis, D., 115, 126, 130
Dawson, R., 24
Day, K. D., 143, 144, 145
Dayton, D. K., 140
Decker, P. J., 89
de Groot, S., 142, 151
Deighton, J., 137
Del Rey, P., 86
De Meyer, G., 160
den Brinker, B. P. L. M., 86
Descy, D. E., 24
DeWulf, M. J., 37
Dickie, K., 190
Dille, B., 16
DiSessa, A. A., 95
Dixon, D., 69
Dixon, P., 149
Doherty, S., 81
Donohew, L., 164
Dorr, A., 160
Dow, J. H., 145
Down, K. S., 18
Drew, D. G., 55
Dubin, R., 6, 8, 13, 21, 25

AUTHOR INDEX 241

Duby, P. B., 16
Duchnicky, R. L., 154
Duck, S. W., 142, 150, 151, 152, 153, 156
Dukelow, J. D., 84, 86, 87
Dumestre, J., 155
Duncan, R. C., 136
Dwyer, F. M., 51, 61, 62, 63, 64, 74, 77, 99, 100, 101, 103, 145, 146, 148, 191
D'Ydewalle, G., 155

E

Eakins, D., 46, 47, 60
Ebeling, B. J., 6, 8, 9, 13, 88, 107, 191
Ehrenfeucht, A., 41, 43, 82, 83
Elkerton, J., 92, 93
Ellis, J. A., 77
Ellis, L., 9
Engel, S. E., 154
Evans, S. A., 148, 150

F

Fauconnier, G., 160
Feltz, D. L., 84
Field, D. E., 45
Findahl, O., 53, 55, 56
Finn, J. D., 6, 7, 160
Fischer, C., 45
Fletcher, J. D., 38, 39, 106, 107, 108, 110
Fortune, J. B., 89
Frager, A. M., 88
Freeman, J., 143
Frey, P. W., 76
Fridland, P. H., 89
Friederich, L. K., 160
Friedman, A., 2, 42, 62, 66, 99, 101, 103, 132
Frost, J., 106
Frost, R., 52, 56
Fry, M. A., 63, 64
Fuller, B. J., 114, 116, 117, 119, 120, 121, 122, 125, 126, 127, 130
Fuller, F. F., 88
Furnham, A., 53, 55, 163
Furu, T., 160

G

Gadberry, S., 160
Gaddy, G. D., 160
Gagné, R. M., 191, 192
Gagnon, D., 92, 93
Gale, N., 81
Gallez, D., 143
Gallini, J. K., 70

Gat, I., 45
Gaver, W., 22, 151
Gay, G., 109
Geiger, S., 53
Gersh, T. L., 143
Giannetti, L. D., 120, 122, 123, 124, 126, 127, 129, 130
Gibbons, J., 45
Gibbons, J. F., 18
Gibson, J. J., 49, 73
Giltrow, D. R., 16
Gittelman, S. S., 91
Glass, A. L., 64
Glenn, A. D., 22
Glock, M. D., 61, 68
Golledge, R. G., 81
Gorman, D. A., 63, 64, 100
Gottdiener, C., 152
Gould, G. M., 164, 165
Gould, J. D., 154
Graber, D. A., 52, 53, 54, 57
Granda, R. E., 154
Gray, S. W., 85
Green, A., 75
Greenberg, B. S., 162, 165
Greene, D., 145
Greenhill, L. P., 134
Greenwald, A. G., 150
Gregory, M., 154
Griffin, R., 155
Griffin, T., 143
Grimes, T., 55, 56
Grischkowsky, N., 154
Gropper, G. L., 41, 69, 73, 74, 78, 79, 102, 155
Gross, L., 114, 115, 116, 117, 118, 119, 123, 126, 127, 128, 129, 158, 160, 161, 162
Grundin, H. U., 16, 17, 36, 37, 38, 39
Guba, E., 142, 151
Gunter, B., 52, 53, 54, 55, 57, 139, 163
Gurevitch, M., 163
Guri-Rosenblit, S., 67
Gutman, J., 164
Guzdial, M., 83

H

Haas, N., 109, 110
Haeghen, P. V., 28
Haertel, E. H., 161
Haertel, G. D., 161
Hall, E. G., 86
Hamilton, H. B., 159
Hannafin, M. J., 73, 103, 106, 108, 109, 110

Hannum, W. H., 109, 110
Hansbrough, J. F., 89
Hansford, B. C., 21
Hanson, L., 40, 54
Haring, M. J., 63, 64
Harless, W. G., 136
Harris, T., 89
Harris, W. J., 67
Hartley, J., 66
Hartman, E. F., 44
Hartman, F. R., 51, 154, 155, 157
Haskins, M. J., 85
Hawkridge, D., 25
Hawley, D. E., 38
Hay, D. H., 77, 81
Hayes, D. S., 44, 45
Hays, R. T., 26, 101, 103
Head, G. E., 28
Heath, C., 22, 151
Hedley, R. A., 6, 8, 13, 21, 25
Heestand, D. E., 140
Hegarty, M., 62, 64, 68
Hendriks, A., 160
Herx, H., 22, 34
Hill, R. D., 56
Himmelweit, H. T., 160, 161, 164
Ho, C. P., 109, 110
Hoban, C. F., 75, 134, 136, 137, 138, 139, 142, 143, 145, 150
Hochberg, J., 73, 74, 75, 102, 126, 127
Hodak, G. W., 19, 35
Hoehn, A. J., 77, 79, 94
Hoffman, H. R., 161
Hoijer, B., 53
Holliday, W. G., 61
Holosko, M. J., 164, 165
Hooijkaas, C., 150
Horn, G., 144
Hornik, R., 4, 159, 160
Hosford, R. E., 89
Hosie, P., J. 25
Houser, E. J., 76
Houser, R. L., 76
Hoyt, D. B., 89
Huddleston, B. M., 150
Hughes, C. W., 110
Hunter, B., 99
Huston, A. C., 40, 46, 47, 52, 57, 59, 60, 135, 136, 138, 139, 141, 142, 143, 149, 189, 196

I

Ingersoll, G. M., 23, 24
Isenhour, J. P., 153

J

Jackson, R., 132
Jackson-Beeck, M., 15, 163
Jacobs, N. E., 145
Jamison, D. T., 6, 7, 12, 27, 28, 29, 30, 32, 193
Jensen, L. C., 88
Jeon, U. H., 73, 77, 78, 80
Johnson, J. L., 20
Johnson, M. E., 89
Jonassen, D. H., 108, 109, 110
Jones, L. L., 26
Jorgensen, E. S., 137, 139
Just, M. A., 62, 64, 68

K

Kagan, J., 160
Kanaba, S., 114, 116, 117, 119, 120, 121, 122, 125, 126, 127, 130
Kanner, J. H., 101, 145, 146
Kantor, B. R., 140, 141
Kantra, S., 143
Kaplan, R. M., 144
Karasar, N., 150
Katz, E., 52, 54, 163
Katzman, N., 146
Kaye, A. R., 14, 16
Kazem, A. K. M., 136
Kearsley, G. P., 106
Kelly, S. B., 44, 45
Kernodle, M. W., 86, 87
Kiely, J., 47, 51, 56
Kiesling, H., 28, 29, 31
Kincheloe, W. R., 18
King, W. A., 92, 93
Kini, A. S., 97
Kintsch, W., 82
Kippax, S., 160
Kipper, P., 148, 150
Kirkup, G., 16, 17, 25, 26, 31
Klees, S. J., 27, 28, 29, 30, 32
Klein, C. A., 145
Klein, E. L., 94, 96
Knemeyer, M., 142, 151
Kolers, P. A., 154
Konoske, P. J., 77
Koomen, W., 150
Kopstein, F. F., 91
Koran, M. L., 48, 88
Kozma, R. B., 51, 57, 61, 62, 71, 74, 75, 138, 190, 193, 194, 195, 197, 199, 203, 210
Kraft, R. N., 142, 150, 151, 152, 185
Krendl, K. A., 24, 140, 165, 177, 196

AUTHOR INDEX 243

Kruger, R. L., 19, 35
Ksobiech, K. J., 46, 177
Kulik, C. C., 107, 191
Kulik, J. A., 6, 8, 9, 13, 88, 107, 191

L

La Blonde, J. A., 161
Lacey, L. A., 145
Laesecke, A., 90
Laidlaw, B., 16, 29, 31, 36
Lamberski, R. J., 101, 145, 146
Landers, D. M., 84
Laner, S., 73, 77, 78
Lange, G., 179
Langer, E. J., 168, 169
Lathen, W. C., 194
Latremouille, S. A., 154
Laurion, S. K., 53
Layard, R., 16, 29, 31, 36
Layne, B., 94
Leeded, J. A., 94, 96
Lehrer, A., 44, 47, 51
Leigh, T., 140, 169, 170, 171, 172, 173, 174, 175
Lentz, R., 61, 65, 71
Lepper, M. R., 145
Lesser, G. S., 145
Levenson, P. M., 109
Levie, W. H., 61, 65, 71, 190, 193, 198, 210
Levin, H. M., 27, 38, 39
Levin, J. R., 66
Levin, S. R., 142, 160
Levitt, S. R., 150
Lieberman, D., 160
Light, L., 142, 151
Lin, C. A., 150
Link, J. D., 139, 146
Lipsey, M. W., 106
Little, B. R., 160
Loftus, G. R., 64
Lorch, E. P., 40, 57, 58, 59, 60, 135, 142, 160, 168, 189, 196
Luff, P., 22, 151
Lumsdaine, A. A., 6, 10, 91, 134, 136, 139, 140, 141, 143, 146, 153, 156, 190
Lumsden, K. G., 16, 31
Lutz, K., 91
Lyle, J., 160, 161

M

MacLennan, D. W., 6, 134
Maccoby, N., 140
Mace, J., 28, 29, 31, 32, 39
Mackersie, R. C., 89

Magne, O., 98
Maher, T. G., 13, 14, 27, 28, 29, 32, 33, 35
Mandel, M., 45
Mandell, L. M., 150
Mangelsdorf, J. E., 154
Mann, R., 143
Manning, B. A., 88
Marchant, H., 140
Marchetti, F. M., 154
Margolius, G. J., 77, 79, 94
Markham, P. L., 153, 155
Mascelli, J., 126, 127
Masland, J. L., 145
Mason, R., 14
Masterson, J. W., 85, 138
Mathias, H., 119, 123
Mathis, D., 9
May, M. A., 6, 10, 134, 136, 139, 140, 141, 143, 146, 153, 156, 190, 191
Mayer, R. E., 61, 70
Mayton, G. B., 92
McArthur, L. Z., 185
McCabe, R. H., 28, 30, 32
McCain, T. A., 150
McCullagh, P., 136, 137
McEwen, W. J., 138
McGhee, P. E., 144
McIntyre, C. J., 136, 144, 149, 153
McKeachie, W. J., 194
McMullen, J., 90
McNeil, B. J., 107
McQueen, J., 137
Mechanic, D., 144
Mercer, J., 142
Meringoff, L. K., 45
Merritt, B. D., 150
Metallinos, N., 151
Mewhort, D. J. K., 154
Meyer, G. E., 90
Mezack, M., 16
Michael, D. N., 140
Miller, G. E., 61
Miller, L. C., 48
Millerson, G., 114, 115, 116, 117, 119, 120, 121, 122, 125, 130
Monson, D., 144
Moore, M. V., 61, 63, 64, 73, 92, 93, 98, 101, 103
Moore, P. J., 69
Morgan, M., 158, 160, 161, 162
Morris, B. A., 90
Morris, J. D., 134, 136, 142, 143
Morrow, J. R., 109
Mosier, J. N., 132, 153, 154
Murphy, R. T., 4, 159
Murray, J. P., 160

Murray, M. J., 148, 150
Muta, H., 31
Muter, P., 154
Muylle, P., 155
Myers, S. D., 56

N

Nathenson, M., 16, 17, 25, 26, 31
Nawrocki, L. H., 61, 63, 64, 73, 92, 93, 98, 101, 103
Neidt, C., 143
Nelson, K. R., 107
Neu, D. M., 140, 141
Neuman, S. B., 159, 160, 161
Neuman, W. R., 52
Newby, T. J., 20
Nielsen, T. G., 49, 75, 77, 102
Nugent, G. C., 43, 136
Nyenhuis, J., 146

O

O'Bryan, K. G., 150
Olsen, R. A., 154
Oppenheim, A. N., 160, 161
Orlansky, J., 107

P

Palmer, E., 136
Palmgreen, P., 164
Palmiter, S., 92, 93
Parchman, S. W., 19, 20, 21, 35, 37, 38
Park, O., 91
Parker, E., 160
Parkhurst, P. E., 63, 100
Parknas, L., 98
Parlett, M., 16
Parness, P., 52, 54
Pascoe, G. C., 144
Patterson, J., 86
Patterson, R., 119, 123
Pavio, A., 51
Pearson, P. D., 99
Peeck, J., 61, 66, 71, 100, 103
Pellegrino, J. W., 81
Penn, R., 153
Perez, R. S., 73, 77, 78, 80, 102
Perkins, R. D., 154
Peters, H. J., 92, 93, 94
Peters, O., 16
Petkovich, M. D., 190, 193, 194
Pew, R., 94, 95
Pezdek, K., 44, 47, 51, 56
Phillips, T. L., 73, 103, 109, 110

Piele, P. K., 38
Pintrich, P. R., 194
Pirrong, G. D., 194
Platten, M. R., 21
Pohl, H. S., 136
Poole, R., 136
Post, D. L., 185
Postman, N., 158, 159
Poston, C. O., 20
Potts, R., 40, 52, 136, 138, 139
Poulton, E. C., 154
Pressley, M., 61
Price, V., 160
Proctor, E., 163
Prowda, P., 160
Pudovkin, V. I., 152
Pugh, H. L., 19, 20, 21, 35, 37, 38

R

Radtke, P. H., 23
Raeissi, P., 40, 52, 136, 138, 139
Randel, J. M., 90
Rank, A. D., 160
Rank, D. S., 160
Rapue, R., 86
Rayburn, J. D., 164
Reed, S., 92, 98
Reese, S. D., 53, 55, 154
Reeves, B., 53, 162
Reeves, T. C., 108
Regan, J. J., 101
Reid, F., 154
Reid, J. C., 6, 134
Reider, W. L., 22, 34
Reiser, R. A., 192
Richardson, A., 84
Riches, B., 90
Richie, D., 160
Riding, R. J., 94, 95
Rieber, L. P., 89, 90, 92, 93, 94, 95, 96, 97, 98, 103
Rigney, J., 91
Rikli, R., 86
Rink, O., 143
Ritchie, C., 16, 31
Ritchie, H., 20
Ritter, B. E., 90
Roberts, D. F., 160
Robinson, D. C., 164
Rocheleau, D. J., 90
Rohwer, W. D., Jr., 67
Rolandelli, D. R., 40, 46, 47, 51, 52, 60, 136, 138, 139
Romer, D., 137
Roper, B. W., 164

AUTHOR INDEX 245

Rosengren, K. E., 164
Rosenkoetter, J. S., 150
Rosenstein, A. J., 145
Roshal, S. M., 77, 78, 150
Ross, R. P., 40, 52, 136, 138, 139
Rothkopf, E. Z., 149
Rothstein, A. L., 84, 86, 87
Royer, J. M., 61, 69
Rubin, A. M., 164, 165
Rule, S., 37
Rumble, G., 16, 29, 30, 31, 32, 35, 37, 38
Rupinski, T. E., 20, 21, 31, 38
Russell, J. J., 49, 75, 77, 102
Rusted, R., 68
Rybolt, W., 52, 56

S

Saettler, P. A., 6, 134, 143, 188
Sakamoto, T., 31
Sales, G., 154
Salomon, G., 48, 51, 53, 66, 71, 99, 135, 140, 147, 163, 168, 169, 170, 171, 172, 173, 174, 175, 178, 181, 182, 183, 184, 185, 186, 189, 190, 191, 192, 193, 194, 195, 196, 210
Saltz, E., 69
Samuels, S., 61
Savenye, W. C., 109, 110, 177
Schaffer, L. C., 109, 110
Schallert, D. L., 61
Schank, R. C., 59, 168, 169
Schleuder, J., 52
Schneider, S. L., 53
Schramm, W., 6, 7, 8, 9, 10, 11, 12, 22, 25, 27, 34, 35, 102, 103, 134, 136, 137, 138, 139, 140, 141, 143, 144, 145, 150, 153, 160, 190, 192, 203
Schulkind, M., 143
Schuller C. F., 63, 100, 103
Schwab, R., 89
Schwier, R. A., 140
Scott, D., 161
Scott, M. C., 138, 143
Seidman, S. A., 23, 24, 143
Sellen, A., 22, 151
Shackford, S. R., 89
Shearer, J. D., 86
Sheffield, F. D., 77, 79, 94
Sheikh, J., 56
Sheppe, M. L., 19, 35
Sherriffs, R. E., 114, 115, 116, 117, 119, 120, 122, 128
Shwalb, B., J. 107

Shyu, H., 83
Siepmann, C. A., 158
Signer, B., 109
Silvernail, D. L., 20
Simon, S., 44, 47, 51, 56
Simonson, M. R., 13, 191
Simpson, H., 19, 20, 21, 35, 37, 38
Simutis, Z. M., 63, 64, 92, 93
Singer, D. G., 4, 40, 52, 144, 158, 160
Singer, J. L., 4, 40, 52, 58, 144, 158, 159, 160
Singer, M. J., 26, 101, 103
Skinner, M. J., 69
Smeltzer, D. K., 23
Smith, C. B., 23, 24
Smith, D., 162
Smith, E. E., 106, 108, 110
Smith, G., 86
Smith, J. R., 138
Smith, P. L., 177
Smith, R., 45
Smith, R. F., 19, 35
Smith, S. G., 26
Smith, S. L., 132, 153, 154
Snow, R. E., 48, 88
Son, J., 53, 55
Spangenberg, R. W., 73, 74, 77, 78, 79, 102
Splaine, J., 159
Stacy, E. W., 64
Stauffer, J., 52, 56
Stein, A. H., 160
Steinberg, E. R., 109
Steiner, G. A., 164
Stevens, E., 44, 51, 56
Stickell, D. W., 6, 8, 9
Stine, E. A. L., 56
Stoeckert, J., 47, 51, 56
Stoloff, P. H., 20, 21, 31, 37, 38
Stone, D. E., 61, 68
Stone, H. R., 19
Stowitschek, J. J., 37
String, J., 107
Suber, J. R., 94, 96
Suedfeld, P., 160
Sugrue, B. M., 189, 191, 193
Sulzer, R. L., 91
Suppes, P., 6, 7, 12, 193
Swann, W. B., 48
Swezey, R. W., 73, 77, 78, 80, 102
Swift, B., 164

T

Tamborini, R., 141
Tar, R. W., 77

Teather, D. C. B., 140
Tennyson, R. D., 190, 193, 194
Thies, P., 13, 191
Thompson, G., 162
Thompson, S. V., 94, 95
Tiemans, R. K., 150, 151
Tipton, T. J., 136
Tolliver, D. L., 146
Torres, J., 140
Torres-Rodriguez, J., 148
Travers, R. M., 78, 134, 139, 141, 142, 143, 144, 146, 153, 156, 157
Trenaman, J. M., 139
Treurniet, W. C., 154
Tripp, S. D., 109, 110
Tritz, G. J., 90
Troiano, C., 24
Trollip, S. R., 110, 153, 154
Tsai, S. L., 160

U

Ulozas, B., 23
Unwin, D., 134
Utz, P., 114, 115, 116, 117, 120, 126, 127, 128, 130, 149

V

Van Atta, R., 142, 151
Van Der Drift, K. D. J. M., 28
Vandermeer, A. W., 136, 146
Van Der Voort, T. H. A., 159, 160, 161
Van Dijk, T., 82
Van Kekerix, D. L., 24, 77
Van Mondfrans, A. P., 76
Van Ormer, E. B., 75, 134, 136, 138, 139, 142, 143, 145, 150
Van Rensbergen, J., 155
Velthuijsen, A., 150
Vernon, M. D., 139
Vince, P., 160, 161

W

Wachtel, T. L., 89
Wade, B., 136
Wagley, M., 143
Wagner, L., 29, 31, 34, 35
Wainer, H., 67
Wakshlag, J., 143, 144, 145
Walberg, H. J., 160, 161
Watkins, B., 140, 143, 177, 196
Watt, J. H., 138, 143
Waugh, M. L., 26
Weaver, J. B., 145

Weeks, L. A., 40, 52, 136, 138, 139
Weiner, B., 168, 169
Weintraub, R., 49, 73, 74, 75, 76, 77, 78, 80, 102, 103, 140, 156
Welch, A. J., 138, 143
Wells, R. A., 16, 19
Wells, S. J., 6, 7, 8, 12, 14, 25, 27, 28, 29, 30, 32, 193
Wetzel, C. D., 24, 77, 90
White, B., 94, 95
White, S. E., 142, 148, 150
Whitehill, B. V., 90
Whiting, H. T. A., 86
Whittington, N., 6, 8, 14, 20
Wickstrom, A., 15, 24
Wilde, R. J., 160
Wilkinson, G. L., 27, 32
Williams, B., 138, 145
Williams, J. G., 85, 138
Williams, R., 149
Wilson, D. B., 106
Windahl, S., 164
Wingfield, A., 56
Winn, B., 61, 66, 67, 70, 71, 192
Winn, M., 159, 160
Winn, W., 66, 71, 100
Wolf, M., 138, 145
Wolf, W., 142, 151
Wood, D. N., 114, 115, 116, 117, 118, 119, 123, 126, 127, 128, 129
Woodley, A., 16
Wright, J. C., 40, 46, 47, 52, 57, 59, 60, 135, 136, 138, 139, 141, 142, 143, 149, 189, 196
Wright, P., 154
Wulfeck, W. H., 24, 77

Y

Yesavage, J., 56
Young, J. I., 88

Z

Zadek, A., 56
Zavotka, S. L., 92
Zettl, H., 114, 115, 116, 117, 118, 119, 120, 121, 122, 123, 124, 125, 126, 127, 128, 150, 152
Ziegler, S. K., 141
Zier, M. A., 136
Zigerell, J. J., 6, 14, 17, 25, 26, 30, 32, 33
Zillmann, D., 138, 141, 142, 143, 144, 145
Zuckerman, D. M., 160
Zuckerman, J., 129, 130, 143

Subject Index

A

Animation, 49, 79, 89–98, 130–132, 206,
  see also Motion
Attention and comprehension, 57–61,
  135, 141–142, 168–169, 196
Attention-getting, cuing, or arousal devices, 141–153, 208–209
Attitudes or preconceptions
  educational television, 12–13, 201
  perceptions and mental effort, 163–180
  popular beliefs and claims, 2, 104, 184, 209–210
Attributes of media, 192–199
Attribution theory, 168, 172
Audio-visual, see also Visual-verbal dynamic presentations
  comparison studies, 40–52, 54–57
  classroom or integrated materials, 14, 17–18, 23–24

B

Books, see Visual-verbal static materials

C

Camera techniques, 113–125, 147–151
Camera angle and perspective, 78, 116–117, 127–128, 149–152
Computer-based instruction, see also Participation
  animation, 89–98, 130–132, 206
  instructional designs, 108–110
  interactive videodisc, 39, 80, 82–83, 105–110, 165–166, 177–178, 204
  meta-analysis, 8–9, 105–108, 191, 204

Computer interface design, 132
Color, 11, 49, 101, 124–125, 131, 145–146, 205
Continuity, 73–75, 102, 126–128, 152
Costs, 27–39, 202
  averting travel costs, 36–38
  break-even point, 32
  comparing distance and conventional education, 30–33
  cost-benefit or efficiency, 27
  cost-effectiveness and achievement outcomes, 27, 38–39
  fixed and variable, 28–30
  initial and recurrent, 28–30
  interactive video, 39
  mass education cost structure, 29–30
  Open University, 31, 33, 35–36, 39
  production and delivery, 33–38
  student costs, 36–38
  tapes or films, 34–36, 38
  undermining cost advantages, 32–33
Critical perspectives on media, 10, 188–199, 209–210
Cuts and editing, 117, 125–128, 151–153

D

Distance education, 13–22, 24–27, 29–33, 201

E

Editing and cuts, 117, 125–128, 151–153
Educational television, 6–39, 200–203
  achievement, 6–11, 14–21, 38–39, 200–201
  attitudes, 12–13, 201
  classroom media usage, 23–24

247

248   SUBJECT INDEX

distance education, 13–22, 24–27, 29–33, 201
  dropping out, 15–16
  interactive television, 19–22, 201
  Open University, 16–18, 31, 33
  practical characteristics, 2–3, 24–27, 192, 203
  teaching techniques, 10–11, 22–23, 139–141, 202–203, 207–208
  telecourses, 14–19
  telecourse students, 15
  tutored videotape instruction, 18–19
  video teletraining, 19–22, 201
  videotapes, 14–19, 22–25, 34–36, 201–203
Effect size, see Meta-analysis

F

Feedback with video, 84–89, 204–205
Fidelity, see Realism
Formal features, 57–58, 112, 134–135
Format of presentation, 26, 135–137, 142, 144–145

H

Human factors, 132, 153
Humor, 144–145

I

Illustrated text, see Visual-verbal static materials
Individual differences
  discussion or studies of, 47–52, 56, 71–72, 76, 146–148, 167, 175–176, 186–187, 196–197, 207–208
  other mention of, 41, 46, 63–64, 67, 69, 70, 79, 97, 162, 189
Interaction, see Participation
Interactive television, 19–22, 201
Interactive videodisc, 39, 80, 82–83, 105–110, 165–166, 177–178, 204

M

Media, see also Attitudes or preconceptions
  attributes and capabilities, 192–199
  classroom or integrated materials, 14, 17–18, 23–24
  critical perspectives, 10, 188–199, 209–210
  historical trends, 188–190
  range of capabilities, 183–184, 195–196, 205–207, 209–210, see also Symbol systems
  popular beliefs and claims, 2, 104, 184, 209–210
  practical characteristics, 2–3, 24–27, 192, 203
  as vehicles, 190–192
Mental effort, 158–180, 209
  amount of invested mental effort (AIME), 170
  attitudes and perceptions, 163–180, 184
  commercial television effects, 158–169
  related research on AIME, 177–179
  Salomon's theory, 169–179
Mental model, 69–70
Mental practice, 84
Meta-analysis
  computer-based instruction, 8–9, 107, 191, 204
  educational television, 8–9
  interactive video, 8–9, 105–108, 204
  mental practice, sports, and motor skills, 84–86
  teacher feedback, 9, 88
  visuals in illustrated text, 65–66
Methodological problems, 190–191
Motion, 49, 73–98, 102–103, 125, 205–206
  attributes and functions, 73–75, 77, 89–90, 97, 102
  animated graphics, 49, 79, 89–98, 130–132, 206
  feedback, sports, or modeling, 48, 84–89
  general studies of, 49, 75–77
  hands–on learning, 77–84, 101–102, 109
  procedural learning, 77–84, 150–151
  realism, 100–103
  route learning, 81
  with sound or text, 75–76, 154
  summary discussion, 77, 84, 87–88, 97–98
Motor skills, 84–88, 138
Music, 129–130, 143–144

N

Narration, 156–157, see also Audio-visual comparison studies
News broadcasts, 52–57, 135, 164, 171–172, 209

O

Open University, 16–18, 31, 33, 35–36, 39

P

Pace, rate, or transient nature of video, 11, 17–18, 25, 40, 50, 52–53, 56, 62–64, 74, 78, 85, 120, 126, 137–138, 142–143, 151, 153–157, 195, 197, 203, 208–209
Participation, 10–11, 139–141, 189, 203–205
 computer-based, 108–110, 189, 204
 feedback and modeling, 84–89
 inserted questions, 11, 108–109, 140–141, 177
 interactive television, 19–22
 teaching techniques, 10–11, 22–23, 139–141, 202–204
 videotapes, 17–19, 203
 hands-on learning, 77–84, 101–102, 109
Perception of media, see Attitudes or preconceptions
Procedural learning, see Motion

Q

Questions, inserted, 11, 108–109, 140–141, 177, 204, see also Participation

R

Reading, 159–161, see also Visual-verbal static materials
Realism and fidelity, 62–64, 76, 98–104, 131, 142–143, 163, 172, 183, 205
Route learning, 81

S

Schema, 59, 62, 168–169, 196–197
Shot, 113–114, 126, 148–149, 152–153
Sound or music, 58, 128–130, 142–144
Symbol systems, 181–187, 195
 aiding and cultivating skills, 186
 decoding and elaboration, 185
 field of reference, 181–182
 in film and television, 183–186

 notationality, repleteness, or density, 182–183
 resemblance, 99, 182–183
 wide range of, 183–184, 195–196, 205–207, 209–210

T

Telecourse, 14–19
Text on screen, 130, 132–133, 153–155, 206–207
Text, see Visual-verbal static materials
Theory, 189–190
Tradecraft and learning, 111–113, 133–135, 208–209

V

Video production and learning, 10–11, 111–113, 133–157, 207–209
 attention-getting, cuing, or arousal devices, 141–153, 208–209
 axis of action and continuity, 127, 152
 camera angle or perspective, 78, 127–128, 149–152
 color, 101, 145–146
 dollying, 148
 dramatization, 136–137
 editing and cuts, 142, 151–153
 encouraging participation, 10–11, 139–140, 203–205
 establishing shot, 152
 expository formats, 137, 156
 eye contact, 150
 humor, 144–145
 inserting questions, 11, 140–141
 music and sound effects, 142–144
 narration, 156–157
 panning, 149
 presentation format, 26, 135–137, 156
 presentation pacing, 137–138
 program length, 138–139
 shot length, 148–149
 verisimilitude, 142
 words on screen, 153–155
 zooming, 147–148
Video production and professional tradecraft, 111–133, 208–209
 animation, 130–132
 axis of action, 127, 152
 balance and proportion, 120–121
 camera angle or perspective, 116–117, 127–128, 149–152
 camera movement, 115–116

camera technique, 113–119
color, 124–125, 131
composition, 119–123
continuity, 126–128
cut or cutting, 125–126, 128
craning, 115–116
dollying, 115–116
discussion, 133, 208–209
editing techniques, 125–128
focus, 117–119
framing, 121–122
human factors guidance, 132
jump cut, 117, 126
lens effects, 117–119
lighting, 123–124
lines, boundaries, and vectors, 122–123
movement or motion, 125
music, 129–130
panning, 115–116
picture complexity, 120
reverse angle, 127
rule of thirds, 120
shot, 113, 126, 152
shot duration, 126
shot length, 113–114
sound, 128
tilting, 115–116
tradecraft, 111–113, 133–135, 208–209
trucking, 115–116
words on screen, 130, 132–133
z-axis, 115
zoom, 117–119
Videotapes or videocassette recorder (VCR), 13–19, 22–25, 34–36, 81, 107, 201–203
Video teletraining, 19–22, 201

Visual detail, 62–64, 100–101, *see also* Realism
Visual-verbal dynamic presentations, 40–61, 194–197, 206
 attention and comprehension, 57–61, 196
 audio-visual comparison studies, 40–52, 54–57
 children's stories, 43–46
 equivalence of content, 42–43, 191
 gaining access to, 46–47, 60, 177
 individual differences, 47–52, 56, 196–197
 motion, 49, 75–76, 154
 narration in productions, 156–157
 news broadcasts, 52–57
 order of presentation, 41–42, 155, 157
 summary or discussion, 50–52, 56–57, 61, 194–197, 206
 text in productions, 130, 132–133, 153–155
Visual-verbal static materials, 61–72
 books and video contrasted, 62, 195–197
 generalizations relevant to video, 61–62
 illustrated text, 62–72
 individual differences, 71–72
 types of visuals, 65–67, 98–99, 181–183
 visual detail, 62–64, 100–101

Z

Zoom, 117–119, 147–148, 186, 208